CATS, CARPENTERS, AND ACCOUNTANTS

HISTORY AND FOUNDATIONS OF INFORMATION SCIENCE

Edited by Michael Buckland, Jonathan Furner, and Markus Krajewski

Human Information Retrieval by Julian Warner

Good Faith Collaboration: The Culture of Wikipedia by Joseph Michael Reagle Jr.

Paper Machines: About Cards & Catalogs, 1548–1929 by Markus Krajewski, translated by Peter Krapp

Information and Intrigue: From Index Cards to Dewey Decimals to Alger Hiss by Colin B. Burke

Indexing It All: The Subject in the Age of Documentation, Information, and Data by Ronald E. Day

Bibliometrics and Research Evaluation: The Good, the Bad, and the Ugly by Yves Gingras

Search Foundations: Toward a Science of Technology-Mediated Experience by Sachi Arafat and Elham Ashoori

The Information Manifold: Why Computers Can't Solve Algorithmic Bias and Fake News by Antonio Badia

Documentarity: Evidence, Ontology, and Inscription by Ronald E. Day

The Infographic: A History of Data Graphics in News and Communications by Murray Dick

The Typographic Medium by Kate Brideau

Power of Position: Classification and the Biodiversity Sciences by Robert D. Montoya

Picture-Work: How Libraries, Museums, and Stock Agencies Launched a New Image Economy by Diana Kamin

Cats, Carpenters, and Accountants: Bibliographical Foundations of Information Science by Wayne de Fremery

CATS, CARPENTERS, AND ACCOUNTANTS

Bibliographical Foundations of Information Science

WAYNE DE FREMERY

The MIT Press
Cambridge, Massachusetts
London, England

The MIT Press would like to thank the anonymous peer reviewers who provided comments on drafts of this book. The generous work of academic experts is essential for establishing the authority and quality of our publications. We acknowledge with gratitude the contributions of these otherwise uncredited readers.

This book was set in Adobe Garamond and Berthold Akzidenz Grotesk by Westchester Publishing Services. Printed and bound in the United States of America.

Library of Congress Cataloging-in-Publication Data

Names: Fremery, Wayne de, author.
Title: Cats, carpenters, and accountants : bibliographical foundations of information science / Wayne de Fremery.
Description: Cambridge, Massachusetts : The MIT Press, 2024. | Series: History and foundations of information science | Includes bibliographical references and index.
Identifiers: LCCN 2023030410 (print) | LCCN 2023030411 (ebook) | ISBN 9780262547598 (paperback) | ISBN 9780262377973 (epub) | ISBN 9780262377966 (pdf)
Subjects: LCSH: Bibliography--Methodology. | Information science. | Big data. | Artificial intelligence.
Classification: LCC Z1001 .F74 2024 (print) | LCC Z1001 (ebook) | DDC 010—dc23/eng20231103
LC record available at https://lccn.loc.gov/2023030410
LC ebook record available at https://lccn.loc.gov/2023030411

10 9 8 7 6 5 4 3 2 1

The pages that follow are presented with a deep sense of gratitude to the many people with whom I have had the privilege to work. You know who you are. Thank you.

The book is dedicated with love, and an even more profound sense of gratitude, to those who have sustained me while I have been at work: Hailey, Payden, and Sukja. You are my foundations, and everything, and more.

Contents

Preface

What do cats, carpenters, and accountants have to do with bibliography? How might bibliography serve as a foundation for the sprawling diversity of practices associated with the phrase "information science"? Partial answers will follow. But, at the outset, I wish to begin from the beginning and focus our attention on what organizes the cats, carpenters, and accountants: a list. It is easy to overlook. The role that it plays is ordinary—so much so that it can be difficult to notice. It asserts, as if it is a natural fact, that cats, carpenters, and accountants belong together, and the groups' members have some relation. It becomes the ground for what it foregrounds: the cats, carpenters, and accounts. Importantly, it is embodied, which is to say formulated materially by blank space and commas (in this case) with their distinctly shaped bodies and feet. It contributes to the descriptive function of my title, hinting, I hope, at the essence of the argument that I aim to put forward: enumeration (list making) and description, along with other bibliographical tools such as analysis and critique, serve foundational roles in the diverse and distinct practices of information science. Bibliographical formulations, like the list of my title and the title's descriptive function, can be difficult to see and consider because they are so ordinary and so obvious. Like the sheet of paper or screen that has this sentence, the list and how it serves a description are easy to see and hard to notice. My simple suggestion is that these bibliographical infrastructures be acknowledged and considered for the ways that they serve and, sometimes, frustrate us.

I use the word "us" hesitatingly. I have not always thought of myself as an information scientist, or as a bibliographer. Nor, as I describe in this book, do I feel the terms "bibliography" or "information science" comfortably encompass the plurality of what they index. For a decade, I taught Korean literature and topics related to the digital humanities in South Korea as part of a Korean studies department. My doctorate concerned Korean poetry, a degree that I paid for by typesetting books and having them printed at shops in Chungmuro, a district in Seoul. My BA is in economics, a degree that I helped to pay for by working for my parents' small construction and publishing businesses. The carpenters and accountants of my title reflect central themes developed in the pages to come concerning the built nature of bibliographical accounts and the importance of accounting for them. They also reflect my nostalgia for the smell of sawdust at my father's worksites, the taste of stamps licked and placed on mailers advertising one of my parents' new publications, and the quiet of the home office that my mother made in our basement while she handled the accounts for both businesses. A proven failure as a carpenter, I would eventually inherit my parents' publishing business, a business that I promptly led into financial ruin and have more recently attempted to resurrect as a software company. Now I direct an innovation center and work as a professor of information science and entrepreneurship in northern California, near the house where I grew up.

Like Kipling's cat, invoked by A. W. Pollard (1859–1944) in a 1932 issue of *The Library* featuring an important debate about the nature of bibliography, I have arrived at bibliography and information science by ever bargaining to walk by myself amid fields and communities of warmth and comradery far afield. The cats in my title are meant to acknowledge my own marginal position relative to whatever might be considered central to information science, but also, and more important, another central theme of the book: the paradoxically foundational work that bibliographers and bibliography perform at the margins of disciplinary practices that have come to formulate, however loosely, information science as a field.

The protagonist in Ch'oe Yun's "The Gray Snowman," a short story that I taught frequently in my Korean literature classes, similarly hesitates to use inclusive pronouns when describing her participation in a circle of pamphleteers in 1970s South Korea. The story describes how Kang Hawŏn, a young South Korean woman who had dropped out of college to work at a clandestine printshop, gains a sustaining sense of purpose while editing antiauthoritarian treatises, despite the fact that she never feels committed to the ideological views of the authors that she risks prison to edit, nor entirely included in the community of men printing screeds. A central tension is created by Kang's lack of loyalty to any particular program or ideology, programs and ideologies that were central to the identities of the men with whom she worked. It is to the work and the people that Kang is devoted, not their ideologies or any metric used to describe the impact of what they did together. Like Kang Hawŏn, I use the words "we" and "us" in what follows to suggest my sense of solidarity with people hard at work on questions associated with information and those questions' many ontological, epistemological, social, mathematical, practical, and personal challenges. "We" and "us" are meant to suggest the close kinship that I feel with the people with whom I have been privileged to work on challenges that have been framed, in one way or another, by information.

The challenges presented by this work are all the more profound, interesting, and important because information is so difficult to pin down as a thing or idea. Although the ends pursued are distinct, the work of working with information, I've come to believe, is similar to what is undertaken in other fields of practice organized, always loosely and often in self-contradictory formulations, around an object of study rather than a set of disciplinary methods. In my own experience, I have seen how "Korea" can organize the disciplined work of linguists, historians, literary scholars, anthropologists, economists, political strategists, trade organizations, and businesspeople, as well as, of course, librarians, bibliographers, and information scientists. Korean studies is a growing and vibrant field despite, and perhaps because, there is little consensus about what "Korea" might mean, even among those who self-identify as Koreanists.

In the contexts of specific disciplinary practices and objectives, different working definitions of "Korea," unproblematized assumptions, or both productively guide work. A working assumption of the arguments presented in this book is that information science can be considered a broad field of practice—one that is diverse, scattered, and, depending upon how one thinks about it, productively incongruent. Rather than assuming that information science is a discipline, scientific or otherwise, with a coherent set of overarching methodologies, I assume that "information" orients diverse kinds of work, done by diverse kinds of people in distinct places and times, with diverse aims and aspirations. When I suggest that bibliography is a foundation of information science, I mean to suggest that, as modes of thinking and action, it supports this diversity of work in an expansive field of activity, including debates over how the field's orienting object, "information," might be formulated, and if the field itself should even be considered a science.[1] I also mean to suggest that bibliographical theory and modes of attention provide rich intellectual legacies and ways of looking that can be employed by those working in some relation to the field. These are hypotheses that I support by describing the ways that bibliography sustains work in and enables reflection about a few regions of the broader field, primarily regions that might be associated with knowledge organization as it overlaps with information ethics and information retrieval if information retrieval includes, as Johnathan Furner suggests, research foci affiliated with data science.[2] These are hypotheses that I hope others will be provoked to test by considering the ways that bibliography supports work and reflection in other areas of practice that, due to the limitations of space and my own learning, I could not include.

Acknowledgments

Pieces and parts of this book have appeared in various publications in the past, including "The Future of Adan Mun'go's Digital Archive: Big Data and Artificial Intelligence at Adan Mun'go," *Muncha wa sasang* 3 (2018): 107–115; "Twenty-First-Century Pleasures—Some Notes on Form, Media Transformation, and Korean Literary Translation," *Translation Review* 108 no. 1 (2021): 78–103; "Copy Theory," *Journal of the Association for Information Science and Technology* 73, no. 3 (2022): 407–418 (with Michael Buckland); "Context, Relevance, and Labor," *Journal of the Association for Information Science and Technology* 73, no. 9 (2022): 1268–1278 (with Michael Buckland); "What Counts as Deep Learning in Korean Studies?" *Korean Studies* 47 (2023): 300–311.

INTRODUCTION

This book is a partial answer to a question posed by the librarian and information scientist Michael Buckland: What might be gained by reinvigorating bibliography? The question was premised on the idea that bibliography has faded into obscurity. The contrarian truth that I am pursuing is that bibliography could hardly be more integral to our intellectual and creative lives than it is now. A mode of intellectual and cultural accounting, bibliography serves a diversity of foundational roles in the sprawling field called *information science.* It seems to have passed into obscurity only because it has become so integral to our work that we do not notice how it supports what we do. I argue this while concomitantly suggesting that there is an urgent need to reinvigorate bibliography as we copy our many scientific findings and cultural heritages using recently developed systems of reproduction. Like all infrastructures, bibliography as an idea and a constellation of material practices undertaken across the academy and beyond needs maintenance. The need for this maintenance is urgent because we are building new representational structures and systems at such an accelerated pace that we are losing track of our ability to account for what we have built and the things that our systems are producing.

Bibliography?

It is a plain word that would seem to suggest little more than a list of books. But its plainness belies its many identities and the vital roles it plays in the sciences and humanities. A form of intellectual and material accounting with a long, rich history, bibliography is the study of representations and the practice of producing them. This is to be literal about the word *representation*. Bibliographers in their many guises establish what has been presented to us as records of what has been known, experienced, and desired. They work to make those presentations available again in other places and times. They enable us to assess the many facts, opinions, and expressions of aesthetic or emotional truth represented to us through an expanding array of media technologies. Bibliographers are responsible for assessing and safeguarding what has arrived in the present and for reproducing what has been deemed worthy to be made available elsewhere—the data of science, the expressions of culture, and the records of personal witness.

To say that bibliography concerns representation and representations is to say simultaneously that bibliography concerns data. This is because it concerns objects and ideas that have been taken as given. My assertion will give pause. An etymology will help clarify. Like the word "bibliography," "data" as it is used today conjures only a portion of what it can mean. We usually use this word to mean the bits and bytes arranged on the storage devices of our information systems. But its history associates data with a much wider variety of meanings. Data's etymology suggests gifts from neighbors, gifts from God, mathematical premises, evidence, and attributed values, in addition to bits and bytes. Bibliography as I explore it concerns what has been represented as gifts from God or neighbors, as mathematical premises and evidence of facts, as well as attributed values stored as bits and bytes. "Bibliography" as I proffer it concerns what has been considered worth making available in other places and times and the host of complex historical, epistemological, ethical, sociotechnological, and aesthetic considerations of copyists attempting to represent a friend's kindness or God's grace, the evidence and assumptions of calculation, and the bits and bytes that we value as data.

Understanding bibliography and data from these broader perspectives begins to crack open the paradox of bibliography's strange unobserved centrality in intellectual and creative work and why a new book about bibliography will contribute to the science of curating and communicating the information and knowledge that result from our intellectual and creative endeavors. It also helps put limits on what can be associated with bibliography. Because bibliography concerns objects that have been presented and represented, nothing arrives *ab ovo*, even when what is presented or represented is unprecedented. What might so arrive is left to philosophers and perhaps theologians, at least until they give shape to their thoughts in sound, on paper, or through electronic transmission, at which point their work also becomes bibliographical.

This book is part of a larger project that situates bibliography in medias res as a means for thinking and making in the arts and sciences. This book primarily addresses bibliographical enumeration and description. It explores counting and what counts, lists, and how things are related to one another through description. It argues that bibliography has many identities and that bibliography's plurality conceals the ways that it serves as infrastructure girding the diversity of work done under the many banners of information science. It lays out a case for understanding bibliographical enumeration as a tool for drawing material and conceptual boundaries that articulate objects and their contexts, as well as the usefulness of drawing up unfamiliar lists to test assumptions about what has established an object and its context. I show how a singular phenomenon has been enumerated differently by humanists and scientists to establish a plethora of textual objects and contexts that enable them to work productively at cross-purposes to understand what is called the *Archimedes Palimpsest*. As one example of the many integrative roles played by bibliography in information science, the book concludes with chapters showing that machine learning (ML) in general and deep learning specifically are forms of bibliographical description. I show how deep learning concerns representation and the ways that representations are put into relation with each other through recursive processes to form descriptions that provide useful predictions. I also demonstrate how bibliographical theory provides information and data scientists with rich intellectual legacies that can be used to theorize the descriptive powers of ML's increasingly ubiquitous and persuasive descriptions. Hinting at topics taken up in a companion volume concerning bibliography and humanistic practice (being prepared separately), I also suggest that ML and its outcomes are ripe for humanistic analysis and critique.

By positioning bibliography as shifting centers of gravity—as barycenters—articulated by the orbits of diverse disciplinary pursuits in information science, the book is polemical. It could be understood as a manifesto and be read to suggest that bibliography is at the center of modern information science. Indeed, it does suggest this, but only if "the center" is conceived of as the excluded middles in logic propositions—what is excluded by the idea that a proposition of logic *or* its opposite must be true.

This book urges that attention be paid to the useful paradoxes of representation and reproduction that inform us by forcing us to reconsider the logic of our propositions in the face of some material particularity, and conversely the particularity of our materials in the face of our logical propositions. The book is not a call to rush to any ramparts (real or imagined) under the banner of Bibliography. Rather, it urges a quiet revolution of attention and communion in diversity—one focused on the means that we use to pursue our intellectual and creative ends and how we account for what we take as givens and, by taking them, what we forgo.

KURT GÖDEL, YI SANG, AND BIBLIOGRAPHY'S ORDINARY TOOLS—ENUMERATION AND DESCRIPTION

In November 1930, a young logician living in Vienna named Kurt Gödel (1906–1978) submitted a paper for publication. The paper and the theorem that it proposes provide useful examples of how the ordinary bibliographical tools of enumeration and description can be used to reveal and test the foundations of the systems that we use to know and understand things. Gödel set out to test arithmetic and, by extension, classical mathematics. To do so, he made a list of mathematical propositions and assigned each a number. He then used these numbers, which are now called *Gödel numbers*, to describe classical mathematics as a system. To test the affordances of the system that he described, Gödel used a mode of paradoxical self-reference enabled by his numbering system to prove that formal systems, such as those of mathematics, will have true statements that are unprovable if the system can be shown to be complete. This head-scratcher is now commonly called *Gödel's first incompleteness theorem.*

Similar methods of enumeration and description have also profoundly shaped the computational methods that we theorize, build, and use in our work as information scientists. Alan Turing (1912–1954), for example, used a similar method of enumeration and description in his famous 1937 paper on computable numbers to suggest that there are definable numbers that are not computable. His paper acknowledges Gödel on its first page.[1]

Gödel's first incompleteness theorem and its relation to ideas such as Turing's help us to see how basic bibliographical practices and processes such as enumeration and description provided Gödel with a foundation for investigating the foundations of mathematics. Gödel, like Turing after him, could identify what is afforded by rudimentary systems of knowing such as arithmetic by enumerating mathematical propositions so that the list could be used, along with a useful paradox, to describe mathematical systems. Turing, whose abstract machine relies on the metaphors of printing, reading, and writing, would do something similar to describe the affordances of computation. We see how foundational thinking in mathematics and logic, themselves arguably foundations for the science of information, are formulated by bibliographical enumeration and description.

Roughly a month before Gödel's paper was published in December 1931, if the date on extant manuscripts is to be believed, Yi Sang (né Kim Hae-kyŏng, 1910–1937), a slightly younger, mathematically gifted Korean poet who had been trained as an architect, composed a poetic analog to Gödel's theorem: "Diagnosis 0:1." I risk presenting a poem in the introduction to a book about information science because Yi Sang's poetic analog to Gödel's incompleteness theorem reveals how bibliographical enumeration and description, even when presented in artistic forms, can help to diagnose systems articulated by foundational thinking that suggests, for example, that information science concerns "the transmission of . . . human knowledge in recorded form, centering on manipulation (representation, organization, and retrieval) of information"[2] rather than "knowing information."[3]

Like bibliography, especially those aspects of it that we examine most closely in this book—enumeration and description—"Diagnosis 0:1" is about list making and description. Conveniently, the poem also helps begin a conversation about the relationships between 0 and 1 that govern our digital technologies and the things that we count as information. Yi Sang's poem first appeared in Japanese in the July 1932 issue of *Chōsen to kenchiku*

(Korea and architecture) as part of a series of poems called *Kenchiku mugen rokumengaku tei* (Constructing bodies of infinite hexahedral angles). Born the year that Korea was formally annexed by Japan as a colony, Yi Sang composed in both Japanese and Korean. Gödel's paper diagnosed a central condition of formal systems—namely, that if a formal system can be proven complete, it will have true statements that are unprovable. Yi Sang's poem diagnosed poetry and a problem concerning a "patient's condition." Their diagnostic methods share a striking similarity, a method of self-reference similar to what the mathematician Georg Cantor (1845–1918) called a "diagonal argument."

Figure 0.1 presents a black-and-white copy of Yi Sang's poem as it was initially published.

And here is one way to render it in English.

◇ Diagnosis 0 : 1

An apparent problem concerning the patient's condition.

1 2 3 4 5 6 7 8 9 0 .
1 2 3 4 5 6 7 8 9 . 0
1 2 3 4 5 6 7 8 . 9 0
1 2 3 4 5 6 7 . 8 9 0
1 2 3 4 5 6 . 7 8 9 0
1 2 3 4 5 . 6 7 8 9 0
1 2 3 4 . 5 6 7 8 9 0
1 2 3 . 4 5 6 7 8 9 0
1 2 . 3 4 5 6 7 8 9 0
1 . 2 3 4 5 6 7 8 9 0
. 1 2 3 4 5 6 7 8 9 0

Diagnosis 0:1

26 . 10 . 1931

As above physician in charge Yi Sang

If we read the presentation of the whole numbers in Yi's poem from left to right and top to bottom, they suggest a formal system like those studied by Gödel. They also suggest a recursive rule for inference: divide the number in the line above by 10. Recursively performing this operation within

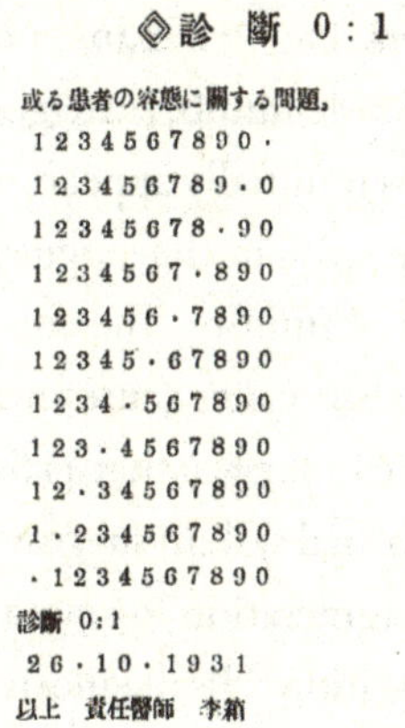

◇診 斷 0:1

或る患者の容態に關する問題。

1234567890·

123456789·0

12345678·90

1234567·890

123456·7890

12345·67890

1234·567890

123·4567890

12·34567890

1·234567890

·1234567890

診斷 0:1

26·10·1931

以上 責任醫師 李箱

Figure 0.1

"Diagnosis 0:1" in the July 1932 issue of *Chōsen to kenchiku* (Korea and architecture). Photo by author. Courtesy of the Seoul National University Library.

the system of integers in Yi Sang's poem produces a regression toward 0. This operation, where substitutions are performed along a diagonal, is like what was proposed by Cantor a few decades before Yi Sang and Gödel were born—something that makes it possible to compare infinities with a "diagonal argument" by testing their cardinality—the number of elements in their sets. Paradox is again useful as a diagnostic. One that is important for our purposes has been called *Richard's paradox*, after the French mathematician Jules Richard (1862–1956). As in Yi Sang's poem, Richard investigated the properties of numbers in relation to writing systems, and by extension language. Richard's paradox concerns sets of numbers, their definitions in language, relations to each other, and, like Cantor, recursive methods that create useful, if contradictory, statements. The sequence presented by Yi Sang's poem suggests these same things. It does this by suggesting an infinitely large set of real numbers produced by recursively dividing the number that preceded it by 10 and adding it to the list.

In this sense, Yi Sang's poem presents a formal system and a rule for transforming the symbols in the system that will arrive logically at 0:1, where 0 suggests the cipher toward which Yi Sang's regression progresses and 1 suggests an infinity that can be associated with an infinite set of real numbers. At the same time, the problem concerning the patient's condition also suggests a set of real numbers that, in a manner of speaking, can be thought of as larger than the set of whole numbers suggested by the poem's integers, "0 such that 1." As cryptic as it initially appears within the systems of poetic expression, 0:1 makes some sense in the language of set theory and discussions about different kinds of infinity. The contradiction 0:1, if the colon is read to equate 0 and 1, also makes sense in the context of Gödel's first incompleteness theorem. It can suggest that Yi Sang's diagnosis may be true, but it is unprovable in the formal system suggested by the integers presented in the poem. Yi Sang uses enumeration to craft a description of the problem concerning his patient's condition. His diagnosis of the problem suggests the vexing problem of accounting for the truth statements provided by the formal systems that Gödel critiqued, their authority in the sciences that we use to diagnose our conditions, and the infinities of descriptive statements that mathematics, science, and literature generate as information and knowledge. Rather than using his lyric to express or evoke an emotion, Yi Sang uses it to diagnose the logic of systems and the cultural logic that articulates what counts as a lyric poem. The argument that I pursue in the following pages is that, by attending to bibliography as recursive modes of enumeration and description, we can better diagnose some of the problems concerning our conditions.

At nearly the same time in the 1930s, from opposite sides of the world in mathematics and poetry, Gödel and Yi Sang use bibliographical tools of enumeration and description to diagnose the foundations of the systems within which they work. Helpful to an argument about the diverse ways that bibliography serves information science, they both suggest how bibliographical tools such as enumeration and description facilitate diverse investigations of logic, knowledge, knowing, and their limits. They each simultaneously assert the power of logical abstractions and the limits of logical systems. They do this in ways that presage how we use logical abstractions and their limits in the computational systems that have become essential tools for pursuing so many of our goals. They also acknowledge, each in his own way, the social and material circumstances that condition how the abstractions of formal systems can be communicated and experienced as human knowledge in recorded form.

Gödel acknowledges the social and material circumstances that help formulate his abstractions when he sends his paper for publication, as well as when he repeatedly registers, as his biographers describe, his disappointment that so many misunderstood what his proofs, in his opinion, meant. Yi Sang registers the social and material infrastructures of the publishing apparatuses that express the abstractions of his thinking in much of his work, including another poem in the *Kenchiku mugen rokumengaku tei* series called "Publication Law (Shupanhō)." His poem formulates quirky laws of publication. It also comments, it would seem, on the historical and oppressive Japanese publication laws that articulated the systems of print media in which Yi Sang could express himself. The "abstract" laws of publication described by his poem and the historically specific publication laws create a tangle of contradictions when it comes to becoming informed and knowing, at least according to the speaker of the poem: "Because, at the very center of things carried out against me, I couldn't know, while coming to know I know things, I couldn't not know something new again."[4] Coming to know, Yi Sang's speaker suggests, means knowing something new again. It is unclear if the something new has been learned before, or if the process of coming to know is one by which something new would be manifested repeatedly. We find a paradox, which might be called an *epistemic paradox,* to complement the set-theoretic paradox[5] articulated by "Diagnosis 0:1": "I couldn't know . . . I couldn't not know."

We also see that, despite or because of the paradox, something new is known. Bibliography attempts to account for both the new thing known and the self-referential processes that generate the new thing. It girds the work of attending to "recordable information and knowledge"[6] and the work of defining information and knowledge, "the enumeration and description of information-related phenomena"[7] and the "enumeration and description of ways in which people interact with information and with information-related phenomena."[8] It supports work in relation to what has been called a "reasonably stable consensus about the identity of those areas of concern that collectively form the central core of information studies."[9] These have been identified as "the nature of information, of information-related phenomena, and of human-information interaction . . . , the identities, purposes, motivations, intentions, needs, desires, and actions of people engaged in interaction with information"; the design and construction of "systems, services, and structures that help people to meet their goals when interacting with information"; and the development of "policies and institutions that enable and/or constrain people's interactions with information."[10] It also facilitates the work of information scientists who define "the scope of information studies and/or the information sciences . . . [as well as] the relationships among that broad category and its various overlapping subfields and related professions, such as library and information science, archival studies, social informatics, information retrieval, knowledge organization, information management, documentation, librarianship, [and, of course] bibliography . . . in very different ways."[11]

Apropos of the publication laws that Yi Sang describes and those that governed his ability to publish, especially their material forces as concepts and conceptual forces as material practices, bibliography also attempts to account for processes of knowing carried out against our will, a condition of being informed that information scientists, as well as media and social theorists, psychologists, and cognitive scientists of all types, have also pondered. This is to suggest that bibliography is the practice of accounting for conceptual-material processes "at the very center" of diverse ways of knowing, including the complex conceptual-material processes that shape the diverse ways that we as information scientists know. By attending to the ways that bibliography supports work in information science as infrastructure, we are better able to learn about the means that support the ends that we pursue with our learning, and to enumerate the boundaries drawn in our field between what counts as "a record of knowledge" and what counts as "knowing," for example. We can describe what is afforded by these boundaries and what is forgone.

BEGINNING TO ACCOUNT FOR THIS BOOK

The disciplinary and geographical scope of this book may seem impossibly large and strange: mathematics and computation, their limits and infinities; poetry composed in Japanese by a Korean architect stress-testing the cultural logic of poetry. I wish to emphasize that this book is not about mathematics, computation, or poetry. It is about information science and its bibliographical foundations. Specifically, it is about the powers afforded by drawing enumerative boundaries and creating descriptive shapes, the information that these shapes and boundaries produce, and the opportunities to become informed that they enable. I start with Yi Sang and Gödel because their divergent backgrounds and pursuits suggest the diversity of infrastructural roles that bibliography plays in creating, communicating, and accounting for information, knowledge, and their records. By focusing on how enumeration and description facilitate practice in information science, this book is rather narrowly cast in fact. It largely forgoes, for example, a discussion of bibliographical analysis and critique, a topic that I take up in a companion volume being prepared independently.

OUTLINE OF THIS BOOK

The chapters that follow are organized in two parts. The chapters in part I focus on enumeration and those in part II on description. Collectively, the chapters incrementally build a case for understanding how bibliography is foundational in information science, integral to artificial intelligence (AI), and a potent critical tool for reflecting on information science and AI. Building on each other, they may present a slow climb for those most interested in how bibliography girds current practice in ML or data science, for example. For those wishing to descend rather than climb the arc of the book's argument, I have written the final chapters so that they can be read first if desired. Previous chapters can then be consulted to understand how I arrived at a particular point of view.

Chapter 1 enumerates a definitional framework for understanding how bibliography provides an infrastructural foundation for information science. It is modeled on the work of the Welsh cultural critic Raymond Williams (1921–1988), who used his investigation of words and their histories to frame and support his cultural critiques. I borrow Williams's playbook, and a few of his keywords as well. Exploiting the histories of words such as "bibliography," "copy," "enumeration," "description," "data," "document," and "information," I use a list of keywords to establish my exposition about bibliography and advance my arguments about its importance as infrastructure in information science.

Apropos of its topic (lists), chapter 2, "Lists as Infrastructure: An Infrastructural Inversion," begins with a list enumerating some of bibliography's many names. It helps unravel the apparent paradox of my claim that bibliography girds information science even if few information scientists would call themselves bibliographers. I argue that the apparent paradox of bibliography's importance and concomitant invisibility can be usefully unraveled by understanding bibliography's marginality. It is marginal in at least two senses. It is marginal in the sense that bibliography is only rarely an end in itself. Most often, bibliography is a means serving what is considered a more powerfully important end. Focused on the ends that we pursue, we often overlook how ordinary bibliographical infrastructures serve as means.

Bibliography is also marginal in the old sociological sense of having multiple identities and affiliations. This is one reason bibliography has had so many names and has faded from view. Except for certain kinds of engagements with manuscripts and printed books, bibliography is infrequently known as bibliography. It has gone by many other names instead: "epigraphy," "chirography," "diplomatics," "informatics," "data management," and "data science." Understanding bibliography's marginality in these two senses helps to illuminate bibliography as a shared infrastructure embedded in all kinds of investigatory and creative actions in information science and beyond. By revealing bibliography as a difficult-to-see infrastructure that is integral to much of what we do, chapter 2 participates in a form of "infrastructural inversion." This is what Geoffrey Bowker and Susan Leigh Star call efforts to reveal the many invisible material and categorical infrastructures that support work.[12]

Chapter 3, "The Powers and Pleasures of Lists and the Coordination of Context," continues my discussion of lists. It focuses on their pleasures and powers and explores some of the human motivations that can be discerned by assessing what has been brought within the boundaries of lists and what has been left beyond their boundaries as context. It also looks at the objective force of lists and what is lost to lists and the contexts that they create when objects are not counted. As ordinary as many of them seem, lists, I argue, create and coordinate contextualizing systems as banal as our shopping lists and as sophisticated as those created by John Dewey (1859–1952) and Paul Otlet (1868–1944). They articulate horizons, generate order, and constitute power. Lists gird the methods and practices of information scientists considering what has counted as knowledge and ways to organize, retrieve, and transmit it. They do this by delineating context and enumerating relationships that serve to formulate recorded knowledge and manners of knowing.

Assessing lists and the contexts they delineate, like noticing infrastructures, is difficult because lists and contexts in their ordinary utility are difficult to see. Like electricity before the room goes dark and the ice cream in the freezer begins to melt, we don't notice how important lists are until they don't work. In chapter 4, "What Unfamiliar Lists Afford," I force the equivalent of a blackout. To assess the ordinary enumerative infrastructures used in information science, I shut off the power to the ordinary ways that we make lists by considering two that are alien to our ordinary practices. I juxtapose two perspectives that help assess our ordinary activities by allowing us to be informed by what is unfamiliar. The first comes from the Baltic-German biologist Jakob von Uexküll (1864–1944), who asks that we seriously investigate the subjectivities of nonhuman creatures to understand how they may enumerate the objects in their worlds. The second is from the media theorist Ian Bogost and the philosopher Graham Harman, who ask that we speculate seriously about objectivity by earnestly considering what it might be like to be a thing. These two unfamiliar perspectives help to reveal how integral our ordinary enumerative practices are to information science and thus make my case for the importance of bibliographical enumeration as productive infrastructure.

Chapters 5 through 11 concern bibliographical description. Chapter 5, "From Enumeration to Description: Knowledge Graphs and Graphing Knowledge," provides a bridge between the discussion of enumeration in part I and the discussion of description in part II. It uses the unusual enumerative perspectives described in chapter 4 to consider the descriptive infrastructures that support information science. Drawing out a rudimentary knowledge graph and then assessing how it has been drawn, the chapter suggests the recursive nature of bibliographical practice, as well as how bibliographical description graphs knowledge by delineating enumerative equivalences while also affording an ability to assess how knowledge has been made known by graphs and other descriptive tools.

Chapter 6, "Describing the Archimedes Palimpsest," provides concrete examples of the recursive descriptive capabilities of bibliography introduced in chapter 5. It suggests how bibliographical description can constructively formulate knowledge for a variety of groups by describing how communities in the sciences and humanities have described the Archimedes Palimpsest. I show how bibliographic description works to coordinate what counts as information for various communities of investigators. The Palimpsest is useful because its complexity as an object helps show how diverse kinds of descriptive data, documents, and texts function as descriptions that inform disparate ends pursued by humanists and scientists.

Chapter 7, "A Descriptive Account of Biological Metaphors in Bibliography," gives an account of some of the powerful ideologies inscribed in knowledge by descriptive bibliographic practices. I consider the close intellectual and ideological affinities between bibliographical description in the Anglo-American bibliographical and Western biological taxonomic traditions. My aim is to begin to account for some of the ideas and practices that have formulated bibliography by presenting a description of how natural history, biology, and biological metaphors have suggested ideological equivalences to bibliographers in the Anglo-European bibliographical tradition. Recounting an early twentieth-century debate that took place among members of the British Bibliographical Society, I show how thinking in biology has shaped bibliographical thinking that served to bind living and nonliving entities into chains of being. Understanding that the ideologies of science and biology have formulated bibliographical description allows us to consider anew what we inscribe when we draw up equivalences and iterate them as descriptions that formulate bodies and bodies of knowledge. Even if it cannot provide prescriptive recommendations for how to create descriptions, a revitalized bibliography offers the opportunity to pause reflectively to consider what has been inscribed with records of human knowledge, how those inscriptions have been accounted for, and what new descriptive accounts might inscribe as we fashion them. As chapter 6 emphasizes, because bibliography provides a means for assessing what has been taken as given when knowledge is recorded and described, including the ideological and conceptual frameworks that shape knowledge creation, it is vital to revitalize bibliography so that we can better consider what has been made to matter and the ways that lives matter.

The remaining chapters continue my description of bibliographical description and how it matters by illuminating the infrastructural role that bibliography plays in AI. I advance my argument about the foundational roles played by bibliography in information science by building a case for understanding the newer kinds of recorded knowledge that we call big data and AI as forms of bibliographical description. I also suggest that the critiques of bibliographical description as an inductive science leveled by bibliographers such as D. F. McKenzie provide a useful framework for a critique of current ML methods.

In chapter 8, "New Bibliographical Description," I begin laying out the contours of my argument that ML is a form of bibliographical description by describing conceptions of bibliographical description as it was pursued by so-called New Bibliographers in the early twentieth century. The chapter focuses on inductive methods imagined as "instruments of thought and investigation" that could "co-ordinate" facts and enable "constant causes"[13] to be traced. Predating moves by Claude Shannon (1916–2001) and others who would productively enumerate messages to exclude their linguistic meanings, the New Bibliographer W. W. Greg (1875–1959) famously wrote: "The bibliographer is concerned with pieces of paper or parchment covered with certain written or printed signs. With these signs he is concerned merely as arbitrary marks; their meaning is no business of his."[14] This manner of enumerating boundaries to isolate arbitrary marks as bibliographical objects distinct from what the marks might signify within linguistic or historical context, Greg believed, would allow ordered data collection and a scientific means for generating more accurate predictions about the past and what caused the bibliographical facts that he wished to understand. As I show, the descriptive methods employed by the New Bibliographers to produce what they believed to be accurate predictions about the past are not dissimilar to methods and assumptions of information scientists working to make predictions with various forms of ML.

Chapter 9, "Bibliographical Description, 'Printers of the Mind,' and the Sociology of Texts," presents a close reading of D. F. McKenzie's essay "Printers of the Mind," a powerful critique of New Bibliographical assumptions and methods that lays the foundations of McKenzie's theory of bibliography as the "sociology of texts."[15] The core of McKenzie's criticism is focused on how New Bibliographers enumerated what counts as bibliographical evidence, their inductive methodologies, and the accuracy of the predictions their descriptive procedures produced. He seizes on statements like Greg's suggesting that bibliographical evidence be limited to the arbitrary physical marks on paper and parchment. He also takes aim at the inductive methods of Greg and his cohort for arriving at descriptive bibliographical statements. Then, with pointed clarity, McKenzie shows how wrong the descriptive statements of New Bibliographers could be for not incorporating more diverse kinds of evidence and more readily using deductive methods to devise descriptive statements. In a manner not unlike how Gödel and Yi Sang laid bare the limits of the systems they described, McKenzie exposed the limits of New Bibliography by suggesting that bibliography attempt to enumerate its assumptions and descriptive systems. He points out that enumerating the line between arbitrary marks on paper and what they might mean is itself a meaningful act that affects the results of bibliographical investigation. McKenzie's critique was a theoretical move to make the simple coordinate system of New Bibliography into a multidimensional apparatus for investigating bibliographical facts and, importantly, how bibliographical facts came to be counted as facts. It was a move to illuminate the ways that linguistic and social systems entangle bibliographers with their evidence and the apparatuses that they use to create it. As I suggest in the conclusion of chapter 8, the bibliographical opportunities and challenges that McKenzie articulates are similar to the challenges and opportunities faced by information scientists building AI systems now.

Chapter 10, "Models, Modeling, and the Socialization of Data," continues to build my case for understanding big data and AI as forms of bibliographical description. Where chapters 8 and 9 focus on bibliographical data collection and description as they might serve literature and history, chapter 10 looks at how data as computer-stored information are organized, modeled, and graphed. It suggests that the work of model building by data modelers, ontologists, and those graphing knowledge stands in synonymic relation with the work of New Bibliographers, and the models that contemporary modelers craft as bibliographical descriptions socialize what has been taken as given (data) in manners analogous to how literary bibliographers socialize literary texts as new critical editions. Juxtaposing approaches to textual editing proposed by Jerome McGann that argue for celebrating the "extreme concrete particularity"[16] of literary art with the theory and practice of data modeling, ontology building, and knowledge graph creation, I suggest that data scientists have produced bibliographical powers through their enumerative and descriptive work that confers the ability to infer personal intentions from private, nonliterary texts with the kind of extreme concrete particularity that McGann associates with literary works. Borrowing and reiterating language from the discourse associated with bibliographical control, I show how bibliographical descriptions developed by information and data scientists facilitate the ability to line up data so they march to one's command (descriptive control) to achieve desired ends (exploitative control).[17] "Bibliographical control" is a phrase most commonly associated with the ability to retrieve appropriate textual resources in a library. Here, I suggest that it can be reconsidered in broader frameworks of power articulated by powerful bibliographical descriptions that serve as forms of AI.

Chapter 11, "Data Science and Machine Learning as New Bibliographical Description," presents a similar case for understanding the inductive approaches of the New Bibliographers and those modeling data with ML technologies as homologous. A brief description of data science and its relationship with big data and AI as these relate to ML situate my contention that, like the descriptive models formulated by ontologists, data modelers, and those who graph knowledge, the inductive approaches of those creating machine-learned models correspond with the approaches of New Bibliographers such as W. W. Greg and Fredson Bowers (1905–1991). Both concern the collection of documentary data to enable the creation of inferencing tools—models that can be used as an ideal against which to compare additional historical data.

Chapter 12, "Bibliography and the Sociology of Data," suggests how the critiques of bibliography as an inductive science leveled by scholars such as McKenzie can help to account for current ML methods. Citing Bertrand Russell, McKenzie writes that induction is "a mere method of making plausible guesses."[18] The "plausible guesses" enabled by machine description have become powerful, but they remain "guesses" afforded by bibliographical power, and what the librarian and information theorist Patrick Wilson (1927–2003) called "descriptive" and "exploitative" control.[19] As many have shown, the inductive guesses produced by ML, as powerful as they might be, can be powerfully wrong and profoundly exploitative. The chapter concludes with a description of creative, counterfactual imagining as a means of assessing, critiquing, and, we might hope, more equitably wielding the exploitative powers of bibliographical description in its newer technological forms.

The book closes with a coda called "Our 'Age of Algorithms.'" It is in the form of a list, of course. The short list that I present hints at the expansive challenge of presenting to future generations the bibliographical objects and processes that inform us now. Manuscript, xylographic, print, electronic, and other reproductive technologies, together with the generative choices of those operating them, have articulated systems that present to us what we might take as given. My discussion concludes by wondering how we do the work of re-presenting what we have received and taken as the givens of our experience to those who may wish to be informed by them and what we have assumed. How, as a bibliographical imperative and large unanswered question in information science, do we build systems that can better account for the great variety and complexity of our rapidly expanding bibliographical universe? How do we present again this universe with all its documents, data, and the many ways that both are described by models leveraged to suggest the books we might read; the movies we might see; the fastest way home from work; whom we might date; how judges might determine our sentences; how human intelligence agencies might do their dance with social media companies to assess threats to voting machines and the idea of democracy; how climate scientists might describe the health of our planet; how oncologists might diagnose cancers; and how epidemiologists might predict the spread of viruses like those that cause COVID-19?

Although lengthy, this list is a litotes, an understatement. It excludes so many of the ways that we present our world again and how these representations inform individual and collective action. But having demonstrated that bibliography is a vital material and conceptual infrastructure that supports the large variety of disciplinary ends pursued in information science, questions like these are easier to articulate. We can better describe and diagnose the problems concerning our condition as information scientists. This is true even if our descriptions must remain incomplete and our diagnoses our best judgments. Recognizing bibliography as a vital infrastructure in information science, we realize that our descriptive and enumerative practices profoundly shape how we experience our culture, spend time with our families, and determine with whom we might build them; calculate and recalculate our sense of justice; attend to our own health and the health of our communities; and safeguard our ideas, our ideals, and even our planet. This illustrates the importance of bibliography, even if it crosses into the vexing form of melodramatic statement peculiar to our time. It suggests some of what can be gained by revitalizing bibliography, and some of what might be lost if we do not.

1 A LIST OF KEYWORDS

The critic Raymond Williams used his investigation of words and their histories to establish his arguments and cultural critiques. His book *Keywords* (1976, 1983, 2015) became a touchstone for what has come to be called *cultural studies*. The list of keywords in this chapter advances my argument about bibliography's importance as an infrastructure in information science by establishing some of the keywords of my exposition. My list also demonstrates the elementary bibliographical practice of drawing up lists. Like the list of keywords that comprise Williams's book, keywords of interest here can be contemplated slowly or browsed quickly and returned to later as needed. One of the many powers of lists is that they make arguments. In fact, a great deal of the argument in this long chapter can be gleaned from a list of the keywords that I will describe and define next:

Bibliography
Copying, reproduction, recursion
Enumeration, description, analysis, critique
Communication and information
Understanding and defamiliarization
Hypothesizing
Science, technology, art
Technical and boundary objects
Culture
Affordance
Data, documents, information (again)

Texts
Information science
Books
Kinds of power

BIBLIOGRAPHY

The definition of *bibliography* proposed by D. F. McKenzie frames many questions that will occupy us in the pages to come. McKenzie proposes in his well-known book *Bibliography and the Sociology of Texts* that bibliography is the "discipline that studies texts as recorded forms, and the processes of their transmission, including their production and reception."[1] Bibliography for McKenzie concerns representation and reproduction, copies and copying. Bibliography, McKenzie emphasizes, concerns texts as *recorded* forms. *Records*, as the word's etymology suggests, concern evidence about past events, accounts and stories, discussion, negotiation, agreement, judgment, and, in several circumstances, the authority of a court or office.[2] *Recording*, the verb, concerns remembering, repeating, declaring, and bearing witness.[3] Records are re-presentations and witnesses that serve as evidence and enable memory. Bibliography accounts for how these recorded forms are created and communicated. Defending the word *bibliography* as a term equal to the many modes of operation that he envisioned, McKenzie writes, "[Bibliography] even has a new felicity in its literal meaning of 'the writing out of books,' of generating new copies and therefore in time new versions."[4] I argue that the literal meaning of *bibliography* still has a new felicity several decades after McKenzie gave his Panizzi Lectures in 1985.

Texts, he suggests, are data given shape through sociotechnical processes: "I define texts to include verbal, visual, oral, and numeric *data*, in the form of maps, prints, and music, of archives of recorded sound, of films, videos, and any computer-stored information, everything in fact from epigraphy to the latest forms of discography."[5] This formulation of bibliography as the study of texts as data woven into social forms is both narrow and quite expansive. It productively narrows bibliographical investigations to studies of data, while simultaneously expanding it to include the myriad ways that data are woven into social forms. It focuses attention on the ways that bibliography is attentive to our assumptions since, as I will describe later in this chapter, we can think of data as things taken as "givens." McKenzie's definition also affords a way of thinking that allows us to entertain the immutability of certain ideas and material objects, even as we attend to the dynamics of how they are fashioned to matter in material, personal, and social interactions.

McKenzie's definition also helps clarify the close relationship between the older bibliographical arts of attending to how manuscript or printed books have been made, circulated, and received and the newer bibliographical arts of attending to how data in their myriad social forms are constituted, circulated, and received. Bibliography as the study of data in myriad media forms is useful at a time when data, taken to mean what is stored as bits and bytes by computational systems, are granted many shapes and considered central to many of our intellectual, commercial, and creative activities. It makes clearer that bibliography as the study of data in social forms is integral to organizing and assessing what we create and capture with our increasingly diverse and sophisticated variety of documentary apparatuses. It clarifies that bibliography is fundamental to documenting and understanding the social forms that these data take as they are articulated by an ever-expanding variety of expressive sociotechnological modes. It also elucidates how bibliography attends to the ways that these data are received (i.e., made computable in systems and meaningful by individuals and communities).

To say that bibliography—defined here as the creation and copying of data in social forms and the study of how this is done—is integral to many of our intellectual and expressive pursuits is not to collapse the distinctions between them. Scientists continue to pursue science. Humanists continue to pursue the humanities. Posthumanist scientists and their alter egos, scientist posthumanists, continue to pursue their hybrid aims. Nor is it to wish that the rich heritages of innumerable communities associated with specific material modes for socializing the "gifts" and "givens" of experience be amalgamated. The opposite, in fact, is desired. The aim of attending to bibliography as the socialization (the copying) and sociology (the study of the copying) of data is to understand and celebrate this diversity so that we can better attend to the diverse ways that we take things as givens, as data, and weave them into the texts that we use in our diverse pursuits. Bibliography does not collapse disciplinary distinctions or usurp disciplinary territory because it sits between academic disciplines as means to disciplinary ends rather than the ends themselves. Although seemly paradoxical, this is true even of bibliography's own diverse disciplinary formulations since bibliographical means have served diverse bibliographical ends.

This focus on means helps explain why bibliography is marginal in the sociological sense of having multiple and mixed identities. It also helps reveal bibliography as a foundational infrastructure in information science. Bibliography's particular identities in information science, as in the humanities and even bibliography's own diverse historical formulations, are formulated by those attending to the particularities of the records that they or their community believe to be important for their goals. In chapter 2, I list some of the many names that bibliography has had to suggest bibliography's many identities. The list is long, I explain, because bibliography often adopts names associated with specific methods of accounting developed to support specific goals. For example, bibliographical methods that help to establish facts derived from manuscript books in their best-known shape, the codex, is known as *codicology*. Bibliographical work done to explicate older methods of writing, especially historic handwriting, is known as *paleography*, a word whose Greek and Latin roots suggest "old" (*paleo*) and "to write" (*graphy*). Bibliographical work to establish predictive truths derived from the bits and bytes that we call data is often called *data science*. As I show in the chapters ahead, understanding bibliography as having many identities helps reveal how bibliography serves as a foundational infrastructure for the many ends pursued in information science.

COPYING, REPRODUCTION, RECURSION

If bibliography concerns the copying of data as texts in social forms, how might we begin to think about copying and copies? It would be an understatement to say that oceans of ink have been spilled on the topic of copies. An obsolete definition of the English noun *copy* suggests the abundance of these oceans and provides a place to begin our discussion. *Copy* is associated with French and Latin predecessors that suggest "abundance, plenty, and multitude."[6] The lifeless lack of originality commonly associated with the term *copy* today is, to borrow a phrase attributed to the Scottish poet John Barbour (1320–1395), cause for "teres full gret copye."[7] I use the word in ways that resuscitate some of its obsolete meanings and etymological history since more contemporary uses of the term elide the profound individual, social, and technical complexities of reproduction I wish to accentuate when I use the term. As I use it, *copy* is meant to connote complex processes of production and reproduction that formulate objects so that they are suitably similar to others. It also connotes the results of those productive processes, where two objects that occupy space and time differently are made to be suitably similar to one another. As Ben Jonson suggests in *Magnetick Lady* (1640), "The copie does confound."[8] He means that abundance confounds us. I take advantage of the ironic puns created by the modern sense of *copy* to suggest that we ought to be more confounded by copies and how they, as particular phenomena, become determinate through interactions that make them suitably similar to other phenomena. If we recognize the plenty of their particularity and the motivations that they record and embody, much can be found in the ordinariness of copies.

Surely one reason that copies have lost their sense of human connection, abundance, and intimate relation is that modern technology has made copying so easy. The methods of copying available to us have never been more powerfully abundant. This seems true even as a sense of loss has attended our ever more powerful means to reproduce what we care about. The well-known bibliophile, translator, and cultural critic Walter Benjamin (1892–1940) has famously formulated this loss as an "aura": that which is lost in mechanical reproduction. The aura of a work of art, he suggests, cannot be copied by mechanical technology. By around 1900, he writes, "technical reproduction had reached a standard that not only permitted it to reproduce all transmitted works of art and thus to cause the most profound change in their impact upon the public."[9] The ability to copy mechanically "substituted a plurality of copies for a unique existence,"[10] Benjamin argued. In addition to transforming art and the public's relation to it, Benjamin asserted that mechanical reproduction has the power to rend traditions by interfering with the authority of objects "imbedded in the fabric of tradition."[11] The threat to tradition was twofold and concerned the presence of objects, Benjamin believed. Mechanically reproductive technologies such as photography, he argued, reproduced aspects of an object through enlargement or other manipulations in ways that were not previously possible, thereby alienating the object from previous customs and habits of perception. Mechanical reproduction also makes copies of objects available where the objects themselves could never have been present. "The cathedral leaves its locale to be received in the studio of a lover of art," he writes, adding that "the choral production, performed in an auditorium or in the open air, resounds in the drawing room."[12]

Whether one is persuaded by Benjamin's arguments or not, bibliography is how we struggle with issues related to authority and authenticity, tradition, and the epistemological opportunities and costs of our expanding abilities to copy and compare. Myriad questions swirl around the centuries of collective work necessary for the creation of our latest reproductive machines, most of which is obscured by the banality of hitting the equivalent of "cmd" or "ctrl-C" on a keyboard. Corresponding kinds of collective work were similarly obscured by the ubiquity of "new media" (especially film) that fascinated Benjamin and made him fear, like Yi Sang's speaker in "Publication Law," the ways that we come to know against our will. My use of the word *copy* is meant to suggest the copiousness and complexity of modern copying and the many reasons why we should revitalize bibliography as a means to account for copying and copies more carefully.

One way to account for copies and their complexity is to recognize that recursive processes play an important role in their production and reproduction. To copy is to employ "repeated procedure[s] such that the required result at each step is defined in terms of the results of previous steps according to a particular rule."[13] This is to adopt a key definition from logic and computer science to suggest that recursion is also a key term in bibliography. As I argue for understanding it, bibliography accounts for the repeated procedures, results, and rules that produce copies. It also provides tools and modes of thinking for manipulating recursive procedures that create copies, lists, descriptions, and other accounts that serve the ends of information scientists as infrastructure. This is to emphasize that bibliography engages the abstractions of logic and mathematics, especially as they inform our work as information scientists *and* the material particulars of the informative objects, processes, and forms of knowledge that we make use of and study.

Recognizing that bibliographical analysis accounts for recursion and bibliographers use recursive procedures to make their accounts also helps to suggest some of the ways that bibliography productively operates as infrastructure in spaces between the subdisciplines of information science, as well as betwixt information science and many other fields. As my discussion of Yi Sang and Gödel in the introduction implied, recursion provides a useful way to think about how bibliography supports what are considered diverse disciplinary ends—the logic of mathematics, its use in the empirical sciences, and modes of human expression such as poetry. In the context of information science, recursion is a key to understanding bibliography as a foundational infrastructure.

Recursion and recursive processes, based as they are on previous events, point toward the material and theoretical a priori conditions that constitute what counts as information. They point, for example, toward constitutional ideas like the belief that there can be a set of all possible messages in a communication system, an idea that enables Claude Shannon, as we will discuss in more detail shortly, to propose information as a measure of those messages. They also point toward physical objects like copies of Shannon's famous paper "A Mathematical Theory of Communication," as well as other papers, library catalogs, and databases that describe Shannon's paper. Bibliography serves information science as a means of accounting for the recursive practices that create and cause physical artifacts like Shannon's paper to recur. It also serves information science as a means of accounting for records made to persist and recur by means of computational technologies that use recursion.

ENUMERATION, DESCRIPTION, ANALYSIS, AND CRITIQUE

In a quirky, recursive turn, recursive patterns can be seen in the overlapping bibliographical processes that serve as infrastructure for information science. As bibliographers in the Anglo-American tradition suggest, these can be summarized as enumeration, description, analysis, and critique.[14]

Recursion as a key term, therefore, also helps to organize a discussion of these methodological processes.

Enumeration To enumerate is to count or ascertain a number of items. *Enumeration* also means to list. This semantic overlap between counting and listing again suggests how bibliography functions as a tool used across disciplines. Bibliography accounts for people, objects, and processes by counting and listing. It serves to theorize and establish the boundaries that define description and the scope of analysis, as well as the ways that we can understand descriptions and analyses. In other words, it delineates what counts, as well as the contexts of counting. As I describe in more detail in chapter 3, lists are etymologically associated with "borders," especially the borders of clothes and textiles. The word *list*, therefore, is not entirely distant from the weaves suggested by the etymology of the word *text*. Lists articulate the borders of our texts by enforcing some selective criteria. As the well-known bibliographer D. C. Greetham suggests, enumerative bibliographical accounts are always selective. Enumerative and systematic bibliography, as bibliographical processes for listing are sometimes called, "use some system of selection."[15] Here and in what follows, Greetham's definitions of enumeration, description, analysis, and critique will provide context for my definitions of the same terms.

Because enumerative systems of selection articulate what count as objects and their contexts, enumeration concerns complex logical, epistemological, and even political considerations. Enumerating books of poetry contained in a particular library, produced by a particular publisher, and coming from a particular region, for example, requires that a system for distinguishing between poetry and fiction be enumerated and that the library, the publisher, and the region be defined geospatially and temporally. The same can be said for enumerating copies of what counts as a single book of poems in a library, produced by a publisher and made in some region. Enumeration requires enumeration. We encounter a quirky, recursive loop that resembles what Gödel and Yi Sang orchestrated. We are confronted again by logical, epistemic, and political issues. What counts as a region? A publisher? A library? By establishing what counts and how it will be counted, enumeration is foundational work because it establishes conditions that articulate what counts as a record of knowledge and rules for making inferences and discerning what counts as knowing, as well as the politics of both.

Description Descriptions are statements, often produced through enumerative processes. Associated with the need to bring relationships among objects into view, they aim to express "the essential nature of a thing or concept."[16] Because they are so closely related, the distinction between description and enumeration often must be drawn performatively. I draw these lines according to the ends pursued. Enumeration and lists concern means of counting and delineating what counts. Description concerns attempts to put what has been enumerated into relations, often in pursuit of a desire to inscribe what can be considered essential.

Greetham helpfully contextualizes my definition. The aim of bibliographical description, as he writes, has often been to "prepare an account of the 'bibliographical nature'"[17] of a book: "Conventionally, descriptive bibliography will address the so-called *ideal copy* of the book (that version intended by the printer for release after all determined corrections had been made) and will list not only the contents but also the format (folio, quarto, etc.), and the collation (the make-up of the folded gatherings of the book), together with any peculiarities—e.g., canceled leaves, misnumbering, etc."[18] To revitalize bibliography so it can better account for data and the many social shapes that they take, bibliographical description as it has been articulated in relation to printed objects can be expanded. Rather than having bibliographical description concern an ideal copy of a printed book as it might be evinced by collation and cancels, I suggest bibliographical description concerns the much larger category of objects that serve as data and their social shapes. Although the category of objects addressed by bibliographical description is broader, my definition of *description* maintains thc useful tension inherent within description as Greetham describes it. This useful tension is created by the descriptive aim of arriving at a categorical ideal through comparative procedures that attempt to account for the sociomaterial particulars of objects.

Analysis Analysis concerns the tensions of critical study. As the term has often meant since the seventeenth century, it ponders resolution and demonstration, reflection and exposition. To come to resolution and provide demonstrations, as well as reflections and expositions, analysis often concerns dissolving things into their elements to solve a problem, as its earlier Latin and Greek associations suggest.[19] As is the case with distinctions between enumeration and description, distinctions between analysis and description pose enumerative difficulties. The *Oxford English Dictionary (OED)* suggests that to analyze is "to differentiate or ascertain the elements of (something complex) in order to determine its structure or nature, and hence to explain or understand it; to examine closely and methodically for the purpose of interpretation."[20] We see how enumeration is also nested in the idea of analysis. The end pursued by analytical enumeration is to determine the relationships that articulate an entity's "structure or nature." Analysis more generally seeks to make the structure or nature of an entity plain in the service of interpretation, which is how I attempt to distinguish analysis from description. Description pursues the aim of enumerating relationships that can serve as statements. Analysis assesses enumerated relationships in the service of resolving interpretative problems. As before, I draw lines between description and analysis performatively according to the ends pursued.

Greetham's description of bibliographical analysis again instructively contextualizes mine. His definition also helps reveal the scientific aspirations of bibliography as a humanistic practice and its close ties to the history of science and, of course, information science. Copies of books enumerated by bibliographical lists, Greetham emphasizes, "are products of a particular manufacturing or technical process." The study of those processes "for printed texts is usually called analytical bibliography."[21] As he describes, *analytical bibliography* is used synonymously with *New Bibliography*. The "newness (in the mid-twentieth century)" of the New Bibliography practiced by W. W. Greg, Fredson Bowers, and others was, as Greetham suggests, "consciously seen as a 'scientific' reaction to the older enumerative, book-collectors' bibliography, as well as to the impressionistic, nonscientific editorial methods of an earlier period."[22] As he summarizes:

> Analytical bibliography begins as a form of "history of science" or "history of technology" and involves the consideration of all those stages of printing

> (from paper, ink, and type manufacture to the habits of the compositor, the press-work, the binding and so on) that might tell us something about how the text reached its present condition. It is therefore closely related to historical bibliography on the one hand (sometimes referred to as the "biology of books," the study of them as part of a Darwinian evolution of a manufacturing process) and descriptive bibliography on the other.[23]

Greetham's description of analytical bibliography emphasizes the scientific analysis of printed books as it might be facilitated by the history of science and technology. Analysis aims to resolve interpretative problems related to the "structure or nature" of a printed book by assessing "all those stages of printing (from paper, ink, and type manufacture to the habits of the compositor, the press-work, the binding and so on) that might tell us something about how the text reached its present condition." As before, my definition of *bibliographical analysis* broadens the scope of objects that can be assessed to include not only the technical processes and manufacturing procedures employed to create printed books, but also the technical processes and creative procedures employed to create and socialize data. My use of the terms *analysis* and *analytical bibliography* will similarly suggest a close relationship between histories of science and technology and analytical bibliography. Indeed, ideas from science and technology studies shape my discussions in many of the chapters to follow.

Criticism and critique Criticism and critique concern acts of judgment, making and acting on decisions and, of course, the plethora of ethical, moral, aesthetic, and other kinds of contingencies that attend judgment. Ideally, if never completely in any practical sense, criticism and critique are informed by rigorous enumeration, description, and analysis. Practically rather than ideologically, entities of all kinds provide a record, in more or less detail, of the critical judgments associated with them due to their historical interactions with other entities. Understanding bibliographical critiques as acts of judgment reveals how they are woven into the foundations of information science. For example, as we will discuss shortly, we find mechanisms for bibliographical judgment built into Shannon's seminal paper in information science, "A Mathematical Theory of Communication." This definition of *critique* will help elucidate how bibliographical critique is built into new artificial intelligence (AI) technologies such as deep learning and how these technologies are being used to automate critique in both productive and dangerous ways.

COMMUNICATION AND INFORMATION

Influential concepts of communication have suggested that communication concerns reproducing a message produced initially in one place at a different location. Information has many meanings, of course, several of which I will discuss in more detail soon. In the formulation that I consider now, information is a means of measurement that facilitates the reproduction of messages with sufficient fidelity for a given purpose. It concerns copies and copying, and hence bibliography. Recognizing that information and communication are (given Shannon's mathematical and highly technical sense of these terms) formulated by bibliographical processes is key to understanding the role that bibliography plays as a foundation of information science. To suggest how bibliography is woven into the foundations of information theory, I perform what might be thought of as a close reading of Shannon's landmark 1948 paper. My argument is that his theory of communication employs methods and modes of thinking that correspond to the fundamental bibliographical methods and modes that we have just discussed—enumeration, description, analysis, and critique.

Reminiscent of Yi Sang's poem, Shannon's paper reduces "the problem" concerning human communication to an engineering and ultimately mathematical one. Like Yi Sang's, Shannon's diagnosis can also be written with a 0 and a 1. Unlike Yi Sang, Shannon was much clearer about the relationship between 0 and 1 in his diagnosis. For Shannon, the idea that 0 can be considered distinct from 1 provided a diagnostic means for measuring messages. This new means of measurement helped to establish information science as a science and is fundamental to the representative and reproductive processes associated with our digital age.

Shannon's use of the term *communication* suggests its etymological roots while simultaneously isolating *communication* from *meaning*. The etymology of the verb *communicate* in English suggests the idea of making "common to many," of "imparting."[24] By the fifteenth century, an object made common could be referred to as a *communication*.[25] These concepts were extended in the seventeenth century to suggest lines of communication and their related physical facilities, and then, in the twentieth century, to media such as "the press and broadcasting."[26] As we will see, the fundamental problem of communication as Shannon conceived it concerns how to make an object—a message—common to entities inhabiting different places or times. As I have been suggesting, Shannon's problem is also a central concern of bibliography since bibliography produces and attempts to account for messages inhabiting different places and times.

To focus his analysis on communication as an engineering problem, Shannon excluded a discussion of what a message might mean. A message may have meaning, Shannon famously writes, but the meaning of the message is unrelated to the "fundamental problem of communication."[27] "The fundamental problem of communication," he suggests, "is that of reproducing at one point either exactly or approximately a message selected at another point. Frequently the messages have *meaning*; that is, they refer to or are correlated according to some system with certain physical or conceptual entities. These semantic aspects of communication are irrelevant to the engineering problem,"[28] which concerns reproducing a message created in one place at a different location with sufficient fidelity.

We notice that Shannon's definition of *meaning*—a reference to or relation with some physical or conceptual entities made possible by a system—is significantly different from the etymology of *meaning*, which suggests the idea of intention, having something in mind, of holding an opinion.[29] We also notice how Shannon engineers the word *communication* for his purposes, which is to describe a communication channel mathematically. Information becomes the measure that he uses to put entities in mathematical relation to each other and to a theorized channel.

To make his measure, Shannon first selects one meaning from the semantic range of communication: message. He imagines a set of discrete messages as things or events selected from a finite set of possibilities. Then he equates "message" with information: "If the number of messages in the set is finite then this number or any monotonic function [a function that preserves or reverses order] of this number can be regarded as a measure of the information produced when one message is chosen from the set, all choices being equally likely."[30] From there, having selectively reduced *communication* to mean *message* and *message* to mean *information*, he suggests that information is a measurement—specifically, a logarithmic measure of likelihood that he calls "entropy." Information is a measure meant to suggest the certainty of an event occurring in an information channel. Events concern a message being sent from the information source or how likely that message was to be affected by noise, which is defined, like messages, as a random variable. High uncertainty equates with high amounts of information. Low uncertainty is equated with low quantities of information.

Shannon was not the first to suggest limiting the connotations of communication to solve the communication problem of enacting similar physical phenomena at two locations. Ralph Hartley (1888–1970), whose work Shannon builds upon and cites, had begun envisioning communication as a physics problem rather than one concerning intentions twenty years earlier.[31] Of course, others since Shannon would articulate information differently, as we will discuss shortly.

This discussion of what Shannon meant by *information* and *communication* is important for our discussion of bibliography as being foundational in information science because it shows his foundational theory of communication to be essentially a theory of representation and reproduction, which is to say again a theory of copying.[32] Importantly, the four essential bibliographical modes just described facilitate Shannon's theory. His diagnosis of his engineering problem uses methods that correspond with bibliographical practice. He starts with a list: information source, message, transmitter, signal, noise source, received signal, receiver, message, and destination. This list delineates the boundaries of his discussion and his description of the engineering problem.

The repetition of *message* in the list describes the engineering problem. It also begins to articulate a pattern that bibliographers and literary scholars will recognize, one that creates a sense of sameness despite change, of transposition. This is especially true after they realize that *transmitter* and *receiver* can be called the same thing—a "discrete transducer."[33] It is also a pattern that neatly summarizes copies, the idea that they are somehow the same although in alternate places, that they are *transpositioned*. The literary term for this pattern is *chiasmus*. Its basic definition is "a placing crosswise" that produces an ABBA pattern.[34] Although he may not have had chiasmus in mind while working on his mathematical description of communication, Shannon's enumeration and description of his engineering problem present a nice account of copies and their chiasmatic structures, as shown in Figure 1.1: information source, message (A), discrete transducer (B)—signal, noise source, received signal—discrete transducer (B), message (A), and destination.

Indeed, Shannon's work also neatly describes what bibliographers would call bibliographical analysis and criticism (critical editing). As we have discussed, bibliographical analysis concerns dissolving things into their elements to solve a problem, especially as this concerns the material and technical details of reproduction. Critical editing concerns critical judgments about whether and how to reproduce an object. In Shannon's model, these bibliographical processes are couched in the language of transmission. The variables presented by materials are what he calls "noise": "Since, ordinarily, channels have a certain amount of noise, and therefore a finite capacity, exact transmission is impossible. This, however, evades the real issue. Practically, we are not interested in exact transmission . . . , but only in transmission to within a certain tolerance."[35]

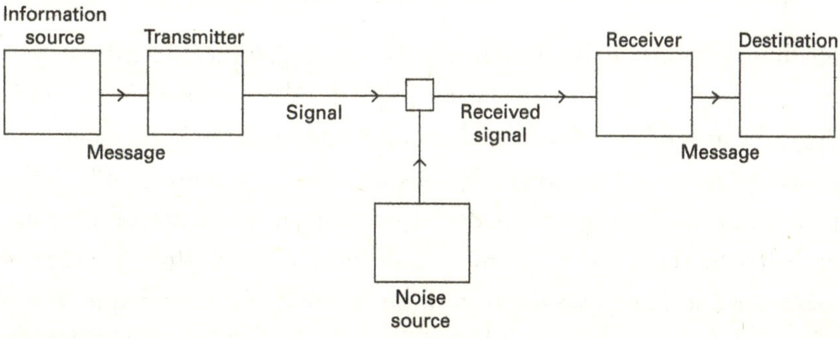

Figure 1.1

Schematic diagram of a general communication system. Based on figure 1 in Claude Shannon, "A Mathematical Theory of Communication," 381, accessed January 3, 2020, https://archive.org/details/bellsystemtechni27amerrich/page/n9.

As with copies, no two messages can be exactly the same when transposed in space or time. The real issue, Shannon asserts, is to create a copy of a message that is sufficiently similar to its source for a given purpose. The aim in telephony, for example, is to reproduce vibrations in the air made by someone speaking in California with sufficient fidelity that air vibrating in Seoul can be considered usefully, if not materially, equivalent to the air in California. His attention to the materials of reproduction (the channel), along with his measurement for information, suggest to him methods for editing messages based on the probabilities of events occurring while messages and materials interact. Shannon's editorial solution was typically to intervene in messages, to edit them, by repeating part or all of them. His aim was to ensure that what was created as message "A" would be usefully similar to its copy, "A," even though the process (B [transduction] [signal-noise-signal] [transduction] B) of creating them in alternate locations entailed their transformation. Information theory as Shannon created it is bibliographical in its concern for copies and its methodological approach to them—enumeration, description, analysis, and critique. This is true even before we address the bibliographical task of attending to the many copies of Shannon's paper that have been made available at many locations around the world through processes that his paper helped to make possible.

UNDERSTANDING AND DEFAMILIARIZATION

Shannon's definition of communication, although it excludes a discussion of the semantic meaning of the messages that he considers, hints paradoxically at a fundamental condition for understanding. *To understand* comes from the Old English *understondan*, literally to "under stand."[36] The preposition *under* suggests a spatial relationship and the action of standing, or of having standing, the primary definition of *stand.* Thus, the verb *to understand*, although we use it to mean "perceive the intended meaning of words"[37] or to "infer something from information received,"[38] has, as its precondition, the experience of "standing" in relation to words and other objects. Shannon's definition of communication concerns the ability to have some standing in relation to phenomena that can be considered usefully the same as another, even when particular material manifestations of each must necessarily be distinct. In Shannon's model, the sender of a message can believe that the phenomenon being created at the other end of a transmission channel is usefully the same as the message sent; the receiver of a message can understand the message received as being usefully similar to the sent message. Understanding, however, is distinct in this case from perceiving an intended meaning.

Shannon took an unfamiliar stance that helped him create a theory for how to produce usefully similar phenomena at alternative places or times. By excluding a discussion of meaning and formulating them as discrete sets of things or events, he made messages unfamiliar. This intellectual move to defamiliarize ordinary things and ideas was one made by many in diverse realms of thinking in the twentieth century. Shannon's unorthodox stance with relation to messages, like Greg's and Bowers's stances toward arbitrary marks as bibliographical objects (discussed in the introduction and chapter 8), is similar to stances taken by modernist artists such has Yi Sang and linguists who studied and advocated for modernist poets such as Roman Jakobson (1896–1982). Each was interested in isolating experiential phenomena from semantic meaning.

Major aspects of their collective projects, especially as they concern art, are often summarized by the word *defamiliarization* (*ostranenie*): the practice of making the familiar unfamiliar. The purpose of defamiliarization, textbooks tell us, "is to impart the sensation of things as they are perceived, not as they are known."[39] This term will be important for us since some foundational definitions of information science are premised on distinctions between information as it is perceived and "knowing information."[40] It will also be important because defamiliarization can be a powerful tool for evincing processes and phenomena that are ordinarily difficult to see, such as the infrastructural roles played by bibliography in information science. As I have done with my reading of Shannon's theory of communication, in many of the chapters that follow, I will attempt to defamiliarize what are now ordinary ideas and practices in information science to suggest how bibliography sustains and supports them. The hope is that my defamiliarizing moves will position us to perceive the foundational roles played by bibliography in information science and provide "standing" to reconsider what are now ordinary ideas and practices in the field.

HYPOTHESIZING

"Hypothesizing" has to do with "placing,"[41] often as part of an attempt to have standing with and an understanding of phenomena. That is, like understanding, hypothesizing concerns positioning. Since bibliography is centrally concerned with copies and how they and their observers are positioned in space and time, hypothesizing is also central to bibliography. Indeed, bibliographers such as D. F. McKenzie argue for understanding bibliographical description as a means for hypothesizing rather than a means of presenting unequivocal truth statements. By attending to the infrastructural roles that bibliography plays in information science, my argument is that we are better able to hypothesize information science and our work as information scientists. Being reminded by bibliography that lists position boundaries is useful. Understanding that description is positional and selective is similarly useful, especially when descriptions become so familiar that they obscure potentially useful positions from which to view phenomena. As Donna Haraway has suggested, positioning is a "key practice grounding knowledge organized around the imaginary of vision."[42]

Arguably, as the etymology of hypothesis suggests, positioning is a key practice that grounds knowledge organized around the many imaginaries used to situate ourselves in relation to what is taken as recorded knowledge, what is known, and what is assumed as common sense. By situating and resituating us through enumeration, description, analysis, and critique, bibliography helps hypothesize information science and what has been imparted and held in common as knowledge and its records.

SCIENCE, TECHNOLOGY, ART

Despite recent historical shifts that would more strictly delineate them, the etymologies of *science*, *art*, and *technology* suggest that the words can be used somewhat interchangeably. Since I use them in this way, a few words about their etymologies will help avoid confusion. *Science*, its etymology suggests, has to do with study, reflection, and knowledge. These practices, products, and states of being have been known as arts since they had to do with skill and craft, which is also at the root of technology: the study and knowledge of *tekhne*, craft, or art.[43] As I have been arguing for understanding it, bibliography serves as means for scientific, artistic, and technological ends. As a means of serving these ends, bibliography has been and continues to be a science, an art, and a technology. Attempts have been made to draw hard boundaries through bibliographical methods of investigation and understanding using the terms *science*, *art*, and *technology* in the past. This is another reason why bibliography has had so many names. Using the terms *art*, *science*, and *technology* interchangeably facilitates my argument that by recognizing the art and science of bibliography as a technology for understanding what has been represented to us, we can better account for what we take as given while we pursue our various intellectual and creative ends as information scientists.

TECHNICAL AND BOUNDARY OBJECTS

One reason that bibliography can be positioned as an art, a science, and a technology is that it crafts and assesses technical objects. These objects are things that enable measurement and facilitate the drawing of boundaries. Whether they are modes of thinking or the material characteristics of objects, technical objects are the yardsticks that facilitate inquiry. They are the scales of music, the metrics of poetic meter, and the many measures used to articulate how we know historical people and the periods that they inhabited. They are card catalogs, metadata and encoding standards, and deep learning frameworks. The sociologist Madeleine Akrich suggests that technical objects "participate in building heterogeneous networks that," as embodied measuring tools, "bring together actants of all types and sizes, whether human or nonhuman."[44] They *coordinate* description by enumerating relations through measurement. The Hinman collator as a technical object, for example (although it is less frequently used now), still supports beliefs about Shakespeare because it provided information about differences between the folios by usefully ordinating them. It did this by enabling two folios to be situated proximately and by facilitating the double vision demanded by comparison. The card catalog organized librarians, library resources, and patrons in relation to Shakespeare and other authors through its standard size and standardized inscriptions. International standards for encoding digital documents, such as Unicode, coordinate the relationship between what I type into a window when I search for Shakespeare and the results that are retrieved.

As Akrich suggests, each of these technical objects points to an "end, a use for which they have been conceived . . . [;] they also form part of a long chain of people, products, tools, machines, money, and so forth."[45] As I emphasize, bibliography both documents and creates these technical objects as it contends with accounting for the copiousness of copies and considers how to usefully produce more.

Once technical objects are stabilized, as Akrich describes, they fade from view. They become so common that they can be hard to see and begin to function as what Susan Leigh Star, an important thinker in many fields,

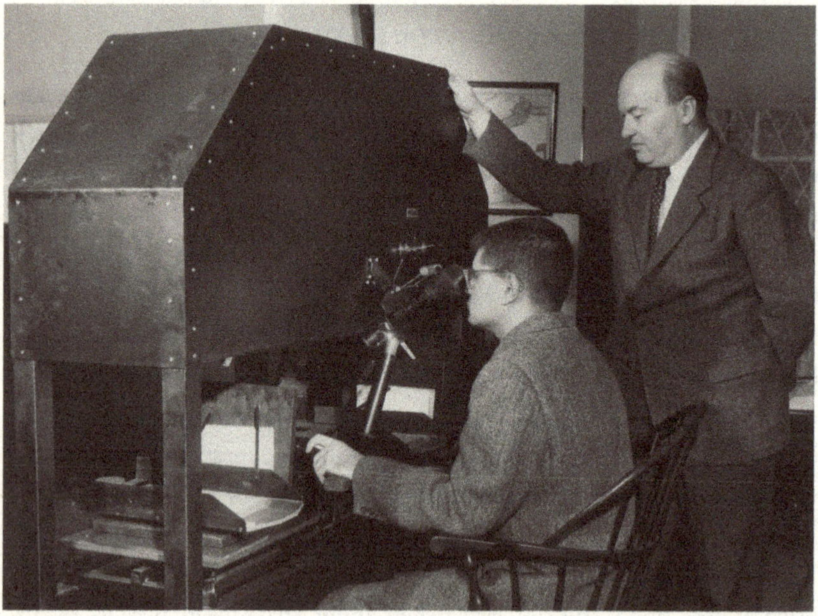

Figure 1.2
Fredson Bowers supervising graduate student Matthew Bruccoli working on a Hinman collator. Albert and Shirley Small Special Collections Library, University of Virginia.

including sociology, information science, and science and technology studies, would call "boundary objects." Boundary objects, as Star conceives them, are objects that support collective work as infrastructure. Technical objects functioning as infrastructure "become instruments of knowledge" by enabling data to be drawn from networks and transmitted elsewhere.[46] An electrical grid, for example, enables people to turn on lights in their homes but also enables an economist to measure the relationship between the cost of energy and the gross domestic product of a country. Unicode enables us to type digital documents, but it also allows computational linguists and statisticians to make, as I describe, claims about lexicography, the evolution of grammar, collective memory, the adoption of technology, the pursuit of fame, censorship, and historical epidemiology. This "conversion of sociotechnical facts . . . into facts pure and simple," such as units of energy and measures of gross domestic product, depend, as Akrich describes, "on the ability to turn technical objects into black boxes." As technical objects become "indispensable," they "also have to efface themselves"[47] and simply become part of the infrastructure that enables work and thinking.

Incredulous bibliographers of all varieties study technical objects and the black boxes of boundary objects because they mistrust "pure," "simple" facts. They need to know what is in the black boxes not only because they wish to know the impure complexity of facts, but also because they are responsible for maintaining the boxes. Bibliographers of all types are among the most stubborn defenders of facts because they have cultivated a deep sense of the complexity of objects and the systems that produce them. As Akrich says:

> Disciplines such as economics and technology studies depend on the presence of a self-effacing apparatus that lies outside their domains. Economists extract one kind of information from technical objects, technologists another. They are able to do this because such objects function in stable situations. The introduction of a new device can thus be assimilated—for example, by economists—into the price/consumption relationship. The economy is not cut off from technology; there is no radical disjunction.[48]

Bibliographers are marginal figures who reside inside and outside disciplinary domains. They are domain experts who double as construction workers, personal assistants, data entry personnel, and software engineers to stabilize and maintain "situations" and the technical objects that produce the boundaries that formulate the objects we use and study. Marginalized as infrastructure, technical objects, if not always those who maintain them, have great political "strength." They not only "change social relations," but perhaps more powerfully, "stabilize, naturalize, depoliticize, and translate these into other media."[49] Understanding that bibliography studies and enacts these "translations" helps to elucidate the vital role played by bibliography as infrastructure in information science, as well as the need to revitalize it as an art and a science.

CULTURE

Another reason that bibliography can be positioned as an art, a science, *and* a technology is that it is performed as an expression of culture. Because it concerns the ways that we account for the things that we and our communities care about, bibliography expresses and reproduces commonly held beliefs about what counts and should be accounted for, even if the methods of accounting and the communities doing the accounting can be described differently using our contemporary nomenclature as scientific, artistic, or technological. Of course, bibliography also expresses the choices of the individuals and communities doing the work of accounting, as well as the material, historical, and cultural contingencies that articulate the circumstances within which they work. As before, we can gain some standing in relation to these complexities by looking at the history of the English word *culture*. A comparison with the word for culture used in East Asia will also helpfully position us to see how bibliography serves as a means supporting the many ends pursued by diverse communities, including the many that we associate with information science.

Raymond Williams suggests that the word *culture* is one of the most complicated in the English language.[50] He traces its origins to the Latin *colere*, meaning "inhabit, cultivate, protect, honor with worship," and *cultura*, which suggests "cultivation or tending," through French forms of *cultura* that passed into English by the early fifteenth century to mean "husbandry, the tending of natural growth."[51] It is not until the eighteenth century that *culture* came to describe the three broad categories that we associate with the word's current meaning: "a general process of intellectual, spiritual and aesthetic development," "a particular way of life," and "the works and practices of intellectual and especially artistic activity."[52] *Culture*, then, has come to suggest the ways that we tend, protect, and honor the things we make and care about, as well as how we cultivate ourselves to inhabit the places where we live. Bibliography in its enumerative, descriptive, analytical, and critical modes expresses and contributes to culture as we understand the newer and older senses of the term. As enumerative, descriptive, analytical, and critical processes, bibliography helps us organize the things we care about and assess how we have used them to cultivate our sense of ourselves and the world. This is true whether these things are the products of processes associated with art, science, or the technologies that we use to do both. Bibliography in its expressive modes also helps us to think about how we might wish to represent the things we care about to others, whether the things we care about are the findings of science, a well-known or recently rediscovered work of art, or the specifications of a machine that fascinates or is crucial to our livelihoods.

In contemporary East Asia, *culture* is now frequently represented with the following: 文化, pronounced *munhwa*, *bunka*, and *wenhua* in Korea, Japan, and China, respectively. The glyph 文 can be traced to oracle bone and tortoiseshell inscriptions of the Shang or Yin dynasties (ca. 1300–1100 BCE), although its meaning at that time is uncertain. The character also appears in the *Analects* and other Chinese classics, where it frequently suggests notions of "culture," "civilization," and certain kinds of embellished writing.[53] By about 100 CE, we have a formal definition of 文 that includes the following definitional description: "文 *wen* [consists of] intersecting strokes, representing a criss-cross pattern."[54] The glyph 化 suggests "transformation" or "becoming." Although the two-syllable word 文化 is likely of recent coinage in East Asia and is roughly equivalent to its English counterpart in contemporary use, the individual characters of the compound are helpful for thinking about copies, copying, and their relationships to culture.

Although *culture* would probably not be articulated in this way by many in East Asia, the idea that culture has something to do with the emergence and transformation of crisscrossing patterns is a useful abstraction for thinking about bibliography and the ways that we might articulate its identities to help us better account for our new computational and communicative technologies. Remembering the recursive transformations and diagonals created by Kurt Gödel and Yi Sang, as well as the crosswise pattern that Shannon created to solve his communication problem, we recognize with more ease that the expressions of culture in our age, whether they be artistic or scientific, manifest and use crisscrossing patterns and their transformations. Placing manifestations of the things that we care about crosswise with the many forms taken by their copies informs because juxtaposition enables us to be surprised by the useful similarity of copies and the copiousness of their particularities. Serendipitously, by placing the definitions of the English word *culture* crosswise with rough equivalents from other regions of the world, we return to the important idea that copies concern transposition. We see more clearly how copying also concerns hypothesizing since hypothesizing, like copying, concerns positioning. And we find again the figure of chiasmus, a placing crosswise with the crisscross pattern: 文. When I use the term *culture*, I will have these definitions and ideas in mind since they help reveal the bibliographical infrastructures that serve as means for the many ends pursued by information scientists.

AFFORDANCE

Words and concepts like *culture*, as I hope to have just shown, have affordances. They allow certain kinds of actions and ways of thinking, and disallow others. Like culture, affordance is an especially important but complex concept when juxtaposed to bibliography because affordances are what bibliography in its enumerative, descriptive, analytical, and critical modes account for and create. The transitive verb *afford*, from which James Gibson fashioned the noun *affordance*,[55] means "to give, provide, contribute; to grant, bestow, confer (a privilege, benefit, gift)."[56] Bibliography accounts for what has been conferred and, while doing so, creates something with what has been granted.

Obsolete meanings of *afford* include "to further, advance; to promote the well-being of (a person or thing); to perform, carry out (a task, order, etc.);

to accomplish."[57] Affordances then can help to achieve an end, as well as promote the well-being of a person or thing. Bibliography as a means to many ends, like affordances, helps to achieve them. Indeed, *afford* can mean "to have means." Affordance is thus semantically aligned with what bibliography provides as means to ends. Bibliography is also aligned, in what it produces through its operations, with the notion of affordance as utility in the social sciences, which concerns means and their benefits. Benefits associated with certain means are determined transactionally. Their measure is called *value*. In psychology, largely after Gibson, an affordance is "a property of an object or an aspect of the environment, esp. relating to its potential utility, which can be inferred from visual or other perceptual signals; (more generally) a quality or utility which is readily apparent or available."[58] In economics, marginal utility is the extra benefit (value) that an extra thing provides. Bibliography makes these benefits evident through the many ways that they can be drawn up and plotted. Doing so, bibliography in its enumerative, descriptive, analytical, and critical modes affords measures of utility, of value. Understanding the close relationship between bibliography and affordance also positions us to better see how bibliography supports the ends pursued in information science. A few additional descriptions of affordance will help to suggest how.

Leah Lievrouw, a professor of information studies at the University of California at Los Angeles, suggests that affordances have three key qualities, which include both the physicality of substances and what they come to mean in systems and to individuals: "They are functional (enable and constrain action), relational (link actors with the world of objects), and learned (repertoires of uses and relations with objects gained through experience according to culturally and socially sanctioned concepts and values)."[59] The philosopher Rom Harré emphasizes that affordances are context-dependent complexes. "Affordances are contextually sensitive, dispositional attributes of complexes,"[60] Harré writes with Jean-Pierre Llored. As examples, he presents wolves and elk in the Yukon: "'Wolf-walking' is an affordance of a local 'wolf-ice' system, but not of an 'elk-ice' system. . . . What the system affords a wolf as an action program there is no such a program available to an elk."[61]

The book artist and bibliographer Johanna Drucker interweaves and puts these qualities and complexes in motion through a dialectic that attempts to account for "the physical, substantial aspects of production as well as the abstract and system-defined elements."[62] She proposes that materiality combines the two in a dialectic relation where "neither presence as substance nor absence as difference can ever be left fully alone."[63] Each, she suggests, "continues to irrupt into the domain of the other and interfere in the happy play of signifiers and in the dismal insistence on self-evident appearance."[64]

Bibliography is recursively imbricated in this dialectic, reflecting through its accounts what has been learned, put in relation, and made functional. It accounts for "the force of stone, of ink, of papyrus, . . . of print," of "wolf-ice" and "elk-ice" as they are recorded by complexes that support "wolf-ice" and "elk-ice." It does this while also accounting for how these forces function as signifying activities "not only because of their encoding in a cultural system . . . but because these values themselves come into being on account of the physical, material properties of . . . different media."[65] At the same time, bibliographers fashion the records that they create with the "durability, scale, reflectiveness, richness and density of saturation and color, tactile and visual pleasure"[66] of their materials in mind because what they afford will either enable or disable the ends that they and their communities pursue and wish to enable for others.

Understanding that bibliographical practices and products enable and constrain action, link actors "with the world of objects," and produce repertoires of use according to culturally and socially sanctioned values provides a useful way to think about how bibliography functions in information science.[67] Similarly, realizing that what is afforded by bibliographical work and its outcomes continually interrupts and interferes in objects' "dismal insistence on self-evident appearance," and the "happy play of signifiers" positions information science in a productive place for thinking again about objects and signifiers and how to most usefully interrupt and interfere in their relationships.

Cognizant of the tangled relationships among the affordances that bibliography accounts for, employs, and creates, when I use this term, I will be careful to situate the word etymologically and in the dialectics that Drucker, Harré, Lievrouw, and Gibson collectively articulate. Thus, when I use *affordance*, I will enumerate which repertoires of use have been sanctioned by the materials and ideas that I am discussing, what actions they enable or disable, and which relationships they create or clarify.

DATA, DOCUMENTS, AND INFORMATION (AGAIN)

If for us affordances concern the complexities of giving, providing, bestowing, and conferring, data will concern the complexities of what has been taken as given, provided, bestowed, and conferred. You will notice my imperfect attempt at chiasmus. Enumerating data in a list with documents and information will help clarify what I mean by *data* and further elucidate the foundational roles played by bibliography in information studies.

Attempts have been made to untangle concepts of documents, data, and information. Johnathan Furner, for example, has done work to establish a relationship between data and documents. He presents a detailed historical survey of the use of the word *data* in English (which has informed my use of the word) and then uses his survey to argue for the idea that data should be thought of as documents. He shows that *data* is derived from the Latin *datum*, "that which is given,"[68] and relates what he calls the "nine lives of data."[69] He organizes these roughly chronologically. Data are related to gifts in classical Latin (100 BCE–200 CE); a very early form of *metadata* (glosses indicating when and where something was written, ca.100 BCE); gifts given by God in the writings of clergy and poets such as John Donne (1572–1631) in the late sixteenth/early seventeenth century; geometric premises in the works of Euclid translated into English in the second half of the seventeenth century; mathematical premises related to geometric principles by the start of the eighteenth century; epistemic interpretations related to "any premise," also by the eighteenth century; attributed values related to the rapid growth of statistical and social science work with their plethora of numerical tables in the second half of the nineteenth century; bits in the mid-twentieth century; and "distinctions, differences, 'lacks' [*sic*] of uniformity," most recently by Luciano Floridi at the University of Oxford.[70] Furner concludes from this review that "a dataset is made up of documents; and the dataset is a species of document."[71] Others, such as Michael Buckland, would not draw such categorical taxonomic distinctions between data and documents.[72]

One reason why it is difficult to know whether and how to draw distinctions between data and documents, especially in relation to information, is that neither constitutes "simple, positive material facts,"[73] as Drucker has said of documents. Given shape by sociotechnical processes, data are formulated in relation with what informs the people and mechanisms that record them. At the same time, distinctions can be, have been, and perhaps should be drawn. To draw them in a way that reveals the bibliographical infrastructures of information science, we can define data, documents, and information as functions of each other in their interactions—interactions that we come to understand within specific procedures for hypothesizing. To suggest the usefulness of thinking about data, documents, and information in this way and how it helps to understand bibliography as a foundational art in the science of accounting for and creating data, documents, and information through enumerative, descriptive, analytical, and critical practices, we can compare conceptions of documentation and experimentation presented by two important thinkers from the twentieth century, Niels Bohr and Michel Foucault. Part of this discussion will loop us back to our discussion of communication.

In a 1958 essay, Bohr describes experimental procedures associated with atomic objects in this way:

> By . . . "experiment" we can only mean a procedure regarding which we are able to communicate to others what we have done and what we have learnt. . . . In actual experimental arrangements . . . it is also essential to remember that all unambiguous information concerning atomic objects is derived from the permanent marks—such as a spot on a photographic plate, caused by the impact of an electron—left on the bodies which define the experimental conditions.[74]

We see that Bohr is thinking here of experiments as bibliographical procedures that concern accounting for and communicating what has been done, as well as how the results of certain procedures might be informative. An *experiment* is a procedure that enables researchers to become informed by arranging the interaction of phenomena with the materials of a specifically designed apparatus. The information that is gained, according to Bohr, is derived from the "marks" left on the bodies that "define the experimental conditions"—through their interactions. The consequence of this, as Bohr and others since have understood, is that the experimental apparatus for measuring phenomena is difficult to untangle from the phenomena, the nature of the information created in the process, or the observer of the arrangement. Nor can it be freed from the communicative procedures that enable learning, procedures that are also enmeshed with the ideas that led to the experiment in the first place. It is a tangle, or to use Harré's term, a "complex." Documents, data, and information are entangled in Bohr's conception of an experiment. Importantly, we can use what seems like a Gordian knot by recognizing that data, documents, and information are serving alternative functions in relation to each other within the experimental apparatus.

Where this tangle of data, documents, and information in modern sciences is often used to produce facts in support of theory, modern historians and cultural critics frequently use the tangle to suggest theories for refiguring facts and how we should understand them. The literary scholar Stephen Owen quipped in a lecture that I attended that Aristotle would call the products of modern historians "poetry." He meant that modern historians are fond of fashioning Aristotelian plots—recognizable beginnings, middles, and ends—from documents and the complexities of time.

Michel Foucault suggests something similar. In *The Archaeology of Knowledge and Discourse on Language* he writes, "The document . . . is no longer for history an inert material through which it tries to reconstitute what men [*sic*] have done or said, the events of which only the trace remains; history is now trying to define within the documentary material itself unities, totalities, series, relations."[75] He suggests that methods used by historians to inform us about the past are no longer concerned with concrete documents as traces of action in the past, what they might say, and whether these utterances should be considered trustworthy. Rather, he suggests, "history now organizes the document, divides it up, distributes it, orders it, arranges it in levels, establishes series, distinguishes between what is relevant and what is not, discovers elements, defines unities, describes relations."[76]

As I describe, documentalists such as the Belgian Paul Otlet (1868–1944) make a science of dividing up, distributing, ordering, and attempting to distinguish what is relevant in documents. In Foucauldian terms, modern librarians and information scientists are remarkably like modern historians. The difference, of course, concerns the ends being pursued. For modern information and data scientists, the work of dividing up, ordering, and distributing is an end pursued in support of the library patron, a historian perhaps, or a business client attempting to use data to tell a story—indeed, anyone working to fashion meaningful plots and useful ways of knowing from what has been enumerated, organized, and disseminated. This is to suggest that documents as evidence of historical phenomena can be used to formulate history as much as report on it. Documents are evidence of facts that can inform. Depending on how they function as methods for informing, they also constitute facts.

I use a moving middle ground to situate my thinking in relation to scholars such as Furner, Buckland, and Foucault, bibliography's own history, and Bohr's notion of complementarity by enabling key terms such as *data*, *document*, and *information* to articulate the shifting ways that they function in particular interactions.[77] For my purpose of elucidating bibliography's many roles in information science, whether to call objects information, data, or documents will hinge on their interactions with other phenomena and observers. Information, as its etymological roots suggest, will concern interactions that accentuate form, both material and conceptual, and enable *acts* of informing.[78] As Buckland has written, information can be intangible, procedural, and concrete. Buckland uses the terms "information-as-knowledge," "information-as-process," and "information-as-thing," respectively.[79] We will take advantage of this framework, as well as some of the other meanings of *information*, such as Shannon's suggestion that information is a measure of surprise and, when associated with knowledge, as Buckland suggests, belief and understanding.[80]

Data will be what can be taken as given in interactions. My play on words—data as what can be *taken* as *given*—is meant to suggest, as Drucker has pointed out, that data are only "given" after they have been initially captured by an idea, a measurement, or some other enumerative boundary-making process. Thus, data for us will be those things that are assumed to be "given," even if only momentarily, to enable investigation and understanding facilitated by the nine lives of data. This definition will enforce the need to test our assumptions about the nature of our givens, since data will only be those things understood and measured as given in ongoing interactions. This means that data can always be reformed as different conceptual/material assumptions, such as when measuring tools or beliefs about the ways that data have been granted the status of assumption change.

Objects will be considered documents when their interactions provide evidence of facts, where evidence concerns making things evident, "obvious to the eye or mind,"[81] recognizing that it is not easy to delineate where the eye ends and the mind begins. In this configuration, evidence is created through interaction. This aligns nicely with the fact that facts, as the Latin roots of the word suggest, are the result of action.[82] Documents teach. They are proofs to be learned from, lessons, as the French and Latin antecedents suggest, that enable surprise (information) in a process that changes what a person knows or the way that a computational system behaves.[83] As bibliographers remind us, documents are also physical evidence, what Buckland equates with information-as-thing.[84] "Every artifact, every physical object made by human beings," according to G. Thomas Tanselle, "is a record of human effort at a particular time and place, as well as a tangible link to all the succeeding moments of its life."[85] In this sense, documents are physical evidence of human exertion. They can also, of course, be evidence for various other facts associated with nonhuman interactions.

TEXTS

As we have defined them, data, documents, and information are "fields of shifting relations momentarily stabilized in an artifact that exists in a continuum of temporal and spatial and quantum dimensions."[86] Having considered these fields, we can return to my initial definition of texts as data given social shape, as well as copies and the crisscrossing patterns of culture. When one understands data, documents, and information as shifting fields momentarily stabilized by experimental acts of intervention, it becomes easier to see how texts can be understood as what has been woven together by individuals in community with sociotechnical processes from what has been taken as given. To bring these shifting fields into relation, something must be taken and assumed as a gift. A boundary must be drawn somewhere to enable counting and methods for determining what counts. This initial thread in the weave of the social form of what has been taken as given lends shape. It begins to articulate a text that we might call a document, information, or even data, depending on how this initial strand is woven with materials and ideas in interactions of community and their technologies. As D. F. McKenzie writes of the word *text*, its "primary sense is one which defines a process of material construction. It creates an object, but it is not peculiar to any one substance or any one form."[87]

The assumption of an initial boundary enables enumeration, description, and opportunities for analysis, as well as critical judgments about the initial gift and its social form. It provides the opportunity for re-presentation: ways of presenting what has been enumerated, described, analyzed, and critiqued—again. Ideas, actions, and procedures can be reproduced, copied into distinct material shapes that are usefully similar. When methods of re-presentation are repeated and used by members of a community, they help to form and strengthen the crisscrossing weave of culture and articulate what is afforded by situations and objects. We call the things produced again *documents* when they are socialized to teach or represent evidence, *information* when they inform, and *data* when they can be taken as given. They can be called other things, of course, but we see better how, collectively and individually, texts are stabilized by processes that are abstract and material, repetitive, frequently recursive, and, in their complexity, often paradoxical. We also see better how these texts can be materialized in a great diversity of forms depending on how they are woven.

Understanding texts as formulations woven in a community and through interaction with technical and other objects also helps one to better see the roles that bibliography and bibliographers play in stabilizing and refiguring texts in their great diversity. In its enumerative and descriptive modes, bibliography helps draw boundaries around the great diversity of things that can be texts and sketch out relationships among the entities that have been enumerated. In its analytical modes of accounting, bibliography assesses the dynamics of interactions that contribute to creating texts that we might call *books*, *databases*, or *deep learning models*. In its experimental expressive modes, bibliography constitutes the repeated rules, definitions, and procedures for drawing boundaries and articulating what is to be woven into a shape with what has been taken as given. In its critical modes, it enforces judgments. These rules, definitions, procedures, and acts of judgment, of course, are affected by the happenstances of being situated in the middle of things—history, the mechanical forces of physical phenomena, and the intellectual and emotional horizons of those performing bibliographical work. Texts as data, documents, and information are constituted, as Drucker writes, "through the framing acts of intervention."[88] Or, as Donna Haraway says succinctly in a way that resonates with bibliographical practice as the study of objects and their copies, "objects are boundary projects."[89] Individual choices and social custom, knowledge and beliefs, tools for measurement and mechanical laws, and serendipity all figure into what might constitute the boundaries of objects and situations, between copies and what has been copied. Recognizing bibliography's contribution to this complexity is another reason to illuminate the ways that it facilitates foundational theoretical ideas and material practices in information science.

INFORMATION SCIENCE

Understanding data, documents, and information as texts in shifting relations momentarily stabilized by acts of framing will help to reveal some of the ways that bibliography girds the thinking and practice associated with information science. As I have said before, this is not to suggest that we should conflate information science and bibliography, despite the tangled historical relationships between these amorphous fields. Rather, it is to advocate for the idea that bibliography serves as the means for many ends pursued in information science, including ends suggested by widely acknowledged definitions of the field and recent critiques suggesting that information science is not actually a science, nor is it really about information.[90] It is also to point out again that perspectives from bibliography can provide useful opportunities for reflection.

To see how bibliography might provide these opportunities and serve as means for the many ends pursued in association with information science,

D. F. McKenzie's well-known definition of *bibliography* can be compared to definitions of *information science* highlighted by the Association for Information Science and Technology (ASIS&T), arguably one of information science's more powerful institutions. Remember that McKenzie suggests that bibliography is a discipline that studies texts as "recorded forms," "the processes of [texts'] transmission, including their production and reception." In "What Is Information Science?" on ASIS&T's web page, we find the following:

> Information science is . . . concerned with the body of knowledge relating to the origination, collection, organization, storage, retrieval, interpretation, transmission, and utilization of information.
>
> —Borko, H. (1968). Information science: What is it? *American Documentation, 19*, 3.
>
> Information science brings together and uses the theories, principles, techniques and technologies of a variety of disciplines toward the solution of information problems. . . . They are brought to bear in solving the problems with information—its generation, organization, representation, processing, distribution, communication and use.
>
> —Williams, M. E. (1987/1988). Defining information science and the role of ASIS. *Bulletin of the American Society for Information Science, 14*(2), 17–19.
>
> Information science is the science and practice dealing with the effective collection, storage, retrieval, and use of information. It is concerned with recordable information and knowledge, and the technologies and related services that facilitate their management and use. More specifically, information science is a field of professional practice and scientific inquiry addressing the effective communication of information and information objects, particularly knowledge records, among humans in the context of social, organizational, and individual need for and use of information. The domain of information science is the transmission of the universe of human knowledge in recorded form, centering on manipulation (representation, organization, and retrieval) of information, rather than knowing information.
>
> —Saracevic, T. (2009). Information science. In M. J. Bates (Ed.), *Encyclopedia of library and information sciences* (3rd ed.) (pp. 2570–2585). New York: Taylor and Francis.[91]

The repetition in these definitions of the idea that information science concerns the generation, collection, organization, storage, retrieval, interpretation, distribution, and utilization of information makes the relationship between information science and bibliography clear, although perhaps not in a way that we might expect initially. It would seem that bibliography is information science when texts are framed as information and information science is bibliography when information is framed as texts. Indeed, this is a useful way to think about the relationship so long as the distinctions between bibliography and information science are usefully maintained. As I have been arguing, bibliography has many identities because it serves as a means to many ends. It is often called *information science* when it serves ends oriented by information, even if information is used only as a nominal marker of concern.

Even if we consider, as we should, assertions by those such as Jonathan Furner, who suggest that information science is neither a science nor about information, it is possible to see how bibliographical acts and modes of thinking support activities in the broad field currently known as information science. Interacting with what might be considered the same object—a book, say—communities and individuals in information science draw its boundaries differently because the ends that they pursue are distinct. As a consequence, they use bibliographical modes of thinking and production differently. Depending on their disciplinary aims, some will likely use methods of enumeration, description, analysis, and critique to understand "the ways in which people act in relation to information"[92] that a book might present. Others will use these bibliographical tools to create organizing descriptions of the book and its relationship with others and concepts such as authorship to enable the book's retrieval from a library. Yet others will investigate the ethical entailments of the ways that people act in relation to information: who counts and has been counted; how the accessibility of a particular book to a particular person or group of people may, or may not, be equitable; and who should have access to information about how a particular person has interacted with a particular book.[93] Indeed, it is possible to see how bibliography as a mode of study that attends to texts as recorded forms could be considered a candidate answer to Furner's question concerning what to call the "productive area of inquiry"[94] known as information science if information science is neither a science nor actually about information.

But, as tempting as it might be to do, rather than investigating these relationships to build a case for seeing information science as a historical derivative of bibliography, information science as a more advanced evolutionary descendant of bibliography, or bibliography as an answer to what else information science might be called, I wish to focus attention on a boundary that can be drawn between bibliography and information science. As entangled as they are, one can be drawn. Bibliography serves as means for diverse ends through its recursive accounts. Information science is formulated by those in the field using bibliographical means to pursue diverse ends.

The biologist Jakob von Uexküll, who will be discussed in chapter 4, provides a useful metaphor. An oak tree, he suggests, can serve as an important environmental support for a fox by providing a burrow. The same oak tree supports an owl by providing a branch as a perch. A wasp is sustained by the oak tree's soft bark, which provides it with a place to lay its eggs. But the fox and the owl and the wasp will not perceive the oak tree as an oak tree, according to Uexküll. The oak tree will not be an oak tree for them; rather, it is a burrow, a branch, or soft bark that serves the particular ends pursued by their species. By arguing for understanding bibliography as a foundational infrastructure in information science I am suggesting that bibliography and its primary enumerative, descriptive, analytical, and critical modes are like the oak tree. Bibliography supports the various forms of intellectual life that we call information science, even when those intellectual forms interact with and understand bibliography according to the ends they pursue. As if to make my point about the ways that bibliography almost imperceptibly supports information science, the "About" page of the ASIS&T website presents its history as the "Bibliography of the History of ASIS&T."[95]

As a mode of attention, bibliography provides resources for self-reflection in information science not because bibliography is guided by any philosophical imperative, nor because it is inherently directed toward answering questions in or about information science. Rather, bibliography gains its power as a mode of attention because, as a means serving reflection in information science (and elsewhere), it recursively contextualizes, positions, and attempts to account for what has been accounted for through additional acts of enumeration, description, analysis, and critique.

BOOKS

According to our definitions thus far, books can be many things, depending upon how we draw their boundaries. They are texts when they are data woven into social forms. They are data when they are taken as given. They are documents when they provide proof and evidence of facts. They are information when they serve as measures of surprise and things that inform and when they contribute to processes that inform and establish knowledge. When they are usefully similar to each other, they are copies, bountiful evidence of myriad desires to transcend the particulars of time and place that have already transcended those particulars to be available in other places and times. The following describes books in relation to poetry, but what the editors of the *Princeton Encyclopedia of Poetry and Poetics* say of the book in relation to poetry can also be said of books in relation to history, mathematics, or ecology—pick a topic:

> Applied to cuneiform tablets, papyrus rolls, bound objects, and electronic devices, [book] refers both to historically specific literary technologies and to writing in general. This combination drives the book's paradoxical relationship to poetic form and lit[erary] hist[ory]. On one hand, books are simply material objects, vehicles for the ostensibly more primary artistic and intellectual works they contain. On the other, their format implies a poetic dimension, a trope for writing, a shaping force, and a silent collaborator in reading. Similarly, books are at once marked by the time of their construction and transcendent of that time, able to project the human imagination across centuries. The poetics of the book derives from its ability to span these contradictions, to figure paradox as unity and thus to sustain the fragmentary, fissured nature of representation as a coherent whole. . . . Book is an inclusive term, then, not only because it encompasses multiple technologies of inscription but because it is a jointly material and discursive object of figural representation.[96]

Noting that the paradoxes that the editors of the *Princeton Encyclopedia* describe resemble those with which we began the chapter, we come full circle. We learn that the term *book* can be understood to be inclusive of myriad recorded forms. Books can be all these things because their boundaries will be drawn differently according to the purposes for which they are used, the context in which they are used, and who (or what) is using them. Bookworms are nourished differently by books according to their species. The idea that a book can be so many things leads to logical paradoxes, many of which can be resolved by shifting positions, by hypothesizing the many ways that the boundaries of books can be drawn. Bibliography accounts for these boundaries—and draws them.

As we learn "to cipher and to sing," "to study reading-books and history," and to "be neat in everything,"[97] we use enumerative systems that draw out the borders that we need between songs and reading-books and history. Tidy distinctions are useful, indeed necessary. Yet we can also wonder, along with poets like William Butler Yeats (1865–1939), about what our labors of separation and enumeration have enabled as methods for describing our world, analyzing it, and passing judgments that determine the ways that we experience it. "O chestnut tree, great blossomer, / Are you the leaf, the blossom or the bole?"[98] asks the elderly speaker in Yeats's poem "Among School Children." He is wondering which of the boundaries best constitute his chestnut tree, his great blossomer. He asks a similar question about the body moved by music: "O body swayed to music, O brightening glance, / How can we know the dancer from the dance?"[99] The elderly speaker in the poem is asking an old, fundamental question about our labors to distinguish. The poem answers its speaker's question in a manner reminiscent of scholars and theories that I have used to mount my argument for the many roles played by bibliography. It suggests that answers come from the work of drawing boundaries rather than any particular partition: "Labour is blossoming or dancing where / the body is not bruised to pleasure soul, / Nor beauty born out of its own despair, / Nor blear-eyed wisdom out of midnight oil."[100] It is "labour" that blossoms, that "is dancing" where the materiality of a body is not damaged to please an immaterial soul, where beauty and wisdom are not born from despair or late nights but from the labor of delineating them. This detour into poetry (one of the last in this book, I promise) is meant to suggest the ways that bibliography serves information science as the means supporting the labor done in pursuit of the ends sought by information scientists. To do this, I labor to enumerate boundaries that help to clarify the ways in which bibliography serves as means in information science.

KINDS OF POWER

To conclude my lengthy list of keywords and the preface to the chapters to come, I return to McKenzie to make a few final juxtapositions. In his seminal 1969 essay "Printers of the Mind," he makes an important observation about observation. When put crosswise with a theory of bibliographical power set forth by Patrick Wilson, it helps summarize my definitional framework. Wilson's book on bibliographical control, *Two Kinds of Power*, appeared in 1968, a year before the publication of McKenzie's essay.

When McKenzie writes the following, he is grappling with central notions of power, both bibliographical and other kinds, the affordances of specific materials and ideas as well as positions and stances—that is, hypotheses: "To observe at all is to bestow meaning of some kind on the thing observed; to gather particular pieces of evidence is to seek those relevant to some preconceived notion of their utility."[101] Wilson explores similar notions of utility, relevance, and the dilemmas of determining which descriptive observations will be useful when all observations must be premised on expectations of utility, not verifiable usefulness. He is interested in this problem because he is trying to discern a method for assessing value, which he sees as the central issue of bibliographical control. Where McKenzie works to formulate the powers of bibliography to establish texts, facts, and useful hypotheses when descriptive observations cannot be untangled from acts of observation, Wilson works to formulate what constitutes the ability to discover "the valuable" in a "mass of the mostly worthless or uninteresting"[102] documents, the "power to obtain the knowledge recorded in written form."[103]

The central issue of bibliographical control, as Wilson sees it, concerns how to gain enough control through description—where description is meant to suggest enumeration, description, analysis, and critical judgment—to make it useful while pursuing some end. Although he does not articulate his problem in these terms, an economist, taking a cue from McKenzie's use of the term *utility*, might rephrase Wilson's problem of bibliographical control this way: What is the marginal utility—that is, the extra benefit derived—from extra bibliographical description when it is not possible to know what textual end the description might serve? Wilson recognizes, like McKenzie, that observing bestows meaning. He also understands that the work of documentation must be based on beliefs about the relevance of what is being documented, even if such beliefs do not ensure the utility of documentary efforts in the future.

Wilson attacks this problem by proposing two interdependent means of gaining control over a mass of mostly worthless and uninteresting documents. He calls these interdependent means "descriptive control" and "exploitative control." "Exploitative control," he explains, "is a deliberately somewhat rough or severe term for the ability to make the best use of a body of writings," or what he calls the best textual means to an end. He adds, "'Descriptive control' is a not very adequate term for an ability to line up a population of writings in any arbitrary order, to make the population march to one's command."[104] Wilson sees exploitative control as the "greater power" and descriptive control as the "lesser power," adding, "That we cannot have knowledge without hard study does not show knowledge less valuable than hard study. . . . And if we were able, by a miracle, to have the one without the other, most of us would gladly take the knowledge and let the study go."[105] But, he argues, "the inferior power is . . . necessary, as a precondition of the possession of the superior power, that I cannot have supplied the best textual means unless it is known (to someone, at some time) what are all the available means, and therefore unless there is descriptive control (possessed by someone, at some time)."[106]

We take up bibliography in relation to philology in more detail in chapter 2, but we can note here that Wilson's articulation of descriptive control is strikingly similar to the German philologist August Boeckh's famous definition of philology: "Die Erkenntnis des Erkannten (The knowledge of what is and has been known)."[107] In the information theoretical terms articulated by Claude Shannon, descriptive control concerns the level of detail needed to describe events at an "information source," statistically, given a certain channel of transmission, so that description can be exploited to create something sufficiently similar in a different location.

As a useful example of the idea that bibliography constitutes means to ends and is not defined by specific practices that have been called *bibliography*, Wilson understands it to be specific kinds of work and study that do not need to be built into his theory of bibliographical control. "Bibliography," he writes, is "a name for a kind of work, namely the making of lists of a certain sort; it is also the name of a kind of study, primarily the study of the history of books and printing."[108] But Wilson does not integrate these specific modes of work and study into his notion of bibliographical control, just as I have not suggested that these specific kinds of work encompass bibliography. The connection between bibliographical control and bibliography as list making "of a certain kind" and the study of printed books is "contingent rather than necessary, a matter of fact rather than meaning."[109] Bibliography, as I am arguing for understanding it, is similarly contingent and a matter of fact. It is a matter of fact that those who have listed and studied printed books have been called *bibliographers*. But bibliography means more than the study of printed books or the listing of them. It is constituted by practices of enumeration, description, analysis, and critique that create and account for knowledge and its records. Work that does not assess what has been taken as given and contribute to knowing what has been woven into the myriad social shapes that we call texts cannot be called *bibliography*. As McKenzie emphasizes in "Printers of the Mind," bibliography can have "nothing to do with bibliographies."[110] Bibliographies that do not facilitate the acquisition of useful knowledge, Wilson might say, have no bibliographical power. Wilson and McKenzie use similar bibliographical means to serve different ends, which they both call "bibliography."

Collectively, Wilson and McKenzie formulate ways of thinking about efforts to attain and account for knowledge as written records and data in their many social forms. We can call the utility of these efforts the *affordances* of bibliographical methods. The ways that lists are compiled, descriptions are composed, analyses performed, and judgments passed determine their utility for different ends—that is, what they afford. This is to acknowledge that bibliographical work, like economics, is also a "dismal science" despite the bounty that it provides. For all that is afforded by the informative surprises of our boundary-making practices, descriptive statements, detailed analysis, critical judgments, our copies, documents, evidence, and data, much will not be afforded. Knowledge and its records will be lost to acts of knowing. Often, we will not see the oak tree for our burrow or the dance in the arc of a dancer's legs descending into a plié. "We shall never" have "complete *mastery* of a body of texts," writes Wilson, for complete control would require a knowledge of not only their contents and "the historical and other relations among texts" but also the uses to which texts can be put "by all the possible users in all the possible circumstances."[111] Such control is beyond us. And even if it were, as McKenzie suggests, we would not be afforded all that texts might provide because we will have already remade them (if never entirely) to suit ends already determined to be meaningful.

The remaining chapters of this book draw and redraw boundaries to reveal their affordances, some of which we have lost sight of because of how we have positioned ourselves, and the ways that bibliography supports the many ends pursued in information science. We will see how bibliographers such as McKenzie seek ever-greater descriptive control so they can line up populations of texts to reveal historical people, processes, and materials during attempts to validate or invalidate hypotheses and gain knowledge. We will also see how, as information scientists, we have sought and gained descriptive control through descriptive bibliographical practices of increasing power we call "machine learning (ML)." Further, we will touch upon some ways that these descriptive powers are being used to predict our pasts, futures, and desires, as well as how they have begun lining us up as populations to march to the commands of various bibliographical authorities. Taking advantage of the definitional framework presented in this chapter, we position ourselves to see how bibliography facilitates ML and much else that we associate with information science, as well as the power of bibliography to account for information science and what it produces.

2 LISTS AS INFRASTRUCTURE: AN INFRASTRUCTURAL INVERSION

This chapter begins by enumerating some of bibliography's many names. The aim is to continue unraveling the apparent paradox of bibliography's foundational importance and concomitant invisibility in information science. As I describe here, understanding bibliography's marginality helps to make sense of the apparent contradiction. Bibliography is marginal in at least two senses. It is marginal in the sense that bibliography is infrequently an end in itself. Most often, it is a means supporting what is considered a more centrally important goal. Ordinary bibliographical infrastructures that support our work go unnoticed as we focus on the ends that we pursue. Bibliography is also marginal in the sociological sense of having many identities and affiliations. This is one reason why bibliography has had so many names, a few of which I list in this chapter. Indeed, bibliography is rarely known as bibliography except for certain kinds of engagements, usually with manuscripts and printed books, and sometimes involving how to responsibly reproduce them in digital form. It has had and goes by many other names instead.

Recognizing bibliography's marginality in these twin senses illuminates bibliography as a shared infrastructure embedded in all kinds of investigatory and creative actions in information science and elsewhere. By revealing bibliography as difficult-to-see infrastructure integral to much of what we do, this chapter attempts what Geoffrey Bowker and Susan Leigh Star call an "infrastructural inversion." It is an "inversion" that struggles "against the tendence of infrastructure to disappear" by providing a way to "look closely at technologies and arrangements that, by design and habit, tend to fade into the woodwork."[1]

BIBLIOGRAPHY'S MANY NAMES—A LIST

Bibliography has had many names. It has many names now. Here are a few:

Philology
Textual criticism
Textual scholarship
Bibliographing
Library
Librarianship
Library science
Subject bibliography
Information science
Informatics
Information retrieval
Bibliometrics
Enumerative bibliography
Systematic bibliography
Descriptive bibliography
Analytical bibliography
Historical bibliography
Textual bibliography
Textual analysis
Textual studies
Textual editing
Documentary editing
Social textual criticism
Epigraphy
Paleography
Codicology
Diplomatics
Historical criticism
Higher criticism
Lower criticism
Writing about books
The science that deals with literary productions
Science of books
Book arts
Bibliology
Bibliognosy
Nature of the book
Technical bibliography
Library service
Book collecting
Old books
Unusual writing
Information
Chirography
Hieroglyphics
Medals
Languages
The universal science
Book history
Digital scholarship
Digital studies
Digital humanities
Big data
Geographical information systems (GIS)
Media archaeology
New media
Media studies
Software studies
Critical code studies
Platform studies

Computer games
Digital memory
Archive
Media technology
Format studies
Publishing
Comparative textual media
Cognitive science
Computer science
Sociology
Artificial intelligence
Linguistics
Library and information science
Cybernetics
Information theory
Psychology
Economics
Systems theory
書誌學 (서지학, しょしがく)
文獻學 (문헌학, ぶんけんがく)
文獻情報 (문헌정보, ぶんけん じょうほう)
Literature
History
Religion

This list helps to reveal the power of lists as bibliographical tools. It also clarifies how bibliography serves as foundational infrastructure in information science. To say that bibliography is infrastructural, like the lists that support it, is to recognize that it is embedded, transparent, learned, built, modular, and has reach—key elements of what Bowker and Star call "infrastructure." The organizing structure of the list fades from view as we wrestle with what is or ought not to be included on it. As we grapple with the expansiveness of what is suggested by this particular list, we lose track of the great reach that lists have. The ways that listing and enumeration are learned as part of membership in a community and linked to conventions of practice are made apparent, I hope, by the initial oddity of mine. Which community would make such a list? Contradicting the expectations of any particular community of practice has the benefit, in this case, of enabling me to suggest some of the diverse ways that enumeration supports diverse communities as infrastructural means.

My list demonstrates how specific bibliographical practices, like specific lists, are enumerated by fixed modular increments. The list itself is a modular structure. Items can easily be added, removed, moved, rearranged, and replaced. By beginning to account for my specific list, we begin to see how enumeration serves as infrastructure for diverse individuals and communities and, in a small way with a single list, begin to perform a kind of "infrastructural inversion"[2] that allows us to see how enumeration facilitates so many diverse practices.

As Kurt Gödel and Yi Sang remind us, enumeration can create useful paradoxes. Indeed, lists themselves can be usefully paradoxical. Their incompleteness suggests expansiveness. Numberlessness enables enumeration and randomness creates formal order.[3] Separateness insists on kinship.[4] The "flexible structures" of the list that I present here "hold separate and disparate items together"[5] to suggest the marginality of bibliography, where *marginality* is meant to suggest the sociological concept of "membership in more than one community of practice."[6] Codicology (the study of codex manuscripts) is put into relation with one of the list's more audacious items, "the universal science," which is what Gabriel Peignot (1767–1849) called "bibliography."[7] "The nature of the book" is ordered by "diplomatics," which concerns the discerning of documentary provenance and only infrequently has anything to do with diplomats. Each arrangement and the measurements afforded by it are hypothetical because more (or fewer) can be imagined. Even in its incompleteness, my list suggests how enumerative bibliographical processes operate as infrastructure serving diverse ends while concomitantly suggesting bibliography's marginality. Which of the disciplinary or practical ends enumerated by my list could be pursued without enumerative lists? Which pursues enumeration as an end?

Lists and their useful paradoxes also have rhetorical power. Repetition suggests emphasis. Philology appears more than once in this discussion, as do science, information, and criticism. And the list loops like a Möbius strip back on itself as a list of terms for *bibliography* that include the word *bibliography: enumerative bibliography, systematic bibliography, descriptive bibliography, analytical bibliography, historical bibliography,* and *textual bibliography.* The list suggests a historical arc, but not a smooth one. *Philology* begins the list, and digital provinces appear toward the end. Importantly, the complexity of bibliography's memberships is on display. A few Chinese, Korean, and Japanese characters hint at the insufficiency of polyglot as an adjective to describe bibliography's language communities.

And to what intellectual tribe does the list suggest bibliography belongs? The sciences? The humanities? "By virtue of having more than one identity to negotiate," like Robert Park's "marginal man," bibliography has at least double vision.[8] Indeed, the thousand-armed and thousand-eyed Avalokitesvara, a figure who has more than double vision and helps all in their quests to transcend suffering,[9] comes to mind. Although Avalokitesvara as a metaphor suggests the multiple ways that bibliography and bibliographers have enabled quests of all kinds, there is nothing divine about bibliographical practice, of course, and bibliography's practitioners often toil unnoticed in the marginal multitudinousness of their identities. An essence of bibliography is difficult to discern even if, as the list suggests, there is kinship in alienation and contradiction.

Imagining bibliography's many names as markers of ends pursued in different places and times rather than a singular essence helps to make some sense of bibliography's marginality and many identities. *Bibliography* and *philology*, for example, have been used interchangeably. Oversimplifying, philology, that once mighty endeavor that gave birth to the modern humanities and social sciences, served the ends of those that desired to be intimate with the particulars of the past and theorize, usually about language and culture, using texts. *Textual criticism*, a term often used as a synonym for *bibliography* today, often serves those that wish to be intimate with and theorize about individual printed texts (that might have *many* copies). The terms *textual scholarship* or *textual studies* are preferred by some. Librarianship and its many sobriquets, such as *library science* and *information science*, as well as its subdisciplines, such as informatics, information retrieval, and bibliometrics, serve those that are often less interested in the particulars of any one object but endeavor to theorize the laws of the bibliographical universe and information. David Greetham writes of bibliography, which he associates with textual scholarship:

> It is a discipline drowning in a sea of terms: enumerative bibliography, systematic bibliography, descriptive bibliography, analytical bibliography, historical bibliography and textual bibliography, textual analysis and textual criticism, textual editing, documentary editing, and social textual criticism—to say

> nothing of such older dispensations as epigraphy, paleography, codicology, and diplomatics, philology and historical criticism, higher and lower criticism, all of which may still be invoked by textuists. And, as if this cacophony were not loud enough, the recent annexation of the "text" by literary theorists and critics abandoning authors, works, and history has introduced more ambiguities and another struggle over ownership of the terms.[10]

This "cacophony" of terms is indicative of bibliography's plurality and is, of course, formulated in relation to just some of the recent English-language names that bibliography has been given. The German bibliographer Georg Schneider (1876–1960), from his vantage point in the 1930s, provides a succinct summary of the conceptual aims pursued under the banner of bibliography in Europe from the seventeenth century to his present. He does this while pursuing his own theory that bibliography is best thought of as the listing of books, what Greetham would call "enumerative bibliography" or "systematic bibliography." I reiterate Schneider's story of bibliography because it is a useful, if ultimately incomplete, accounting of bibliographical list making that complements Greetham's list, which emphasizes the historical study of books as material objects. I juxtapose these perspectives to evince the variety of bibliographical identities rather than provide a history. What the librarian and information scientist Barbara Hale writes of enumerative and systematic bibliography in 1970, what she calls "subject bibliography," remains true of bibliography's diversity more generally: "A definitive history of subject bibliography has yet to be written and the literature of its development is scattered through many sources."[11]

Schneider calls the use of lists "bibliographing (*Bibliographieren*)" and the lists themselves "bibliographies (*Bibliographien*)."[12] He suggests "all collective bibliographies were originally termed 'library [*Bibliothek*].'"[13] Focusing on the term *bibliography* and not the work of those making bibliographies, such as Conrad Gessner (1516–1565), whose 1545 *Bibliotheca universalis* (Universal bibliography) is often pointed to as the first post-Gutenberg bibliography in the West, Schneider writes that the term *bibliography* was first used in Europe by Louis Jacob de Saint Charles in his *Bibliographia Parisiana, 1645–50*, and "did not come into general use until the eighteenth century."[14] As Schneider conveys the story, bibliography was initially associated with lists of books. By the eighteenth century, especially as it gained popularity in France, bibliography "took on a decidedly different and much broader significance in that it was ambiguously defined as 'writing about books.'"[15]

The German bibliographer Friedrich Ebert (1791–1834) defines *bibliography* as "the science that deals with literary productions."[16] Ebert's assertion, Schneider claims, "culminated in a new definition of bibliography as the 'science of books [*Bücherwissenschaft*].'"[17] This created "a maze of infinitely varied interpretations that are seldom clear" and a flowering of terms such as "'book arts [*Bücherkunde*],' 'bibliology [*Bibliologie*],' 'bibliognosy [*Bibliognosie*],' and many others."[18] These terms applied to scholarly publications and what we would now call *trade books,* as well as the "nature of the book (*Buchwasen*)," which concerned the material aspects of books and what was sometimes called "technical bibliography (*technische Bibliographie*)," in addition to "library service (*Bibliothekswesen*)" and "book collecting (*Bibliophilie*)."[19] Bibliographical societies of all sorts were concerned with all sorts of investigations, and bibliophiles of all varieties—from Thomas Frognall Dibdin (1776–1847) to Denis Diderot (1713–1784) to Paul Otlet (1868–1944)—were using the term *bibliography* to describe everything from "old books" and "unusual writing" to what we would now more commonly call "information."

Like Greetham, Schneider finds himself flummoxed by the "dispensation" of

> paleography and manuscripts, which cannot be sharply differentiated from the "science of books," [and] is occasionally included in treatment of the subject of "bibliography." . . . Chirography [the study of handwriting and penmanship] may not be included without taking into consideration the study of paleography. . . . Peignot included in his *Dictionnaire de bibliologie* treatment of hieroglyphics, medals and languages. He even went so far as to define bibliography, by means of a clever bit of juggling, as the universal science [*Universalwissenschaft*].[20]

Schneider and Greetham are both frustrated by bibliography's cacophony of terms because each pursues a categorical description of bibliographical essences. The ends they pursue, their historical and disciplinary positions, and the objects that interest them most (books and lists of books) position them so that it is more difficult for them to see that bibliography's cacophony of terms suggests the various and overlapping ends served by bibliography as means.

Matthew Kirschenbaum and Sarah Werner suggest additional ends pursued and more contemporary terms for bibliography in a 2014 *Book History* article called "Digital Scholarship and Digital Studies: The State of the Discipline." Their focus is the study of "books" rather than their enumeration. By 2014, having scare quotes around "book" had become obligatory. For the many communities that studied them amid the emerging contexts provided by digital technologies, books were no longer naturalized objects that could be understood using what had been commonsense definitions. Rather, books raised a host of practical, epistemological, and even ontological questions. In this context, Kirschenbaum and Werner write that they are interested in studies of books that "whether theoretical or applied, [do] not posit a transcendental 'digital' that somehow stands outside the historical and material legacies of other artifacts and phenomena."[21] They understood the book in digital contexts as "a messy complex of extensions and extrusions of prior media and technologies."[22] The study of books is pursued, they argue, via questions about "the relevance of digital tools and methods to diverse areas of book history and the study of books as physical objects" and the implications of "the transformations underway in nearly every aspect of contemporary authorship, reading, and bookselling" as they complicate and reconfigure our "notions of textual 'materiality' and dissemination."[23] As Kirschenbaum and Werner describe them, a huge variety of names mark these pursuits, the tools used, and objects discerned, only some of which we have seen before: digital humanities, big data, GIS, media archaeology, new media, software studies, critical code studies, platform studies, computer games, archives, media technology, format studies, publishing, comparative textual media, and textual scholarship.

In addition to juxtaposing the ends pursued separately by those who study books and those that enumerate them, we can investigate any one of the items in the list that starts this chapter to discover a multitude of pursuits marked by an ever-larger number of names. Apropos of this book's topic, we might choose to focus on information and look up work by Fritz Machlup and Una Mansfield, who in the 1980s asked those who studied information to explain what they understood to be the object of their studies. The "interdisciplinary messages" that they received in response came from the fields of information science, cognitive science, informatics, computer science, sociology, artificial intelligence (AI), linguistics, library and information science, cybernetics, information theory, psychology, economics, and systems theory.[24]

Conversely, look outward from the boundaries delineated by the languages of the list, and a constellation of diverse names marks diverse ends associated with bibliography around the world. A quick survey of what bibliography is now called in South Korea and East Asia (areas beyond North America and Europe with which I have some familiarity) is instructive, even if it can only hint at the variety of ways that bibliography is pursued around the world. *Sŏjihak* (書誌學), literally translated as "book-record-study," is the term for *bibliography* used in South Korea today, although my own anecdotal experience suggests that few South Koreans know the word outside of a small cadre of especially bookish collectors and scholars. *Sŏjihak* is a translation of the English and French words *bibliography* and *bibliographie*, which entered into circulation in Korea during the early twentieth century when Korea was a Japanese colony.[25] The earliest use of the term in Korea that I have found is an announcement advertising the first issue of a Japanese journal called *Bibliography* (書誌學) in a Korean daily newspaper, the *Tonga ilbo* (East Asia daily), in February 1933.[26] The same glyphs are used to represent *bibliography* in Japan as well as China, although the glyphs are pronounced differently in Japanese and Chinese (*shyokaku* and *shu zhi xue*, respectively).

Of course, a variety of terms were used for listing and editing texts millennia before the arrival of *sŏjihak* in Korea, Japan, and China. One of Korea's best-known modern bibliographers, Ch'ŏn Hye-bong (1926–2016), traces bibliographical work related to verifying and correcting texts harking as far back as the fourth century, when what are known as the Three Kingdoms (Koguryŏ, Paekche, and Silla) imported a variety of Confucian and Buddhist texts from China.[27] Ch'ŏn calls what was practiced in the Three Kingdoms "*wŏnmun sŏjihak*," which might be awkwardly translated as "original text biobibliography" or bibliography concerned with originals. Ch'ŏn maps the terms *textual bibliography*, as well as *analytical and critical bibliography*, to *wŏnmun sŏjihak*.[28] Currently, *munhŏnhak* (文獻學; *bunkenkaku (J) wen xian xue* (C)) is often considered a synonym for *sŏjihak* (書誌學), although *munhŏnhak* sometimes connotes more philological desires.

Indicative of the ways that bibliography, philology, and information science are often simultaneously conjoined by contemporary institutions while being practiced as separate endeavors, librarians in South Korea study and teach in schools and departments of "Bibliography/Philology and Information" (文獻情報 *munhŏn chŏngbo*). *Chŏngbo* (情報) is a word used in South Korea today to mean "information," although the literal meaning of its two syllables are "emotion" and "report." If one did not know better, rather than in schools of information, one might expect "emotion-reports" to be studied in departments of literature with early twentieth-century classics such Yi Kwang-su's (1892–1950) *Mujŏng* (無情 emotionless). Textual criticism and textual editing, especially as it is associated with what is sometimes called *higher criticism* in the West, is most often studied and taught, if at all, in departments of literature (文學), history (歷史), and religion (宗教).

Placing bibliography crosswise with its doppelgangers in Korean, Chinese, and Japanese contextualizes the words and the work undertaken under the banner of each one. My list of words for *bibliography* is also meant to contextualize it by positioning us in a way that makes it easier to see bibliography's many identities and the diverse ends that it serves as means. This is to acknowledge that my list also serves my own rhetorical ends by showing the power of lists to support the goals that we pursue, in this case the presentation of a convincing argument about the infrastructural roles played by bibliography in information science.

LISTS AS INFRASTRUCTURE

Having gained some standing in relation to bibliography's plurality and marginality by means of lists, we are better positioned to see how, as means to ends, lists are good infrastructure. We can return to Bowker and Star's notion of infrastructure in more detail here. They present their definition of infrastructure, yes, as a list:

- Embeddedness
- Transparency
- Reach or scope
- Learned as part of membership
- Links with conventions of practice
- Embodiment of standards
- Built on an installed base
- Becomes visible upon breakdown
- Is fixed in modular increments, not all at once or globally[29]

Lists are "embedded," as Bowker and Star use the term, in the diverse work associated with the field of information science. Just as their enumerative form supports their definition of infrastructure, lists support the various kinds of work done in information science as infrastructure. Borrowing from the etymology of *infrastructure*, they write that "infrastructure is sunk into, inside of, other structures, social arrangements, and technologies."[30] Bibliographical lists are "sunk into" a huge variety of social structures, arrangements, and technologies associated with information science, including the dual-entry list 01 that is so important to digital information. Along with Shannon, Gödel reminds us that list making is embedded in the mathematics that supports many disciplines associated with the science of information. Yi Sang reminds us that lists frequently formulate the cultural texts organized by information scientists.[31] The impossibility of imagining a modern library without a list of its holdings suggests how thoroughly lists and list making are "embedded" as infrastructure-supporting conventions of practice associated with collecting, storing, retrieving, and using information. Indeed, we can return to the lists used by some to define information science to suggest lists' embeddedness and links with convention. Take Borko's, Williams's, and Saracevic's definitions of information science (mentioned in chapter 1 and described in more detail in this chapter) and the lists that they use to construct them. For Borko, we remember, information science concerns the "body of knowledge relating to the origination, collection, organization, storage, retrieval, interpretation, transmission, and utilization of information."[32] Of course, it is difficult to imagine attempting to organize, collect, store, retrieve, interpret, transmit, or utilize information without lists. Williams suggests, "Information science brings together and uses the theories, principles, techniques and technologies of a variety of disciplines toward the solution of information problems. . . . They are brought to bear in solving the problems with information—its generation, organization, representation, processing, distribution, communication and use."[33] Imagine investigating the generation, organization, representation, processing, distribution, communication, and use of information without using enumeration as a tool. Saracevic's definitional list includes elements from Borko's and Williams's: "Information science is the science and practice of dealing with the effective collection, storage, retrieval, and use of information."[34] Although they are ordinarily transparent, it is easier to see how lists are linked to conventions of practice in information science and more difficult to overlook how lists like these are embedded, in this case in some of the field's definitions.

Transparency, as Bowker and Star acknowledge, is a matter of perspective and intent. Lists are transparent in use. They do not have "to be reinvented each time or assembled for each task";[35] rather, they support work invisibly. They are ready to hand as tools supporting the work of organizing, collecting, storing, retrieving, interpreting, transmitting, or utilizing information, and they fade into the woodwork, sometimes literally, as is the case with the lists organized on library cards in standardized wooden cabinets. They are similarly ready to hand as tools for those like Furner, who carefully enumerate work done in association with information science to build his case for the idea that the field does not frequently concern information and, in most cases, should not be considered a science.[36]

The reach and scope of lists are both spatial and temporal. They are shared across space and time. Borko's list describing the fundamental concerns of information science appeared in the 1960s in the journal *American Documentation*. Williams's list appeared in the late 1980s in the *Bulletin of the American Society for Information Science*. Saracevic's list was published in the late 2000s in the third edition of the *Encyclopedia of Library and Information Sciences*. I made repeated use of them in a small town north of Seoul while composing this book between 2019 and 2022 so you might have them in some other place and time. Presenting them again here suggests the spatiality and temporality of lists and the ways that they serve as infrastructure.

Lists and list making are learned as part of membership, and they embody standards. Reiterated by community institutions such as the Association for Information Science and Technology (ASIS&T), the lists created by Borko, Williams, and Saracevic are learned by members and embody standards in the field. The same can be said of the list provided by Bowker and Star that defines infrastructure. Even as these standards are debated, the enumerative shape of these lists and the items that they include support debate and shape learning in information science. They also help to formulate the enumerative standards that I am employing to make my argument about the infrastructural role that enervative practices play in information science. I emphasize my own rhetorical strategies because, like the enumerative structures that facilitate the definitions of Borko, Williams, and Saracevic, the list that I am using to support my argument can slip from view. Its enumerative shape can be taken for granted and overlooked, for example, as the organizing structure of these paragraphs. Yet, "the taken-for-grantedness of artifacts and organizational arrangements" articulated by these lists "is a sine qua non of membership in [our] community of practice,"[37] which is to suggest again that they serve as infrastructure.

Lists do not arrive *ab ovo*. They have "an installed base," to use Bowker and Star's term. "Infrastructure does not grow de novo; it wrestles with the inertia of the installed base and inherits strengths and limitations from that base."[38] And they write, "Optical fibers run along old railroad lines"[39] as a metaphorical summary. Similarly, we can track the ways that lists are built on one another and the ways that newer lists run beside older ones. Take Borko's 1968 definition. He suggests that it is "derived from" three definitions of information science presented by Robert Taylor in 1966.[40] A reading of Taylor's article "Professional Aspects of Information Science and Technology" does not reveal three specific definitions but rather a review of many definitions of information science within a framework of three "professional aspects" of information science, especially as they might concern pedagogy. Among the lists and definitions that Taylor presents, we discover the lists beside which Borko laid down his own. Informing Borko's is a list of recommendations made by participants at the symposium "Education for Information Science" sponsored by the American Documentation Institute and held in Washington, D.C., in September 1965. The definitional list from 1965 is in turn informed by definitional lists created by participants at conferences held at the Georgia Institute of Technology in 1961 and 1962.[41] A comparison of these lists with Borko's definitional 1968 list reveal the "installed base" of the lists that serve as the definitional infrastructure in information science as it is reiterated by community institutions such as ASIS&T on their website. The differences between the lists also reveal changing perspectives and emphases. We can notice, for example, that the recent posting of Borko's definition on the ASIS&T website excludes a great deal of not only Borko's definition, but also the history of the lists that informed his list.

Here is how Taylor presents the definition of information science that resulted from the conferences held at the Georgia Institute of Technology in 1961 and 1962:

> The science that investigates the properties and behavior of information, the forces governing the flow of information, and the means of processing information for optimum accessibility and usability. The processes include the origination, dissemination, collection, organization, storage, retrieval, interpretation, and use of information. The field is derived from and related to mathematics, logic, linguistics, psychology, computer technology, operations research, the graphic arts, communications, library science, management, and some other fields.[42]

Here is the definition negotiated at the American Documentation Institute symposium held in September 1965, as represented by Taylor: "Information Science is particularly concerned with stored or recorded messages, their creation as distinguishable marks or documents, their propagation and use. The discipline has two characteristics of science: a pure science component which inquires into the subject without regard to its application, and the applied science component which develops into services and products."[43]

Here is Borko's definition from 1968:

> *Information science* is that discipline that investigates the properties and behavior of information, the forces governing the flow of information, and the means of processing information for optimum accessibility and usability. It is

> concerned with that body of knowledge relating to the origination, collection, organization, storage, retrieval, interpretation, transmission, transformation, and utilization of information. This includes the investigation of information representations in both natural and artificial systems, the use of codes for efficient message transmission, and the study of information processing devices and techniques such as computers and their programming systems. It is an interdisciplinary science derived from and related to such fields as mathematics, logic, linguistics, psychology, computer technology, operations research, the graphic arts, communications, library science, management, and other similar fields. It has both a pure science component, which inquires into the subject without regard to its application, and an applied science component, which develops services and products.[44]

Finally, here again is how Borko's definition is represented on the ASIS&T website: "Information science is that discipline that investigates the properties and behavior of information, the forces governing the flow of information, and the means of processing information for optimum accessibility and usability. It is concerned with that body of knowledge relating to the origination, collection, organization, storage, retrieval, interpretation, transmission, transformation, and utilization of information."[45]

The recursive bibliographical desire to collect and compare these lists provides an opportunity to see how lists function as part of the definitional infrastructure of information science but also the opportunity to reflect on that infrastructure. Somewhat like what Gödel and Yi Sang did when they used enumeration and description to diagnose the foundations of the systems within which they worked, we can enumerate some of the definitional lists of information science to describe some of the field's definitional formulations and gain a perspective from which to diagnose how they have come to be what they are and how they can be different. This recursive bibliographical instinct reveals the quirky recursive processes that serve to establish these definitional formulations as an installed base in the field. For example, Taylor's 1966 annual review, which Borko used to formulate his definitional list in 1968, is formulated in part by Borko's own May 1965 report, *The Conceptual Foundations of Information Systems*.[46] Infrastructures, like these lists, are the result of complex interactions, as Bowker and Star suggest.

To continue a detailed, point-by-point explication of how bibliography and its enumerative lists function as foundational infrastructure in information science and a means for reflection would belabor my point. We could continue and discuss how lists become visible when they "break down," as when items that should be on them are left off, or when lists as physical objects are not accessible despite the redundancies that might have been put in place to make them available. I could describe how lists are always local, created and used in specific places and times, such as the conferences in Georgia or the symposium in Washington, even if they are distributed through space and time. I could emphasize that lists are modular by pointing out that all-encompassing lists are an oxymoron, even if such lists have frequently been attempted. But hopefully I have made the case for how bibliography and its enumerative tools serve as foundational infrastructure in information science, as well as a means of studied reflection.

INFRASTRUCTURAL INVERSION

To have focused so much attention on the infrastructural roles played by lists in information science is to have performed what Star and Bowker call "infrastructural inversion." To foreground bibliographical lists as integral material and conceptual technologies in information science is to suggest "the depths of interdependence of technical networks and standards" created by lists on the one hand, "and the real work of politics and knowledge production"[47] that they perform on the other. As material and symbolic objects, lists instantiate the categories integral to the material-conceptual infrastructures that Bowker and Star describe, as well as provide a means of interrogating classifications and classificatory systems as objects that are similarly and simultaneously "conceptual (in the sense of persistent patterns of change and action, resources for organizing abstractions) and material (in the sense of being inscribed, transported, and affixed to stuff)."[48] To use a central metaphor from Bowker and Star and reiterate one that I have been employing, lists are woven into and feature classificatory textures, the threads of which touch people's lives. They formulate and situate work done in relation to information science and also provide opportunities to reflect on the work done in the field.

The many manifestations of bibliography have faded from view as naturalized structures of our everyday life and intellectual work. To cast our gaze intently on bibliography is to scrutinize our assumptions about the means that we use for the ends that we pursue. Taking a page from the playbook of Star and Bowker, I lend bibliography and its technologies "causal prominence in many areas usually attributed to heroic actors, social movements, or cultural mores"[49] to bring them to our attention. In chapter 3, to better understand the work that lists do and the "real work" of "knowledge production," we delve more deeply into the powers and human pleasures of enumeration.

3 THE POWERS AND PLEASURES OF LISTS AND THE COORDINATION OF CONTEXT

In chapter 2, we established bibliography and lists as important infrastructure. This chapter investigates the powers and pleasures of enumeration—powers and pleasures that help to coordinate contexts by ordinating the boundaries of objects. It examines some of the human motivations that can be discerned by considering what has been brought within the boundaries of lists and what has been left beyond their boundaries as context. It also explores the objective force of lists and what is lost to them and the contexts that they create when objects are not taken into account. Ordinary as they are, lists create and coordinate contextualizing systems as banal as the contact lists in our phones and as sophisticated as those fashioned by the world's largest libraries and repositories of knowledge. They generate order, formulate horizons, and constitute power. By delineating context and enumerating relationships that serve to shape recorded knowledge and manners of knowing, lists enable information scientists to consider what has counted as knowledge and construct mechanisms for organizing, transmitting, and retrieving it. Through the boundaries they draw, the lists that bibliographers create while inhabiting their many identities coordinate context—the weave of connections suggested by the etymology of the word *context.* Their boundaries "ordain" what will be positioned "together" to create "order, rank, or division,"[1] which is to suggest the meaning and etymology of the verb *coordinate.*

Lists create pleasure too, and they are powerfully pleasurable tools to operate. In his preface to *The Order of Things,* Foucault famously confesses the bodily pleasures, as well as the intellectual and other powers, afforded by lists:

> This book first arose out of a passage in Borges, out of the laughter that shattered, as I read the passage, all the familiar landmarks of my thought. . . . This passage quotes a "certain Chinese encyclopedia" in which it is written that "animals are divided into: (a) belonging to the Emperor, (b) embalmed, (c) tame, (d) sucking pigs, (e) sirens, (f) fabulous, (g) stray dogs, (h) included in the present classification, (i) frenzied, (j) innumerable, (k) drawn with a very fine camelhair brush, (l) *et cetera*, (m) having just broken the water pitcher, (n) that from a long way off look like flies." In the wonderment of this taxonomy, the thing we apprehend in one great leap, the thing that, by means of the fable, is demonstrated as the exotic charm of another system of thought, is the limitation of our own, the stark impossibility of thinking *that*.[2]

As this passage suggests, we create order and manifest control—power—by making lists. This is true even if the lists that we make and lend authority to are fictions, as Jorge Luis Borges's is, and reinforce, as Foucault's passage does, various dogmas through jest, specious bibliographical inuendo, or careless assumptions about what we might know about the bibliographical context of assertions. The italicized *that*, an important bibliographical detail and mode of textual expression traceable to Renaissance printers, punchcutters, and scribal copyists such as Aldus Manutius (?–1515), Francesco Griffo (1450–1518), and Niccolò de' Niccoli (1364–1437) emphasizes the hurtful alienations of this list and the powers and pleasures of lists more generally.

As Foucault's passage clarifies, it is crucial to recognize that these efforts to make boundaries are artful, often cunning, and always motivated by the pleasures that they provide and the powers that they facilitate. Indeed, lists are etymologically associated with "borders," especially those of clothes and textiles. As I have mentioned, the list is not entirely distant, therefore, from the weaves of the words *text* and *context*. The Old English *liste*, Middle Dutch *lijste*, and Old High German *lista* suggest hems and selvage, or a bordering strip of cloth and the materials of which they are made.[3] Lists are also etymologically associated with the "art, craft, [and] cunning" of making them and the boundaries that they suggest.[4] The *Oxford English Dictionary (OED)* list of the meanings of *list* suggest that the term can be associated with the Old Saxon, High Olde German, and Middle High German for "art" and "wisdom," the Dutch for "cunning," and the Gothic for "stratagem" and "wile." Finally, the word *list* also has etymological associations with "pleasure, joy, [and] delight," as well as "appetite, craving, desire, and longing."[5] This is to suggest for our purposes the human joys and cravings associated with giving bounded shape to the world's overwhelming plenty. These etymologies are meant to make evident the power of lists to articulate and contain, as well as exclude. They are also meant to suggest that list making is artful and strategic, and lists are indicative of the appetites and delights of those who have drawn them up.

Recognizing the human impulses at play in list making is not to suggest that any determination that results from the formulation of a list is necessarily subjective and, hence, somehow unscientific. Indeed, list making is a key to objectivity. List making produces lists, objects that can be used to measure. This is made plain most expediently by considering again the two-item list that formulates Claude Shannon's measure of information, 01, or the kinds of infinities that Kurt Gödel and Yi Sang pondered. Indeed, lists allow us to measure the impossibly large, such as the infinity of natural numbers and the infinity of real numbers. As we have discussed, the infinity of real numbers can be enumerated to suggest that it is larger than the infinity of natural numbers. We know this because there are more real numbers than can be listed with natural numbers. These powers of measurement provided by lists serve as means for gaining some control of the infinities with which we work in information science.

The two-item list provided by Patrick Wilson that I repeat frequently in this book similarly exploits the power of lists to organize a description of bibliography and gain control of it as a topic. When he writes that *bibliography* is "a name for a kind of work, namely the making of lists of a certain sort; it is also the name of a kind of study, primarily the study of the history of books and printing,"[6] he creates order by providing a categorical boundary. His distinction between work related to list making and work related to the history of books is helpful because it simultaneously distinguishes the "list makers" from the "studiers," while at the same time coordinating their relationship by means of the boundary that they share. Wilson, of course, was not the first to enumerate the field of bibliography in this way. W. W. Greg had created a similar boundary in 1912, as I discuss in more detail in chapter 7.[7] With the boundary in place, we can compare the work, stratagems, and desires of diverse groups traditionally associated with bibliography as Wilson, reinforcing boundaries drawn by scholars such as Greg, has organized them.

The power of Wilson's list is derived from how it divides and elides. It divides, for example, the roles played by historical individuals, now often called *librarians*, who worked at both studying books and listing them. His axiomatic category of bibliographers as studiers of printing and book history elides the fact that many among the "studiers" fashioned a great many lists. Revealing this elision and some of the divisions of Wilson's list helps to show its cunning and Wilson's own intellectual predilections and allegiances to the group concerned with making lists, a group that has come to be organized around librarianship and, more recently, concepts of information and information science.

To acknowledge the cunning and art of Wilson's list is not to deny its power or usefulness. With just two entries, Wilson's list organizes, however imperfectly, a long and complicated history of bibliography. His list shows how lists support the organization of information science as a discipline of bibliographical list makers. It is also its own example of bibliographical control. It lines up elements of a complex history and has those elements march in an orderly fashion according to categorical orders created by his list. His list is also a powerful example of how lists serve as means to ends in information science—Wilson's end being a description of bibliographical power and control. For the ends that I pursue, his list coordinates my arguments. By providing a way to create boundaries and borders, it enables me to contextualize the roles played by bibliography in information science. By means of the shared boundary that Wilson draws, studiers of books in the humanities provide context for the "list makers" of information science, and vice versa.

UNIVERSAL DECIMAL CLASSIFICATION AND THE CREATION OF CONTEXTS

By the early years of the twentieth century, as Wilson's list usefully conveys, bibliographers were divvying up the work of bibliographical accounting. Remembering William Butler Yeats's poem "Among School Children" from chapter 1 (How can we know the dancer from the dance?), we can say that certain communities of bibliographers were focusing their attention on the dance that books suggest, while others paid more attention to the books as dancers. With the possible exception of John Dewey, it is difficult to think of a historical person more enthralled by the dance that books suggest than the Belgian librarian and systematizer Paul Otlet. He reveled in the infinities of books. To cope with their abundance, he, like Dewey, fashioned enumerative practices that would enable him to assign a number to *every* document considered significant. The word *book* was shorthand for the "ever-expanding landscape of information in which almost any object can serve as a document."[8] Indeed, Otlet pushed to expand ordinary definitions of documents so documents could be not only "graphic and written records [that] are representations of ideas or of objects," but also "*objects themselves* if it is possible to be informed by them."[9] In this latter sense, "natural objects, artifacts, objects bearing traces of human activity (such as archaeological finds), explanatory models, educational games, and works of art"[10] are all documents according to Otlet.

As we see, Outlet does not overlook the materiality of objects in this landscape of information, but he did believe that their materiality often got in the way of making their facts and knowledge ready to hand. He was most interested in what Buckland has called "information-as-knowledge."[11] In a manner not dissimilar from how Gödel enumerated the elements of mathematics to make a statement about the completeness of formal systems, Otlet aimed to make a complete statement about the dance of human knowledge. To do so, he created a numerical coordinate system that would facilitate his description by creating an ordered means of drawing relationships between documents. That is, he created a system for contextualizing documents. It is a method of contextualization that continues to facilitate knowledge and its dance while always, of course, also demonstrating its own incompleteness.

Otlet, like Gödel, had been inspired by the German philosopher and mathematician Gottfried Wilhelm Leibniz (1646–1716), who in a quirky twist of history pondered, like Yi Sang, the infinitely small and the infinitely large. While Yi Sang's meditation concerned his patient and Otlet's concerned a set containing all human knowledge, Leibniz considered the "binary scale in theological terms, wondering whether 'God, represented by the number 1, created the Universe out of nothing, represented by 0.'"[12] The combinatory logic of Otlet's Universal Decimal Classification system enabled a powerfully flexible means of mapping the relationship of not only the topic of books but subsets of topics associated with documentary entities, including information about their physical properties. By creating a list and then assigning a positional identity to documents within the boundaries articulated by the list, Otlet, like Dewey, created an enumerative context that formulated boundaries that could be used to put the world's infinitely large number of documents and their infinity of knowledge into a relational order.

Alex Wright provides a description of Otlet's creation that is worth citing at length since it describes how Otlet's system generated relationships through its enumerative procedures, as well as how it foreshadows the powerful enumerative and descriptive tools of our contemporary database systems:

> Using single characters, such as the equal sign, plus sign, colon, quotation marks, and parentheses, Otlet and [his partner Henri] La Fontaine [1854–1943] created a symbolic language to encode relationships from one topic to another. For example, the plus sign would allow catalogers to assign multiple topics to a single source; colons allowed them to combine classification numbers; additional qualifiers allowed the use of parentheses to denote place and the equal sign to denote language; and quotation marks denoted time periods.
>
> For example: 51 + 53 = Mathematics and chemistry
> 63:30 or 31:63 = Statistics relating to agriculture
> 339.5 (410/44) = Trade relations between the United Kingdom and France
> 35 94(410)"19"(075) = History of the United Kingdom in the 20th Century Textbook
>
> This ability to create symbolic links between multiple topics marked a major conceptual breakthrough, allowing for a theoretically endless series of permutations that could express any number of semantic relationships. It also provided a powerful tool for indexing, permitting highly specific references drilling deep into the contents of books and articles. This ability to create symbolic linkages between entities and interpolate them with one another anticipates the logic of the modern relational database.[13]

As we see, Otlet's notational system creates connections between topics by first enumerating the boundaries between topics. Those using descendants of his schema associate what are considered important elements of a book's content, and to a lesser degree its material details, with categorical ideas. A book concerning the "arts" is labeled with the integer 7. A book concerning language, linguistics, or literature is labeled with an 8. These integers create context by situating that book in relation to others of that type and the system. That is, individual books are contextualized by a mapping to an enumerative apparatus. As Wright suggests, this apparatus allows a book to be situated in a theoretically infinite web of semantic relationships constituted by the positionality of a conceptual vocabulary mapped to integers that can assert statements according to a set of syntactical rules. Books gain identity in the system through the context—that is, the weave of connections articulated by boundaries that also suggest distinction—provided by symbols and their ordered relation to each other. The fluid boundaries of this kind of context are managed by the controlled vocabulary of the system and its operations as they relate to what we might call "content," "news of some fact, subject, or event."[14]

Otlet's system and those inspired by it connect the infinities of books through the intricate boundaries drawn by the system's enumerative procedures. We think of Otlet's system as enumerative and descriptive. As we have defined the terms, *enumeration* concerns lists and *description* concerns the articulation of relationships. But it is important to emphasize, even if it is not novel to claim, that Otlet's system is also generative. It generates contexts through the boundaries that its draws, the concepts that it delineates, and how individuals choose to associate elements of books with the concepts enumerated by the system. The boundaries drawn by the system and how people use it coordinate a weave of connections among books to create *contexts*. These same boundaries determine how books enumerated in the system will be positioned "together" to create order. In this sense, Otlet's system and systems like it *coordinate*.

It is crucial to notice (although, again, not novel to claim) that Otlet's enumerative system also enumerates his own desires and beliefs, as well as those that use it to coordinate documents. Otlet has decided that "art" is a concept that should be labeled "7." Librarians who use the system to gain bibliographical control of the documents with which they work use the numbers and the categories to coordinate their documents and solve the real-world problem of accounting for and making them accessible to those who wish to use them. Doing so, they are making choices about what constitutes a book about art. Library catalogs are a record of these choices. They can be read as not only finding aids but also a record of how books have been contextualized by the art and cunning of librarians, each with individual appetites, desires, and subtly different stratagems for satiating them by means of their enumerative work.

READING BOOKS FOR THE CONTEXTS THEY EVINCE

The shared boundary that Wilson draws to formulate list makers and studiers of books as contexts for one another also has the quirky power to describe how list makers and studiers of books have tended to formulate contexts differently. Where Otlet and list makers have tended to be interested in creating a coordinated system for enumerating a description of the dance of knowledge by formulating contexts, humanist studiers of books have tended to try to know the books as dancers through the weave of contexts that they make available. That is, studiers of books have tended to read books as evidence of the rich, connected weave of contexts that books can be understood to evince. Enumeration serves descriptions of a book's connections to its authors, its printers, the kinds of presses that produced it, its owners by means of marginalia or book plates, the places that provided the materials used to make it, and any indications of how it made its journey to its present location; and any particular qualities that recommend it should be copied and made available elsewhere.

The meticulous research of McKenzie's masterwork,[15] the *Cambridge University Press, 1696–1712: A Bibliographical Study*, situates the books he enumerates and describes in intricately woven contexts to suggest a great deal about what can be known about how each was produced, transmitted, and received. We learn what the books are about, but rather than using aboutness to gird the construction of a context for organizing them, McKenzie builds his detailed enumerative description by coordinating what can be discerned about a press's books through material examinations of the books themselves and an investigation of the press's records. The books provide a context for the records, and the records contextualize the books to enable McKenzie to produce his carefully detailed descriptions. Reading attempts to discover and account for what might count as useful contexts for particular intellectual ends, in this case particular books and records that serve McKenzie's desire to explore what he would later call the "sociology" of texts.

SIMILAR BUT LISTED SEPARATELY

We can say, acknowledging that Wilson's two-item list has framed our thinking, that the kinds of contexts that scholars such McKenzie formulate and explore to describe physical objects are distinct from the contexts formulated to describe physical objects by thinkers such as Otlet. We might associate the former with the humanities and the latter with information science. The same differentiating boundary can also be used to associate these approaches. To bring this chapter to a close and reinforce one of its central ideas—that enumeration formulates distinction through boundaries that connect what has been distinguished—a final juxtaposition will helpfully suggest how bibliography, as practiced by scholars such as McKenzie, and information science share a border that connects and distinguishes them.

What McKenzie says about books in *Bibliography and the Sociology of Texts*, from the 1980s, can be usefully compared to what Lee Pierce Butler (1884–1953) has to say about books in *An Introduction to Library Science*, from the 1930s. Indeed, Butler's statements about books could be used to summarize much of what McKenzie presents in his Panizzi Lectures of the 1980s. That McKenzie may not have read the statements of Butler, which so neatly organizes many of his own assertions about books and bibliography, is an indication of not only the deepening divide between the communities of list makers and studiers of books in the twentieth century, but also their strong connections. Using Butler's statements to summarize many of

McKenzie's assertions about bibliography is not meant to lend pride of intellectual place to Butler or to suggest that we should collapse the hardening distinction between the two communities that we might associate with Wilson's list makers and studiers of books. Rather, I present Butler's description of textual creation as a social act to suggest the shared boundary between the communities, and also the force of enumerative practices that would catalog and contextualize Butler's book under the subject headings "library science; libraries; information science"[16] and McKenzie's under the subject headings "criticism, textual—social aspects; Communication—social aspects; knowledge, sociology of"[17] when they both engage the same topic—books—from remarkably similar perspectives. Presenting an extended passage from Butler's 1933 book clarifies the nuanced relationship between him and McKenzie:

> Society probably contributes far more to the publication of a printed book than does the author who composes it. The mechanical process by which the first manuscript is reproduced in many printed copies has been evolved by the cumulative labors of many men through many generations. The apparatus by which the book is actually printed has also required for its fabrication the cooperative effort of countless individuals in dozens of industries. No single mind has ever planned the coordination but from the miner who excavates the ore to the pressman who sets the finished machine in motion there has been an organization of enterprise and achievement which involves the whole social fabric. Society has used for a final communal purpose what single individuals have intended for ends that are immediate and personal. . . . Society itself has built the printing press.
>
> Where the author working alone might in the course of years make a few copies of his book and circulate them in his immediate circle, his people organized in a society have reproduced and scattered his writing broadcast. But his dependence upon social organization is more complete than this. The language which he uses and the written form in which he records it are not his own inventions. These symbolic sounds and graphic symbols have no meaning except by virtue of social convention. His ideas and the patterns in which he combines them are themselves but seldom more than borrowings from the social group of which he is a member. Though the pen is directed by the writer, it may be said in a very real sense, that usually it can write only what society itself has dictated.

. . .

What memory is to man the graphic record is, in part, to modern society. Memory is a phase necessary to any mental process and itself involves the whole range of intellectual activities. To record in the mind requires perception, to retain requires the creation of a concept, and to recall usually gives rise to an act of volition animated by desire. If remembering were merely a discharge of stored neural forces the act of remembering would be in effect a re-acting of the things remembered in a reverse order of occurrence. It is selective in so far as it is an act of intelligence.[18]

Many aspects of Butler's remarks can be updated by more recent science and thinking about society and social systems. His remarks are nearly eighty years old. But he clearly views texts as manifold potentialities created and enabled or disabled by constellations of individuals, institutions, ideas, processes, and materials, which is what he seems to mean by "society." Writing about printed materials and his idea that they should be studied as social ensembles, McKenzie asserts:

At one level, a sociology simply reminds us of the full range of social realities which the medium of print had to serve, from receipt blanks to bibles. But it also directs us to consider the human motives and interactions which texts involve at every stage of their production, transmission, and consumption. It alerts us to the roles of institutions, and their own complex structures, in affecting the forms of social discourse, past and present. Those are the realities which bibliographers and textual critics as such have, until very recently, either neglected or, by defining them as strictly non-bibliographical, have felt unable to denominate, logically and coherently, as central to what we do. Historical bibliography, we were told, was not strictly bibliography at all.[19]

It is important to notice how similar McKenzie's statement is to Butler's because the similarity helps to reveal the force of enumerative systems such as those created by the Online Computer Library Center (OCLC), which would so forcefully divide their statements into separate categories of knowledge and discourse. There are certainly distinctions to be drawn between Butler's statement and McKenzie's. McKenzie is defining bibliography as a sociology of texts to suggest texts as records of human agency in complex systems. Society is less a kind of unseen force for McKenzie as it is a complex weave of many actors, with various degrees of agency interacting. An author in McKenzie's sociology of texts has considerable agency, more perhaps than Butler might concede, even if s/he is never granted autonomy. Butler's statements, of course, were made in the context of his desire for libraries to play a role in educational reform in Depression-era America while McKenzie was writing against the doctrines of early twentieth-century Anglophone studiers of texts such W. W. Greg and Fredson Bowers, two figures that will feature prominently in the pages to come.

Greg and Bowers believed that for bibliography to be a science, it must constrain itself primarily to the physical traces of activity recorded by books as evidence of bibliographical truths: "A 'sociology of texts'" was meant to contrast and extend "a bibliography confined to logical inference from printed signs as arbitrary marks on parchment or paper."[20] The nuance of the distinctions that need to be drawn between Butler and McKenzie again reveals the force of lists like Wilson's and the list makers at institutions such as OCLC, who presently formulate many of the lists that we see in our libraries, and who would so forcefully divide them into camps: "library science; libraries; information science" versus "criticism, textual—social aspects; Communication—social aspects; knowledge, sociology of." Their division, as I hope to have shown, also provides the opportunity to coordinate the context of each statement by positioning them across boundaries that have been drawn between them.

By focusing on the pleasures and powers of enumeration, I hope that I have suggested some of the human motivations that can be discerned by assessing lists and, by means of my own two-item list (one built upon Wilson's), how lists can generate order and power by articulating horizons of knowing. I hope that the horizons drawn in this chapter can enable us to see how lists help to formulate contexts and how approaches to context can be formulated so differently by diverse practices in information science, distinct from but connected to bibliography as diverse practices in the humanities.

4 WHAT UNFAMILIAR LISTS AFFORD

Assessing lists and contexts, like seeing infrastructures, is difficult because contexts and lists in their ordinary utility are difficult to see. It is difficult to see the similarity between the assertions of McKenzie and Butler from within the organizing contexts provided by information science or textual criticism as they have been organized by those working in those fields and as they are enumerated by classificatory systems such as those provided by the Online Computer Library Center (OCLC). In this chapter, I present less familiar ways of thinking about lists to defamiliarize enumeration. The aim is to step outside our ordinary ways of working and thinking so we might find standing to reconsider enumerative bibliographical practices in information science. These unfamiliar modes of list making are meant to provide a sense for lists and enumerative practices as they can be perceived, not necessarily as we have come to know them. My presentation is not an endorsement of the scientific or philosophical arguments that formulate them. The measures of value that they may provide are not afforded by the validity of the science and philosophy that formulate them, but rather by how they enable us to relate our ordinary learned repertoires of enumerative practices with their culturally and socially sanctioned concepts and with what they enable and constrain.[1] Just as Borges's imaginative encyclopedic list afforded Foucault an opportunity to reconsider relations between words and things (*les mots et les choses*)—"the order of things"—the idea is to entertain alien lists and list-making processes to reconsider how lists and enumerative practices order relations. The odd perspectives enabled by the speculative lists presented in the chapter suggest that our own enumerative practices are likely to create usefully limiting contexts that afford utility and enable action by constraining what can be taken as given. They create contexts that afford the ability to find and organize information about books concerning "library science; libraries; information science" and "criticism, textual—social aspects; Communication—social aspects; knowledge, sociology of," for example. But the affordances of these contexts are simultaneously disabling and thwart efforts to find and organize points of intersection and shared boundaries, such as between library science and textual criticism. Apropos of its title, this chapter suggests that unfamiliar lists afford a means of accounting (albeit incompletely) for the enabling and disabling contexts that enumerative practices produce.

Two perspectives are particularly useful for investigating what is afforded by lists, how they create contexts that can be both enabling and constraining, and the ways that they can formulate what is taken as given. The first comes from the Baltic-German biologist Jakob von Uexküll (1864–1944), who asks that we seriously consider the subjectivities of nonhuman creatures. The second is from the speculative realist and media theorist Ian Bogost and his philosopher colleague Graham Harman, who ask that we speculate seriously about objectivity by earnestly considering what it might be like to be a thing. The works of Uexküll, Bogost, and Harman are useful for exposing bibliographical practices as infrastructure in information science because they disrupt commonsensical enumerative practices in ways that reposition us in relation to things and ideas ordinarily taken as given, such as how to enumerate objects and distinguish between objects and their contexts, by having us consider how this might be done by nonhuman subjectivities and alien objectivities.

UEXKÜLLIAN *UMWELTEN* (ENVIRONMENTS) AND ENUMERATION

How does a tick experience its world? What is an oak tree to a fox or a wasp? How many objects constitute an oak tree? Uexküll, who sees himself as a biologist first and foremost, asks questions like these to understand the biological world. At first estimation, these may not seem to be bibliographical questions. But they are profoundly bibliographical in the sense that they provide a way to consider the affordances of enumerative processes, the contexts that they can generate and reveal, and what can be taken as given.

Uexküll theorizes that every living creature lives in the bubble of its own perceptions. He calls these bubbles "environments" (*Umwelten*), by which he means "all the features accessible" to an organism through its perceptive capabilities. Creaturely environments are delineated by creatures' sensory organs. Each creature has its own *Umwelt*, Uexküll argues, and each is a closed world: "Everything a subject perceives belongs to its perception world [*Merkwelt*], and everything it produces, to its effect world [*Wirkwelt*]. These two worlds, of perception and production of effects, form one closed unit, the environment."[2] This kind of closed-world thinking has profound implications for the objects that can be enumerated by creatures and what they can perceive as context in their environments.

As if he were a systematic bibliographer and not a biologist, Uexküll suggests that organisms create meaning by making lists. Enumeration provides a foundational utility to biological organisms as Uexküll conceives them by providing what information scientists might call "descriptive control." This control is a function of the ability to reduce the complexity of the universe so that courses of actions that promote their survival can be undertaken. As Uexküll understands them, organisms' perceptual systems "embody and measure a set of relations between heterogeneous elements"[3] in the world so that organisms can take these measurements as established facts. In this sense, the sensory organs of biological entities function as biological equivalents of what Madeleine Akrich calls "technical objects" (see chapter 1). As with objects like electrical systems and the sensors that monitor them, the sensory organs of organisms create boundaries that delimit the plentitude of the universe and what counts as contexts. As Uexküll explains, the environmental bubbles within which organisms operate are formulated by perceptual apparatuses that facilitate a conversion of the facts created by their sensory systems "into facts" of their worlds, "pure and simple."[4] To emphasize the bibliographical and information-scientific nature of his thinking, we can notice that perceptions and their effects in Uexküll's conception of the biological world are equated with marks that function as documentation for nonhuman animals. These marks are not unlike the documentary inscriptions made by electrons hitting photosensitive plates which physicists have used as evidence of subatomic particles. Describing the *Umwelt* of a tick, he writes: "The whole rich world surrounding the tick is constricted and transformed into an impoverished structure that, most importantly of all, consists only of three features [*Merkmalan*] and three effect marks [*Wirkmalen*]—the tick's environment. However, the poverty of this environment is needful for the certainty of action, and certainty is more important than riches."[5]

Enumerating the tick's environment as he does, Uexküll provides a means for us to think about the affordances of bibliographical lists and enumerative processes and to consider how they might usefully impoverish the complexity of the world to facilitate the certainty of action toward specific ends. For a tick and its sensory system as described by Uexküll, the end is survival. Enumeration as a form of descriptive control, as we can hypothesize from the odd angle that Uexküll's tick provides, impoverishes the bibliographical universe to facilitate its use for some end or ends. The contexts enumerated by the tick's perceptual systems are limited to what is relevant to its survival. A person seeking a means to some bibliographical end, as Wilson describes, will wish to have an enumerative description just rich enough to exploit the bibliographical universe for some purpose. They will wish to have a context that is only as complex as what facilitates an end. At the same time, Wilson acknowledges that ends and purposes are variable. What is one person's heap of bibliographical flotsam and jetsam is another's treasure trove. Enumeration, because it is always selective, impoverishes complexity. It thus serves certain ends while disabling others by creating variously useful or disabling contexts. Enumerative practices selectively provide means to certain ends while affording none to others. Uexküll's tick provides a usefully unusual perspective on the old problem that Wilson describes while clarifying the infrastructural role of enumeration in information science by suggesting enumeration's inherent trade-offs.

UEXKÜLLIAN OBJECTS

The selective enumeration that is performed by biological subjects means that objects are never fully knowable to subjects in Uexküllian environments. Moreover, alternative methods of enumeration ensure that things are to be taken as givens in different ways. The usefully impoverished contexts of our tick's environment will be impoverished differently from a horsefly's, and differently again from the horse that the horsefly bites. This means that objects are variously formulated by biological subjects. As mentioned in chapter 1, Uexküll gives an example of an oak tree, which is a different object to different creatures. For the fox, the oak's roots become a solid roof that protects it and its family. For the squirrel, the oak's branches are "handy springboards," and for the bird, they are places to land. In the ant's environment, only the furrows of the oak's bark exist, and this bark is "soft" for the ichneumon wasp that is burrowing to feast upon the larvae of bark beetles despite being "hard" in the environments of many other creatures. The enumerative sensory apparatus of each species provides different means for their survival and for impoverishing the complexity of the world for their species-specific ends. Along with objects, what counts as context is articulated differently for each creature, according to Uexküll:

> In the hundred different environments of its inhabitants, the oak plays an ever-changing role as object, sometimes with some parts, sometimes with others. The same parts are alternately large and small. Its wood is both hard and soft; it serves for attack and for defense.
>
> If one wanted to summarize all the different characteristics shown by the oak as an object, this would only give rise to chaos. Yet these are only parts of a subject that is solidly put together in itself, which carries and shelters all environments—one which is never known by all the subjects of these environments and never knowable for them.[6]

The multiplicity of Uexküllian objects provides a vantage point for us to consider how enumerative processes enable objects to matter so differently and provide such distinct affordances. It also help us to consider how, even when objects matter differently, they can coordinate action. Like what Star calls "boundary objects," Uexküllian objects organize diverse actions in and across communities with no need of consensus concerning what objects are. The oak tree usefully facilitates diverse action while also disabling similarly diverse action. From this admittedly unorthodox vantage point, it is easier to see how the same objects can matter so differently depending upon how they are enumerated by the perceptive apparatuses of different individuals and communities, and hence to see more clearly the important roles played by bibliographers (whether they go by that name or not) in formulating contexts through enumerative practices that serve (or thwart) the ends of individuals and communities.

UEXKÜLLIAN MEANING

Uexküll's take on meaning is also productive for thinking about the power and force of enumerative systems as they operate in information science. Meaning, in Uexküll's way of thinking, has force. For him, "meaning bridges the gap between physical and nonphysical processes"[7] so that everything that "falls under the spell of an environment" is "reformed" until it becomes a "useful carrier of meaning" or is "neglected."[8] Uexküllian *Umwelten* are creatively destructive; their "components" are "crudely torn apart without the slightest consideration"[9] for what might have been afforded in an alternative environment or nature's plan. Although Claude Shannon attempted to bracket the meaning of messages, we can express Uexküllian meaning in Shannonian terms. It describes how information sources as discrete sets are formulated in relation to the channels of communication with the world available to a creature. In Wilsonian terms, Uexküllian meaning describes the marginal utility of an extra unit of descriptive control relative to exploitative control that it provides a creature as it acts for its survival. Uexküll explains with a complex conceit that has a "simple" curved glass bowl serving a variety of functions, including as a window. He writes, "I can . . . put the glass bowl on the table and fill it with water in order to use it as a flower vase"[10] or insert it into an outer wall to be "transformed" into a "window." He adds: "The properties of the object are not changed thereby. But as soon as it has transformed itself into a carrier of meaning such as 'window' or 'vase,' a distinction of properties according to their *rank* becomes apparent. For the window, transparency is the 'leading' property, whereas curvature represents a supporting property. For the vase, on the contrary, curvature is the leading property and transparency the supporting property."[11]

Parallels between Uexküllian meaning and library catalogs can be easily drawn. The meaning of Uexküll's own book can be ranked according to its properties as librarians enumerate them from within their environments. The book's title, or Uexküll's name as the book's author, might be "leading" properties. Other properties enumerated as part of what we would call "descriptive metadata" could also be leading properties. Uexküll's take on meaning also provides a means of considering how we in information science often attempt to generate it.

While we as information scientists sometimes attempt to bracket certain kinds of meaning and knowing from definitions of information science and foundational technical definitions of communication (see chapter 1), these definitions and intellectual foci are themselves meaningful in an Uexküllian sense. The inclination to bracket what a message might mean to a person receiving it in order to focus on communication as an engineering problem, and the professional disposition that has us overlook the nuanced meaning of a novel or Shannon's paper in order to catalog it correctly for readers, are themselves meaningful knowledge practices, of course. As Marcia Bates has suggested, our frequent focus on technical problems as they relate to the ways that people interact with the systems that we build helps to constitute what she calls the "invisible substrate of information science."[12] Crudely put in Uexküllian terms, we are diverse species that tend, as we go about work in our field, to enumerate the world in ways that rank the properties of things and ideas differently from others. The useful paradox that Uexküll helps us to see more clearly is that we often understand the ends that we pursue in terms of our work's meaningful utility to others.

Contemplating our work through an Uexküllian lens, we might say that through our own creative-destructive fashioning of the world, we fashion "information science" environments in which we "tear" what we formulate as "leading" properties of books—their titles, authors, subjects, and other features—to facilitate "bridges" that span the "gap between physical and nonphysical processes."[13] We do this, an Uexküllian perspective would suggest, from within our environments such that what falls under the spell of our environment is "reformed" until it becomes a "useful carrier of meaning" or is "neglected."[14]

Again, Uexküllian meaning helps to illuminate this old problem in information science from a new angle while reinforcing the notion that enumeration and description are foundational. What is meaningful to us as information scientists and how we formulate meaning are functions of how we mark, count, and list; the variously useful contexts that we produce with our enumerative practices; and the ways that our enumerative practices cause us to take things as given. These will be distinct from how others mark, count, and make meaning with the systems that information scientists fashion. These potential incompatibilities of meaning are not a problem, so long as what is fashioned by information scientists serves others in their alternative environments. In Uexküll's model, the oak tree grows for the oak tree's sake, but doing so creates forms of utility for other creatures.

The very hard problem is finding standing in relation to these other environments and ecosystems so what we enumerate as the properties of objects helps to sustain and propel others inhabiting alternative *Umwelten*. To borrow from Uexküll's productive metaphor of the oak tree one last time, we have the difficult problem of wishing to sustain the ecosystem enabled by the oak tree without being able, from our own environmental perspective, to know the oak tree as an oak tree, let alone as what the oak tree is to the squirrel or fox. We also have the difficult problem of recognizing other trees in the forest and the ecologies that they inhabit and support. More troubling, we can just as easily degrade the ecosystems suggested by the forest as help them and the forest's cohabitants thrive.

OBJECT-ORIENTED ONTOLOGIES AND ONTOGRAPHY

Purposeful speculation is one way to address this hard problem of finding standing in relation to those that we aim to support and sustain with our work. In addition to our more ordinary empirical approaches, and as a check on the ways that we fashion our world with our disciplinary inclinations, we can consider alien enumerative practices as means of accounting for what has fallen under the spell of the environment that we have created for ourselves, what we have "reformed" through our own practices to be "useful carrier[s] of meaning," and what we have neglected. Bogost and Harman provide a particularly useful method of accounting for what we take as given.

What is it like to be *E.T.* (the computer game from 1982, not Steven Spielberg's movie or the alien that appeared in it)? Speculative realists like Bogost and Harman ask this question as they attempt to understand objects in relation to each other rather than as relations between living subjects and objects. They ask us to empathize with things rather than living beings by asking absurd questions. What is it like to be a bookbinding, acidic paper, or a Unicode value? The aim, they suggest, is to prompt a cascade of additional unfamiliar questions that allow us to write what Bogost calls "speculative fictions." These fictions are meant to provide opportunities to reconsider and contextualize the nonfictions of what we take to be a real book, its binding, its acidic paper, and the Unicode values used to transcribe what appears on its sheets into digital systems. The idea is that such fictions enable us to consider the physical and mental environments that we inhabit by going "where everyone has gone before, but where few have bothered to linger."[15] Bogost and Harman suggest that we can be led closer to knowing what we assume about books and data by attempting to consider what they might be in "their worlds." For our purposes, this kind of speculation affords opportunities to assess enumerative practices for how they draw the boundaries of things, ideas, and our relations with them.

LISTS AND ONTOGRAPHY

As you might expect, list making plays a central role in speculating about what might be taken as real by speculative realists. Harman and Bogost call their brand of list making "ontography," and they associate it with methods of drawing our "attention to the countless things that litter our world unseen."[16] Lists "map" what they call the "basic landmarks and fault lines in the universe of objects" rather than a geography of "stock natural characters."[17] A book is a "landmark" and "fault line" that can be used to distinguish objects, but it also highlights the inadequacy of *book* as a "stock character" and descriptive term for a literary bibliographer or librarian, which is comparable to the inadequacy of the term *forest* for an ecologist. For Bogost and Harman, ontography celebrates worldly detail by honing the virtue of attentive practices that attempt to suspend "anthropocentric narrative coherence"[18] in favor of an object's material or imagined presence. Like many defamiliarizing projects, the aim is to see things for what they are before they are made into a story of what is or should be. There is an imperative to explore what is afforded by quirky lists and the unfamiliar contexts that they produce. Ontography, according to Harman and Bogost, offers fitful contemplative pauses and "an antidote to the obsession with Deleuzean becoming" or any privileging of "continuity and smoothness" over "sequentiality and fitfulness."[19]

Whatever we might feel about Deleuzean becoming or the need for a philosophical antidote to it, for our purposes, Harman and Bogost's ontography suggests opportunities to pause and reconsider what coheres the narrative assumptions that guide our enumerative practices. We do not need to have a philosophical stake in what might constitute anthropocentric narrative coherence or their beliefs about speculative realism. But the oddity provided by ontography provides what reflection from an alternative perspective provides: the possibility of gaining something unexpected—for example, information about our assumptions, how we have positioned ourselves and our work, and what we may have left out.

As a concrete example of how ontography can afford opportunities to reconsider our enumerative practices and, by extension, the ways that bibliography serves as integral infrastructure in information science, we can consider lists that we have seen before: library science, libraries, information science; criticism, textual—social aspects, communication—social aspects, knowledge, sociology of. These are the lists provided by OCLC for the descriptions of McKenzie's *Bibliography and the Sociology of Texts* and Butler's *An Introduction to Library Science*. Pausing over them, we can wonder again what narrative coherence they might suggest. In chapter 3, I suggested that they could be associated with the similarity of Butler's and

McKenzie's assertions about books and societies, even if OCLC cataloged them separately—something that I have attempted to record by placing a semicolon between the two lists.

Suggestive of how ontography can sensitize us to the ways that we enumerate facts that have already been established, we can fret over *things*, small and large. Ontography provides license to fret, as I did, over the semicolon used to conjoin the lists describing McKenzie's and Butler's books. We can wonder what semicolons are and how they might cohere or sunder narrative assumptions. How *truly* different would things be if a carriage return marked the boundary between the two lists?

Library science, libraries, information science
Criticism, textual—social aspects, communication—social aspects, knowledge, sociology of

This admittedly superficial and self-referential question, reflective of my own quandaries over how to punctuate this list, has the benefit of showing the ways that ordinary "stock characters" like semicolons and carriage returns can become "fault lines" capable of repositioning us in relation to the most mundane enumerative procedures. The carriage return creates a vertical hierarchy between the lists. Do I mean to suggest that "Library science" is above "Criticism, textual"? Did I mean to intend anything by having "Library science" precede "Criticism, textual" when ordered by the semicolon?

What defines a carriage return? Is it the idea of the carriage, so integral to the typewriters that helped to formulate the phrase? The Unicode value that can be expressed in decimal form as "10" if I think a carriage return as a "new line" and not a "carriage return," which is encoded with the decimal value "13" by the Unicode consortium? What about the word *semicolon*? The *Oxford English Dictionary (OED)* defines it as follows: "In present use [the semicolon] is the chief stop intermediate in value between the comma and the full stop; usually separating sentences the latter of which limits the former, or marking off a series of sentences or clauses of co-ordinate value."[20] Do I mean to suggest a "stop intermediate in value" between "library science" and "bibliography as a sociology of texts," where "bibliography as a sociology of texts" limits "library science"? How might such an expression sustain or undercut my arguments from the last chapter? Perhaps I mean simply to "mark off a series of sentences or clauses of co-ordinate value." Indeed, this might be a nice summary of my arguments; but the semicolon suggests both ideas.

The larger point is that ontography can help to reveal our ordinary bibliographical practices of enumeration and our own fitful moments considering how to count, recount, and reshuffle what has been counted as information and knowledge so as to usefully formulate them and their relations. It helps us to see how enumerative practices reify and build the contextualizing systems within which they work and also how they provide opportunities to recontextualize those systems by insistently accounting for the objects formulated by systems. An apparently simple enumerative problem unfurls into questions about distinctions that can be drawn between a "carriage return" and a "new line" in the Unicode standard. One commenter on Stack Overflow endorsed by a "green check" indicating the usefulness of her/his suggestion writes: "\n is the newline character, while \r is the carriage return. They differ in what uses them. Windows uses \r\n to signify the enter key was pressed, while Linux and Unix use \n to signify that the enter key was pressed."[21]

Those who have wrestled with data where fields are sometimes delimited by semicolons, and sometimes by something else, know with intimacy the fitful moments of those who have previously attempted to count and recount what has previously counted as information and knowledge. For our particular purposes, the distinction between a "carriage return" and a "new line" may not be of particular import. But attending to it as part of our ontographic example reveals contexts in which the distinction could be important. Along with the capacity to better attend to how lists have been formulated, the ability to reveal contexts is among ontography's powers.

CARPENTRY-ACCOUNTING

To summarize our discussion of what is afforded by the unusual enumerative practices that we have been considering, bring this chapter to a close, and suggest again how bibliography and enumeration are marginal but constructive and constitutive actors in diverse networks of practice in information science, we can dwell momentarily over an additional tool provided by Bogost.

To level an important critique of philosophy (and academic endeavor more generally), Bogost constructs a philosophical tool that he calls "carpentry." "Carpentry," he suggests, "extends the ordinary sense of woodcraft to any material whatsoever,"[22] including philosophy. "To do carpentry is to make anything, but to make it in earnest, with one's own hands, like a cabinetmaker."[23] Bogost's notion of carpentry can be extended to enumeration as a craft of "representation and organization" that we fashion with our own hands by engaging, as Bates has suggested, "fundamentally different talents and skills from those required in other professions and intellectual disciplines."[24] Bogost's basic argument is that making and building are the best kinds of philosophizing. He contrasts this with the philosophy that can be read from books, including, paradoxically, his own: "Like scientific experiments and engineering prototypes, the stuffs produced by carpentry are not mere accidents, waypoints on the way to something else. Instead, they are themselves earnest entries into philosophical discourse."[25] "Carpentry," Bogost's critique suggests, can "offer a more rigorous kind of philosophical creativity" by addressing more than a "human reader's ability to pass eyeballs over words and intellect over notions they contain."[26] He adds:

> Sure, written matter is subject to the material constraints of the page, the printing press, the publishing company, and related matters, but those factors exert minimal force on the content of a written philosophy. While a few exceptions exist (Jacques Derrida's *Glas*, perhaps, or the Nietzschean aphorism, or the propositional structure of Baruch Spinoza's *Ethics* or Ludwig Wittgenstein's *Tractatus*), philosophical works generally do not perpetrate their philosophical positions through their form as books. The carpenter, by contrast, must contend with the material resistance of his or her chosen form, making the object itself become the philosophy.[27]

This claim assumes a great deal about books and about philosophy. Bogost dismisses books themselves as contingencies, along with all the contingent processes that would bring any particular one before the eyeballs of a human reader. These are contingences that Bogost otherwise celebrates, and bibliographers and information scientists, each in their own way as they pursue their own ends, know in their bones the way that a cabinet maker knows the feel of oak and can distinguish it from pine. Even as we might applaud Bogost's attempt to reposition contemporary philosophy to align it with building and the "knowing-how"[28] of old concepts like *technê*, he looks past the "carpentry" of the many people that created and then accounted for what has been made and organized as "books of philosophy." Their carpentry slips from view: not just the carpentry of the publisher raising capital to pay for the carpentry of the press people who ensure that the registers are aligned to constrain pages as proscribed by the carpentry of typesetters picking type or fiddling with a variety of settings in any variety of software packages; but also the bibliographical carpentry of those doing the work of "related matters" like enumerating, describing, analyzing, and critiquing as they facilitate cataloging and describing again, modeling and remodeling as data and metadata "books of philosophy."

If we take Bogost's notion of carpentry and append the idea of insistent recursive, enumerative accounting for what has been carpentered, it becomes a potent means of considering the foundational infrastructural roles played by bibliography and enumeration in information science, not as a kind of philosophy, but as a kind of material-conceptual work. Indeed, it becomes another usefully odd list that affords the idea that bibliography builds enumerative accounts that construct usefully constrained contexts while also providing means of accounting for what has been built. Carpentry-accounting creates one additional unfamiliar list that suggests through its strangeness how integral our ordinary enumerative practices are to work done in information science and how useful they can be as means of reflecting on it.

II

5 FROM ENUMERATION TO DESCRIPTION: KNOWLEDGE GRAPHS AND GRAPHING KNOWLEDGE

This chapter and those that follow shift gears. Where lists and enumeration have been our topic, this chapter and those to come focus their attention on description. They recount some historical approaches to bibliographical description and a way to think again about the cleavages that enabled Wilson to describe bibliography with his two-item list: list makers and studiers of texts. A new history of bibliographical description, however that might be imagined, is not my objective, however. Rather, using the intentionally odd enumerative perspectives provided by chapter 4 and what we learned about the powers and pleasures of enumeration in that chapter, as well as the infrastructural inversion that we performed in chapter 2, I aim to reflect on the less noticed descriptive infrastructures that support work in information science. As a preface to those that follow, this brief transitional chapter describes some of the ways that enumeration and description are distinct but entangled.

FROM ENUMERATION TO DESCRIPTION—KNOWLEDGE GRAPHS AND GRAPHING KNOWLEDGE

One of the many daunting tasks that we have assigned ourselves as information scientists is to construct an account of the records associated with human inquiry and knowledge. Indeed, descriptions of human modes of inquiry inform many of the descriptions that I have presented, such as my description of bibliography as a constellation of barycenters formulating the orbits of different disciplinary planets while also being formulated by them, a metaphorical description that I presented in the introduction and return to in this chapter. The metaphor is enabled by the idea that human inquiry can be categorized according to discipline. A similar descriptive framework girds the introduction to this chapter and ideas considered previously: the idea that "science" and "the humanities" can coordinate diverse disciplinary modes of inquiry. A thought experiment will help to reflect on the descriptive infrastructures that support information science as it goes about its work of supporting diverse modes of human inquiry. We might start with a list, of course, such as the two-item list that frames our discussion and my assertions—science and the humanities—and then create a simple descriptive knowledge graph.

As we begin to describe modes of human inquiry and knowing formulated by science and the humanities, we turn to documents that describe science, perhaps one that specifies how science is currently organized to include formal sciences, such as logic and mathematics; the natural sciences, including the physical sciences and the life sciences; and the social sciences like sociology and economics. Turning to a book about the modern humanities, we might be persuaded that the modern humanistic disciplines of history, literature, linguistics, archaeology, religious studies, and classics have descended from a progenitor mode of intellectual inquiry called *philology*.

The artificial simplicity of these categorical and genealogical lists, as we have been discussing, will immediately disclose how much more could have been included in a description of the disciplinary landscape of our contemporary educational systems, modes of knowing, and their histories. They will also remind us that our initial arbitrary, two-item list has powerfully shaped what has already become a description, and our description is informed by existing knowledge and our access to it. Perhaps less obviously, the list also reveals how lists can be used as technical objects that allow powerful modes of measurement crucial to bibliography in its descriptive modes. As part of our bibliographical thought experiment, we might try to account for these objects and how they facilitate this ability to measure.

My list suggests history, literature, and archaeology are equivalent disciplines in the humanities. My list of sciences assumes similar equivalences.

These initial equivalences allow me to draw out relations among them. For example, my lists can be combined into what is called an "edge list," which allows me to graph their relationships as a network. This can be done because my lists define relationships among entities that are understood to be distinct modes of knowing that are similar in kind (equivalent disciplines within equivalent modes of human investigation in this case). The words *include* and *progenitor* define relationships among the entities. Arrows could be drawn pointing from philology to linguistics, literary studies, archaeology, history, classics, and religious studies. Similar arrows could be drawn pointing from science to the formal, natural, and social sciences.

Once enumerated, these equivalences and the distinctions they enact afford measurement and its powers. Science and the humanities are considered distinct but equivalent. Their subdisciplines are similarly formulated as being equivalent in their distinctions. The ability to assume equivalences of kind and relationship (among enumerated entities and between enumerated entities) enables the calculation of graph metrics such as centrality. We could say that philology has a high degree centrality in our representation of human modes of inquiry, for example. This *high degree centrality*, as it is called in the language of network analysis, would suggest the importance of philology as a mode of human inquiry, even if the word may not be as widely used as it once was. Similarly, we could suggest the obvious fact that science is an important mode of human inquiry. The large number of network connections formulated by our list would provide our evidence.

In both cases, the idea of importance is formulated by equivalences and the ability to count, in this case the ability to count connections articulated between modes of knowledge made equivalent by our initial list. Not surprisingly, our graph reiterates the importance of our initial enumerative choices. Less obviously, we can observe that an ability to assert equivalence has formulated an ability to measure, and the ability to measure, in turn, has helped to extend our initial description. We can also see how my description has been enabled by "mathesis," systems of knowledge premised on the ability to consider equivalences as always repeatable.[1] The ability to assume equivalences of kind and relationship enables the calculation of graph metrics such as centrality. Our newfound powers of measurement and description might cause us to begin to forget the unsurprising fact that these descriptive powers are formulated by the assertions of our initial lists.

As this thought experiment is meant to emphasize in the context of description, the insistent recursive drive of bibliography to account for accounts can also provide a mechanism for accounting for the equivalences and math that enable description. The recursive logic of bibliography means that it can function as a form of what Johanna Drucker has called "graphesis," "a system [of knowledge] in which every instantiation is specific, characterized (however minutely) by individual differences."[2] Bibliography enables an ability to investigate instantiations of equivalence as they might be formulated by mathesis or graphesis and the graphs printed in this chapter. The graphs in figure 5.1 allow us, even if we do not ordinarily avail ourselves of the opportunity, to investigate how their individual shapes affect how we know modes of human inquiry. They also present the ability to investigate how and why we assume that the graph printed in one copy of this book is equivalent to the "same" graph printed in another copy, despite their material distinctions.

My lists and their expression as a simple descriptive network in figure 5.1 (what some might call a "rudimentary knowledge graph") are rudimentary formulations meant to help expose how descriptive practices operate as situated assertions of equivalence that enable measurement and further description, which in turn present the opportunity for building additional descriptions and more measurements that enable distinctions. It is in this sense that descriptive practices can be understood as barycenters in the middle of the knowledge practices, including those of information science, as information scientists collect, store, retrieve, interpret, and transmit records of human knowledge. Existing forms of knowledge shape how those working at these shifting centers can describe knowledge. Simultaneously, the descriptions of knowledge produced at these peripheral centers formulate many of the ways that we can know.

Although overly simplified, my lists and the descriptions that they help to formulate are supported by scholarship and the wisdom of the crowd as expressed by Wikipedia. They rearticulate arguments made by James Turner about philology as a progenitor of an artificially divided modern humanities.

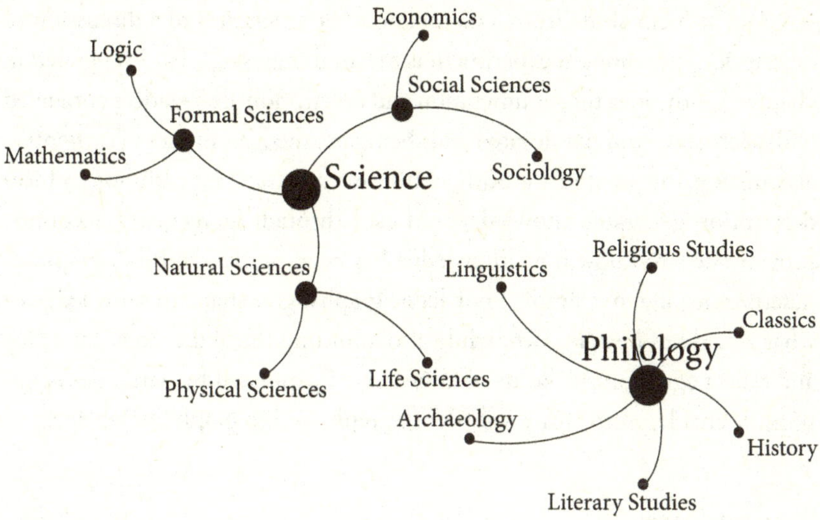

Figure 5.1
A simple graph of knowledge.

He writes, "Today's humanities disciplines are not ancient, integral modes of knowledge. They are modern, artificial creations—where made-up lines pretend to divide the single sandbox in which we all play into each boy's or girl's own inviolable kingdom."[3] Turner is describing the modern humanities, but contemporary scientific disciplines are similarly modern, artificial modes of knowledge. Few are likely to disagree, even if the English-language Wikipedia entry on "branches of science" does not emphasize this fact. And this is not a value judgment. It would be problematic to propose a mode of human inquiry that is not made or produced by human beings—the definition of "artificial."

My simplified network graphs and Turner's proclamation point to the need to make the artificiality of intellectual modes apparent. They also suggest the need to disclose the artificiality and extraordinary power provided by the ability to formulate and reproduce equivalences and distinctions since their artificiality ensures that our modern forms of producing and organizing knowledge are as inherently ideological as they are impactful. We know this already, but the recursive practices of bibliography remind us of it and have us reflect on it again.

As our focus shifts from a discussion of enumeration to a discussion of description, my thought experiment is meant to reiterate what I suggested in chapter 1—the idea that enumeration and description are practices entangled with each other and the situated ends being pursued. As modes of carpentry-accounting formulated by both mathesis and graphesis, bibliographical description generates knowledge and can, through its recursive accounts, provide ways to know how knowledge has been produced. Bibliographical descriptions, like my simple knowledge graphs, give shape to knowledge of what is and has been known, while also affording the ability to account for and reflect again on the kinds of knowledge formulated by particular equations. It enables us to create knowledge graphs and to graph knowledge.

DESCRIPTION

A *description* is a statement that is often produced through a process of enumeration. Here is the first definition of the term, provided by the *Oxford English Dictionary (OED)*: "a statement or account which describes something or someone by listing characteristic features, significant details."[4] Description articulates what has been enumerated, often recursively, through language that aims to express "the essential nature of a thing or concept."[5] Indeed, description and bibliography as the enumeration and copying of texts as data overlap semantically in a variety of ways. The noun *description* has multiple origins, many of which concern enumeration and copying. The Anglo-Norman, Middle French, and French precedents suggest the "action of describing," "enumeration," "census," "inscription," "delimitation," "written definition," "explanation," "or analysis (of an object, process, concept, etc.)," "piece of writing," "text," "picture," "diagram," "figure (in geometry)," and "act of representing in such a figure."[6] Description's association with census taking suggests its authority, and, as Markus Krajewski says, the historical origins of the card catalog.[7] The Latin roots of the verb *to describe* suggest "to represent by drawing, draw, mark out, to trace out, to record in writing, write down, to transcribe, copy out, to represent (in speech or writing), to prescribe, establish," as well as "to write down in a register, enrol."[8] This, of course, is very close to the etymological definition of *bibliography*.

Descriptions, like their enumerative subroutines, are more (or less) conspicuous about what they leave out. They are a function of the same kinds of cunning and desire that constitute list making. Apropos of this relationship, the lists and descriptive graphs with which I began this chapter are conspicuous for what they leave out. As such, they are descriptive visual strategies for articulating a central argument of this chapter—namely, that bibliography, in its marginal multiplicity and multiple roles as infrastructure, is often left out of our descriptions of intellectual communities. My depictions are drawn as part of my argument that, as the community responsible for accounting for and making accessible the records of human knowledge, we reconsider description and our descriptions of knowledge to better account for the roles played by descriptive statements in intellectual and creative work, both our own and those of the communities that we serve. Although description is always performed situationally and incompletely, it has the power to formulate and reify equivalences and distinctions that suggest impossible forms of ubiquity and completeness.

When we account for how data are created and collected, circulated and transformed, received and interpreted as descriptive statements, we can better situate the descriptive practices that formulate the records of human knowledge that we in our variously situated roles as information scientists aim, in turn, to organize and describe.

Again, I am not suggesting that bibliography be thought of (or made into) an "ur-discipline." Rather, my proposition is that bibliographical practice, of which bibliographical description is part, girds the work of attending to the records of our sciences and our humanities. Through its recursive accounting, it also provides opportunities to reflect on the work that we do. The case that I am making is not that bibliography is some all-encompassing discipline, but rather that it is infrastructure that, like all infrastructures, requires attention and maintenance because it situationally formulates, rightly and wrongly, equivalences and distinctions that powerfully affect us by helping to formulate the contexts that we inhabit and the ways that we know the world.

Here, Georg Schneider is helpful again. The close relationship between bibliography and the history of literature, he writes, does "not merely indicate that they both modify or replace a single science; it shows the basic relationship of bibliography to all the sciences."[9] Concerning bibliographical artisanship and the status of bibliography among shifting disciplinary hierarchies, he writes:

> It makes little difference whether bibliography is termed a science or an art, a technique or a skill, or even all of these together. The very limiting term "art" could be borne, if it be taken to mean that the method of performing bibliographic work represents knowing rather than understanding, or practice rather than theory. . . . The determination of the value of bibliography, which is not affected by a name, is of far greater importance than the determination of the title or rank that bibliography should be entitled to bear.[10]

Schneider's point is similar to mine. By recognizing the roles played by bibliography as diverse knowledge practices related to "all the sciences," we gain a clearer view of the complex bibliographical infrastructures that serve our diverse ends. Attending to the knowledge practices of information science, we are better positioned to account for our own ways of knowing as they affect our work and it affects others. In short, by recognizing the infrastructural roles played by bibliography, we are better positioned to know how we are working and if we are doing our work well. Schneider's emphasis on knowing and practice aligns with the idea of bibliography as carpentry-accounting in the sense that we would wish to build useful accounts of records, while also self-reflectively accounting for how we build those accounts to ensure that we are serving communities of which we are not members. I take Schneider's emphasis on knowing and practice to mean something akin to what Richard Sennett has written about artisanship—namely, that it concerns "a dialogue between concrete practices and thinking; this dialogue evolves into sustaining habits, and these habits establish a rhythm between problem solving and problem finding."[11] Bibliographical understanding is shaped into knowing through practices that form theories tested through work aimed to solve problems and, importantly, the discovery of problems that have yet to be theorized. A first step toward assessing the infrastructures crafted by us as information scientists and bibliographers is to attempt to bring them into view.

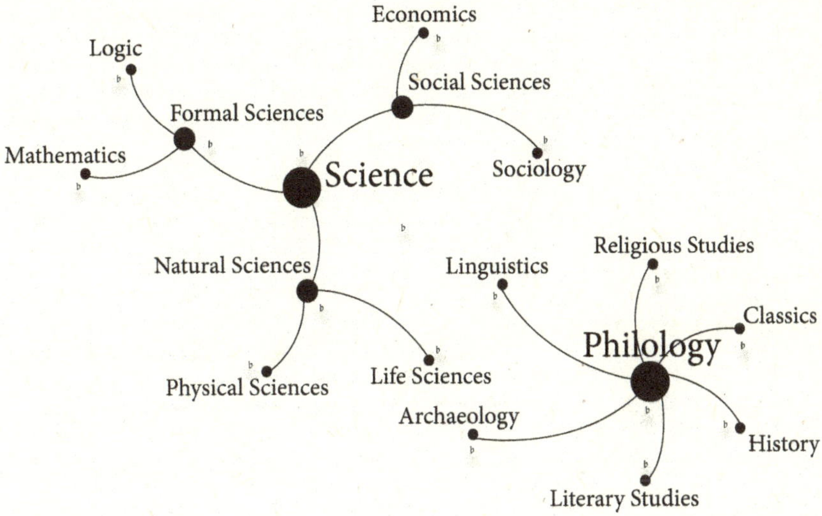

Figure 5.2
A simple graph of knowledge.

Figure 5.2 is a clumsy, similarly simple, and ultimately incomplete graph of knowledge that means to recognize the infrastructural roles facilitated by bibliography and its diverse descriptive practices, including recursive bibliographical opportunities to account for bibliographical description, which I have been emphasizing with my thought experiment. The lowercase *b*s are an attempt to suggest the multiple and plural identities of bibliography. Their positions are meant to suggest bibliography's marginal relationships to particular disciplinary centers and how bibliographical infrastructure can be shared. Their awkwardly oriented shadows suggest my maladroit attempts to make bibliography visible but also, hopefully, demonstrate the dimensionality that bibliography can provide to flat descriptive representations.

6 DESCRIBING THE ARCHIMEDES PALIMPSEST

To expose the infrastructural role played by bibliographical description in a diverse field that has some relation to the generation, collection, organization, storage, retrieval, interpretation, distribution, and utilization of information, we can examine recent efforts to copy what has come to be called the *Archimedes Palimpsest.* The Palimpsest is especially useful because its complexity as a record of human knowledge helps to show how diverse kinds of descriptive data, documents, and texts can be constructed to inform disparate informational ends pursued collaboratively by humanists and scientists at work on creating copies. The example of the Palimpsest suggests how descriptions can be constructed to enable scientists and humanists to work productively, even at cross-purposes, to produce an intellectual weave that is diversely informative.

THE ARCHIMEDES PALIMPSEST

The Archimedes Palimpsest is many things. This is one reason why it is so wonderfully difficult to describe. In what follows, my description is indebted to the description provided by Reviel Netz and William Noel in their wonderful book *The Archimedes Codex.*

The Archimedes Palimpsest is a collection of animal hides that have been treated to make a reusable writing surface called *parchment.* As the title of Netz and Noel's book suggests, the Archimedes Palimpsest is also a codex, a book, since it has been shaped into folios. Specifically, it is a Byzantine prayer book, which is called a *euchologion*. To make the prayer book, scribes took parchment that had been used previously to record seven treatises by Archimedes, the Greek thinker from the third century BCE. The treatises by Archimedes were probably applied to the parchment in Constantinople in the second half of the tenth century. Sometime in the early thirteenth century, the makers of the prayer book scraped the following from the parchment that they were reusing: "The Equilibrium of Planes," "Spiral Lines," "The Measurement of the Circle," "Sphere and Cylinder," "On Floating Bodies," "The Method of Mechanical Theorems," and "Stomachion." They also scraped off texts attributed to the Attic orator Hyperides, commentary on Aristotle's *Categories*, and other texts. Over Archimedes's treatises and the other texts, the scribes copied prayers onto 174 folios, finishing their work in April 1229, probably in Jerusalem. Because it was created with reused parchment, in addition to being a collection of animal hides, a gathering of treatises by Archimedes, a codex, and a prayer book, it is also a *palimpsest*, a word that derives from the Greek to "scrape again."

And this is just the beginning of the list of things called the Archimedes Palimpsest. As the object of intense philological and scientific investigation, as well as a home for some hardy molds, the Palimpsest has also been a fantastically challenging computer imaging problem, an interpretive challenge for linguists, translators, and mathematicians, and a conservatorial test for those wishing to make all of the many things that are now called the Archimedes Palimpsest available in the present and the future. This multiplicity is a useful reminder that even truly unique objects are not self-identical, and we are informed by them according to how we enumerate and describe them. The Archimedes Palimpsest is and has been a function of those who have used it as a physical and conceptual tool for spiritual, historical, mathematical, linguistic, textual, and other ends. The molds are evidence that we humans are not the only ones attracted to the Archimedes Palimpsest.

We can begin our consideration of how Archimedes was copied from the Palimpsest by grappling again with the idea of equivalence associated with the work of copying and how the idea itself has been shaped by bibliographers. Just as it would be difficult to imagine copying without some notion of equivalence, it is difficult to imagine the modern sciences without the ability to inscribe notions of equivalence, such as with the parallel lines that we call the "equal sign" (=). As Reviel Netz suggests, "Silently, scribes have invented the mathematical symbol. By doing so, they paved the way for the modern equation—the most powerful tool of modern science."[1] Of course, humanist scholars interested in the history of science are interested in the same parallel lines in all their variations for what they say about the people who formulated and used this tool of modern science; what they considered equivalent; and the ways that they worked with or as scribes, and later, with or as typesetters, with or as word processors, or with or as technicians who help to store data in ever larger and more complex memory systems that help to tally what counts as equivalent. The Welsh mathematician Robert Recorde (aptly named since we are discussing equivalences and how to copy records) is often credited with being the first to record what we now call the equal sign as a symbol for equivalence. He writes in *The Whetstone of Witte* (1557) that to avoid the tedious repetition of "is equal to," "I will set . . . a pair of parallels . . . of one length, thus: =."[2] He does this "because no 2 things can be more equal."[3] We can note Recorde's descriptive assertion about parallel lines. We can also note the contingency of what we take naturally to mean "equal to." There were at least five other competing meanings for the parallel lines that we now think of as the equal sign among European mathematicians, including one suggested by Francis Vieta meaning "arithmetical difference."[4] And there were, of course, other symbols used to suggest equality before Recorde. The obvious point is that equivalences and how they are inscribed are contingently formulated, even if we come to assume a natural relation later.

The somewhat less obvious point is that equivalences are selective. Contingent formulations of equivalence are premised on the exclusion of what is *not* equivalent. When researchers decide to copy the texts of Archimedes, they formulate how equivalences will be determined and, by doing so, what will not be considered equivalent. They are participating in a variety of processes and engaging with the choices of those who similarly had to decide what counts as equivalent. They choose not to copy the Byzantine prayers or to help the mold to reproduce. This may seem obvious, but many much subtler choices need to be made. Does a pixel formulated by directed radiation, sensors, and software suggest a feature of a Greek letter that can be associated with Archimedes? Dust? An artifact in an image created by the imagining system?

In the case of Archimedes, decisions about equivalence were formulated by enumerating and engaging multiple contexts. For example, philological beliefs about Archimedes's Greek as it would have been rearticulated by his tenth-century scribe, but also a transcription of the Palimpsest made by Johan Ludvig Heiberg (1854–1928), a Danish philologist who recognized Archimedes in the *euchologion* that he saw in the Church of the Holy Sepulchre in Istanbul in 1906, helped to formulate the equivalences that any particular pixel might suggest. Indeed, what came to be considered a copy of Archimedes was arrived at by coordinating philological contexts and expectations and with what could be created with a constellation of various lenses and sensors and software systems.

After spending years *very* carefully disassembling the prayer book containing Archimedes, the pages of the Archimedes Palimpsest were copied by researchers using a variety of imaging techniques that used some thirty-five different wavelengths of infrared, ultraviolet, and visible light, as well as a particle accelerator for some of the trickier pages to reproduce. No one frequency made it possible to read Archimedes. Rather, the imaging specialists used their documentary power to describe most of the Palimpsest pages with a composite of the images captured using different frequencies. Using software, they blended the representations made possible by the energy's diverse frequencies to create an image that modern experts could read as the Greek of Archimedes's tenth-century scribe.

Although the composite images of the Palimpsest made many of its folios legible, four pages of the manuscript that had been covered by a forger with representations of the Christian Evangelists remained illegible. Sometime in the twentieth century, apparently to increase the value of the prayer book, the forger painted over Archimedes with gold, lead, copper, barium, zinc, and many other elements that made it impossible to use multispectral imaging to copy Archimedes. Archimedes's modern copyists decided to use X-ray fluorescence imaging on the four pages that were illegible.

X-ray fluorescence imaging is a technique that causes atoms hit by synchrotron radiation to shed X-rays that are specific to their frequencies. The ink used to copy Archimedes in the tenth century was iron, as mentioned previously; so, the team of Archimedes copyists decided that they were going to attempt to use X-ray fluorescence imaging to look for the iron in the ink used by the tenth-century scribe. The modern copyists reasoned that a map of the iron could be read as the text of Archimedes created in the tenth century.

Since X-ray fluorescence needs powerful light sources, the four uncopied pages of the Palimpsest were taken to the Stanford Synchrotron Radiation Laboratory, a particle accelerator, which provided the synchrotron radiation needed to create the map of the iron atoms arranged by Archimedes's tenth-century copyist. It worked. The map of the X-rays emitted by the iron atoms of the ink laid down in the tenth century could be read as Archimedes's "Stomachion"; this is now thought to be the earliest study of combinatorics.

The combinatory efforts of modern philologists and imaging scientists to generate and coordinate contexts to produce equivalences that could be understood as what was produced by Archimedes's tenth-century scribe are suggested, ironically, by the team's initial failures. Despite all the efforts of the imagining team, initially, the imaging scientist involved in the project "created images with characteristics that the scholars simply did not value."[5] A series of meetings were arranged so that the philologists could explain what they did value, which often surprised the scientists. For example, initially the imaging specialists had digitally "erased" the text of the prayer book because they assumed that it would interfere with reading the Archimedes text. However, as the philologists explained, they needed to know why certain strokes that they thought *might* be associated with Archimedes's tenth-century scribe took the shapes that they did. Were certain strokes truncated to suggest a specific letter or because they were overlain by the prayer book text? In their composite images, the imagers had initially made the prayer book text the same color as the parchment, which confused the philologists, who needed the context provided by the prayer book to know if what they were looking at could be equated with what Archimedes's scribe had inscribed on the parchment in the tenth century.

As those involved in the project acknowledge, the images that were eventually settled on as useful copies of Archimedes were "not images of the Palimpsest,"[6] but rather "synthetic creations made from images of the Palimpsest."[7] As they describe, "They are works of art. Well, they work, anyway. And that's the point."[8] The copies worked to facilitate what the philologists determined to be useful descriptive equivalences. The larger bibliographical point is that descriptions are always formulated by these kinds of selective processes and the coordination of contexts that enable equivalences (as well as distinctions) to be drawn up.

Although the technologies of bibliographical description and copying change through time and affect how we can know the objects we describe, the fact that bibliographical descriptions are selective statements made in medias res does not. With a copy rested on a stand before him (it is presumed), the scribe who copied Archimedes in the tenth century used some sort of flat surface that he placed on his lap as a surface for the parchment, reed pens sharpened on a stone, an ink made of gallic acid and "green vitriol," and his hands and eyes. The Archimedes scribes of the late twentieth and early twenty-first centuries used a variety of experimental scientific imaging technologies, each of which afforded alternative possibilities to know Archimedes. As impressive as the technology used by Archimedes's modern copyists may be, the choices that they made about how to formulate Archimedes were contingent upon the choices made by their tenth-century predecessor. The choice to use X-ray fluorescence to image the Palimpsest, for example, was made in part because the tenth-century scribe used an ink that contained concentrations of iron. None of the documentary technologies that help us to know Archimedes provides transparent access to Archimedes or "his" words. They have all been mediated by his scribes and the technologies that they have employed.

These are obvious points with a less obvious bibliographical consequence: that every bibliographical description itself calls for a bibliographical description. The recursive drive of bibliography to account for previous accounts is a function of the fact that knowledge is mediated by choices and contingencies like those that I have been describing. Bibliography, as I am arguing for understanding it, insistently attempts to account for the choices and contingencies that have shaped human knowledge as it has been presented. When doing so, as Yi Sang hinted in his poetry, knowing becomes combinatory: coming to know, we know something new again. Bibliography is a foundation of information science, as the Archimedes Palimpsest helps to demonstrate, because new, descriptive copies of Archimedes are opportunities to know something new again about the ways that we can know Archimedes.

DOUG EMERY

These ways of knowing Archimedes are described by additional bibliographical descriptions of the new ways that we know him. Metadata were created to describe what was eventually taken as given, as data, by the philologists and imaging scientists copying Archimedes. For instance, Doug Emery oversaw efforts to describe the new digital copies of Archimedes. Now a digital content programmer for Special Collections at the University of Pennsylvania library, during the last few years of the Archimedes Palimpsest project, Emery ran his own information technology company called Emery IT. Before that, he worked for a year as a Java/J2EE developer at a company called Accenture Technology Solutions. Prior to his year at Accenture Technology Solutions, he was a database/systems administrator at Johns Hopkins University, where he worked toward a doctorate in northwest Semitic philology.[9]

I pause to relate Emery's biography to suggest the eclectic skills and work experience of contemporary bibliographers both inside and outside academia. I press my case for understanding bibliography and bibliographers as inhabiting multiple identities, very few of which overlap with the imaginaries articulated by bibliographers such as Fredson Bowers at his Hinman collator (see figure 1.2 in chapter 1) or Paul Otlet in the clutter of his Mundaneum. Like the countless bibliographers who have been marginalized and left out of descriptions of bibliographical projects and of bibliography in the West more generally, such as the women that Cait Coker and Kate Ozment have begun to recuperate with "A Bibliography: Women in Book History"[10] or the black perspectives, bibliophiles, and collectors described by the "Black Bibliography Project" that Jacqueline Goldsby and Meredith McGill lead,[11]

Emery was both central to and at the margins of the Archimedes Palimpsest project. Dubbed "the Lord of Minutiae" by colleagues,[12] he was so centrally marginal to the Palimpsest project that, while he was entrusted with ensuring the future of the digital objects created at great expense by philologists and imaging scientists, his work went essentially unacknowledged in most of the academic and popular books that resulted from the ten-year project. As Emery relates in a talk that he gave at the Library of Congress, William Noel gave him an inscribed copy of *The Archimedes Codex*, a book that Noel and Reviel Netz wrote. Noel's inscription read: "To Doug Emery, whose critical contribution to this project goes unrecorded in this book. Sorry, metadata doesn't sell."[13] Emery quipped in response, "Metadata may not sell, but it pays."[14]

The dividend that Emery's metadata provides is an ability to know, by means of the partial access that description offers, how Archimedes is and can be known in the early twenty-first century. His metadata describes in rich detail, for example, how the composite images produced by the different frequencies of light used to image the Palimpsest folios are registered (i.e., made to line up with one another) so as to be legible as Palimpsest folios. It provides rich descriptions of the people and technologies used, who produced which image, with which technology adjusted to which settings—descriptions that McKenzie might describe as the beginnings of a sociology of the new Archimedes copies. Indeed, he created a metadata standard to support long-term access and use of what he called the "scriptospatial" data associated with the Palimpsest, a standard that he has since used to describe data associated with similar efforts to create digital copies of other historic manuscripts.[15]

The term *scriptospatial* is useful because it emphasizes the need for a coordinated space for the script set down by Archimedes's tenth-century scribe to be legible to philologists and translators such as Netz. It is also useful because it helps to summarize how imaging scientists and philologists produced the equivalences that they arrived at and called a digital copy of Archimedes. Like crisp color prints from an offset press where the distinct impressions made by each of the color plates have been usefully aligned, Emery's metadata helps create a vivid description of how the abstractions of individual Greek letters have been equated by philologists with specific *x,y* coordinates in a digital image created by scientists bouncing diverse frequencies of radiation off of the skins of long-dead animals. Based primarily on the Dublin Core Metadata Initiative Element Set (ISO Standard 15836) and the Content Standard for Digital Geospatial Data (FGDC-STD-001-1998), Emery's metadata description enables what we might call a combinatorics of knowing. Coming to know Archimedes, we come to know something new about how we know Archimedes. And, indicative of the recursive bibliographical need to account for accounts, Emery includes in his metadata descriptions bibliographical descriptions of the Dublin Core Metadata Initiative Element Set and the Content Standard for Digital Geospatial Data standards.

Niels Bohr suggests that what can be known about quantum interactions is a function of the way that the forces of nature are orchestrated to interact with each other so as to produce documents that can be read. The case of Archimedes's more recent copyists shows how the same forces of the universe were made to interact to reveal writings associated with Archimedes and early forms of the mathematical thinking that made the investigations of Bohr and the scientists at the Stanford particle accelerator possible. The process was elaborate but only the latest effort to create a copy of Archimedes, an account of what had been copied before. Although it was some supremely high-powered carpentry-accounting, it was still essentially a descriptive bibliographical exercise—one that helps reveal how bibliography supports information science as infrastructure and information science helps to support diverse groups of people working to know and know again what is and has been.

Understanding the Archimedes Palimpsest project as a bibliographical description, we gain purchase on how we know what we know about what Archimedes knew. It is easier to understand that our knowledge is a function of the properties of iron atoms, the sensors and memory devices at Stanford's particle accelerator, the people and institutions that contributed to the copying of the Greek mathematician's texts, and, crucially, the motivations of all involved to arrive at selectively useful equivalences. A metaphor created by Galileo, one of Archimedes's best-known intellectual descendants, helps to make a similar point:

> Philosophy is written in this vast book, which lies continuously open before our eyes (I mean the universe). But it cannot be understood unless you have first learned to understand the language and recognize the characters in which it is written. It is written in the language of mathematics, and the characters are triangles, circles, and other geometrical figures. Without such means it is impossible for us humans to understand a word of it, and to be without them is to wander around in vain through a dark labyrinth.[16]

The universe is figured by Galileo as a *book*. Learning to read it (the book and the universe) means learning its language (mathematics) and the orthographies used to represent this language (triangles, circles, and other "geometrical figures"). Galileo's suggestion is that science is a representational and interpretive endeavor. The equations that he draws to make his suggestion are somewhat less obvious but can be documented for descriptive emphasis and thoroughness.

Universe = Book

Language = Mathematics

Script = Triangles, circles, and other geometrical figures

Ability to read triangles, circles, and other geometrical figures = Ability to understand the universe

Our discussion of the Archimedes Palimpsest helps remind us that the equivalencies enacted and enabled by the science that Galileo imagines are contingent and formulated selectively in the middle of things, and bibliography's recursive accounts provide at least partial access to a knowledge of how equivalences have been formulated. Triangles, circles, and other geometrical figures may help us to avoid dark labyrinths, but so does knowledge of how triangles and circles have been equated with phenomena and the universe by documentary accounts such as Galileo's. Bibliography is foundational in the work of information science, with its broad aim of making records of human knowledge available, because it insists on recursively descriptive accounts of the documents that record *what* we know and the equivalences that formulate *how* we know it.

7 A DESCRIPTIVE ACCOUNT OF BIOLOGICAL METAPHORS IN BIBLIOGRAPHY

To consider some of the ways that we might reflect on constructed bibliographical descriptions, this chapter focuses on accounting for the scientific ideologies that have guided what has been built and how, as infrastructure, bibliography as means to many ends can inscribe and reproduce ideologies through description. The aim is to begin to account for some of the ideas and practices that have formulated bibliography as an infrastructural power by presenting a description of how natural history, biology, and biological metaphors have suggested ideological equivalence to bibliographers in the Anglo-European bibliographical tradition during a period when list makers and studiers of books were debating and formulating distinctions that enable Patrick Wilson's two-item description of bibliography.

BIOLOGY AND BIBLIOGRAPHERS

Because repeated figures such as circles and triangles have proved to be so helpful, it is tempting to believe, as Galileo's metaphor suggests, that the equivalences produced by science and the bibliographical processes that support it are neutral, natural formulations of the universe, and that the universe is composed of triangles and circles which, once they can be read, provide unmediated access to what we might call the "content of the universe." Galileo's metaphorical "book" is its content, not its parchment, ink, or lettering. Metaphors, like bibliographical descriptions, are selective, and Galileo's excludes any consideration of the sheep or goats that would be slaughtered to provide a parchment surface for the triangles and circles. My admittedly morbid reformulation of Galileo's metaphor is meant to emphasize that bibliographical processes are hardly neutral or inevitable. Indeed, because they are like list making—artful and always motivated by the pleasures they provide and the powers they facilitate—bibliographical processes can sustain many kinds of violence. This potential for violence is one of the many reasons why it is crucial to reinvigorate bibliography and recursively account for how we have been doing our bibliographical accounting. Because our contingent bibliographical practices serve as foundational infrastructure, it can be as difficult to see their potential for violence as it is to see their generative promise as means that support knowledge and reflection.

Where chapter 6 focused on the generative aspects of bibliography as contingent reproductive acts, on bibliography as a kind of carpentry, this chapter presents an account of the scientific ideologies that have guided what has been built and how, as infrastructure, bibliography can inscribe and reproduce ideologies. My aim is to begin to account for some of the ideas and practices that have formulated bibliography in the Anglo-European tradition. By describing the ways that biological metaphors have guided the thinking of those associated with the Anglo-American school, this discussion contributes to the growing body of research that attends to the ethics of cataloging and classification in library and information science,[1] as well as what Michelle Warren has called the "politics of textual scholarship"[2] and Kari Kraus has called "conjectural criticism"[3] in relation to the emerging field of biohumanities. It also begins to formulate bibliography and bibliographical description as a useful accounting tool for critiquing beliefs about bibliographical descriptions produced by artificial intelligence (AI) that assume that they are "rational," "evolved," "ahistorical," "objective," and "neutral."[4] In turn, this begins to contribute to the increasingly important and usefully critical discourse concerning AI ethics. It does so by revisiting a moment in Anglo-American bibliographical history when the aims of bibliography were being debated in ways that helpfully clarify the necessity of these critiques, as well as extend my argument for understanding bibliography as marginal practices that function as means to other ends.

By revisiting the life, death, and ideas of Henry Bradshaw, a Cambridge University librarian, as well as an exchange in *The Library* in December 1932 between Stephen Gaselee (1882–1943), the incoming president of the Bibliographical Society of England, W. W. Greg, the outgoing president, and A. W. Pollard (1859–1944), an influential early contributor to the society, we see how each was advocating for bibliography to serve distinct ends. They are ends that we will be tempted to equate with library science and textual criticism. We will also see how natural history and biology provided metaphorical equivalences that guided their visions for what they called *bibliography*.

I have been arguing that the bibliography and bibliographers are ordinarily "marginal," plural, and at the periphery. Given how the term *marginal* is also often used to connote nonwhite, nonmale experience, it might seem counterintuitive to center Bradshaw, Gaselee, Greg, and Pollard, white men all, in a discussion of marginality. And it would be counterintuitive if we were not interested in how bibliography inscribes ideologies and perspectives into descriptions that can be, and often are, naturalized as representations of reality. The plural and peripheral marginality that I wish to explore here is similar to what Jonathan Furner describes as "ambiguous territory" in the context of bibliographical classification and descriptive systems. How do we understand the marginal, "ambiguous territories" where literary and user warrant intersect with race, gender, and the ideological biases of projected worldviews to create descriptive infrastructures that endure not necessarily because they are productive, fair, or desired, but because they slip from view as infrastructure and become taken as given.

Writing about the Dewey decimal system, Furner suggests that the system is an "ambiguous territory between description and prescription" where classification and bibliographical description are at once "reflective of literary and user warrant, and projective of worldviews."[5] The recursive bibliographical accounting that I pursue here is meant to complement efforts to recuperate marginalized experience by accounting, at least in part, for what was formulated by a small group of white men as they inhabited ambiguous territory between description and prescription. My implicit argument is that the long overdue and necessary bibliographical accounts of "A Bibliography: Women in Book History," created by Cait Coker and Kate Ozment, or the "Black Bibliography Project," by Jacqueline Goldsby and Meredith McGill, can be complemented by accounts of how the descriptive/prescriptive assertions of white men proximate to the centers of power were formulated and have been reiterated as bibliographical infrastructure. Acknowledging the privilege and standing of these four white men is to account for how they have shaped thinking in bibliography proscriptively with their worldviews and the power they were afforded as white men, librarians, scholars, and inheritors of colonial power, sometimes quite directly. That is the case with Greg, whose father-in-law, James Wilson (1805–1860), in addition to establishing *The Economist*, oversaw the East India Company and later went to India as part of efforts to reaffirm British colonial rule following what has been variously called the Sepoy Mutiny or First War of Indian Independence in the late 1850s. By attending to how natural history and biology shaped the ways that these men thought about their work provides some standing in relation to their proscriptive worldviews and how worldviews like theirs have been integrated into bibliographical infrastructures that support work in information science even today.

As just one example of how the biological thinking of the late nineteenth and early twentieth centuries still supports descriptive bibliographical processes in information science, we can look at the Library of Congress in the US, its subject headings, and how they are taught. The example is perhaps too obvious, since the Library of Congress subject headings (LCSH) have been so often singled out for their biases. But looking at how LCSH are taught is instructive of how descriptions and ways of thinking become engrained as infrastructure, particularly when it comes to seeing how biological metaphors continue to operate in and by means of them. In their clear but pedagogically bland "Module 2.1, Structural Overview of LCSH," the Standards Division of the library describes relationships among subject headings using the language of living bodies and biology. Of the three hierarchical relationships between "broader terms" (frequently described as "parent" terms) and "narrower terms" (frequently described as "child" terms), the first is described as "Genus/Species *or* Thing/kind relationships."[6] Attempting to read sections of what the Library of Congress presents as training materials literally shows how deeply engrained biological metaphors remain in the work of bibliographical description. Take the following:

> In LCSH there are three types of broader term / narrower term (or hierarchical) relationships. The first is genus/species, also sometimes called thing/kind, or maybe class and class member. For example, frozen foods are a specific kind of food, and the concept of frozen foods is thus narrower than food in general. Because **Frozen foods** has a parent of **Food**, then logically **Food** must display that it has a child, **Frozen foods**.[7] (boldface in original)

Food is a parent of *Frozen foods*; and *Frozen foods* is the child of *Food*. There is a kind of poetry in the expression "logically *Food* must display that it has a child." It makes me worry about the progeny of the pizza I had for lunch, but the important point to make by highlighting the poetry to be found in Library of Congress training manuals is that the logic of descriptive systems are themselves run through with assumed equivalences that can be very difficult to see and account for. They are frequently reinforced and repeated to create conceptual hierarchies and other kinds of relationships for the sake of descriptive utility. We are told, for example, that "the beauty of hierarchical (or BT/NT) relationships is that we can move up and move down them to find the heading that best suits our needs."[8] This is true at levels of abstraction that elide the plurality of "we" and how communities and individuals differently inhabit a diversity of intellectual and social hierarchies. Another challenge is that descriptive terms are not constrained by the controls of controlled vocabularies, of course, and can be differently productive (or even destructive) depending upon how "we" is formulated by those making "the beauty of hierarchical relationships" used to craft descriptions that classify.

The debate among Gaselee, Greg, and Pollard provides an opportunity to account for some of the equivalencies that formulate the logic of hierarchies in information science at a moment when bibliographer list makers *and* studiers of books, to borrow again from Wilson, were shaping distinctions among themselves. While Bradshaw, Pollard, Greg, and Gaselee all believed biology to be a worthwhile intellectual area for guiding bibliographical work, they were divided about whether the work of enumeration should be considered essential to bibliographical projects. They took strong stances for and against considering enumeration a part of the field that they wished to call "bibliography," and, as Pollard does, for the idea that bibliographers should have the freedom to do one, the other, or both.

Returning to this particular debate illuminates how bibliographical description in information science can be nominally the same but entirely distinct from bibliographical description in what might be called *textual studies* or *textual scholarship*, one with scientific aspiration, another with humanistic aspiration, and a third, which would wish to avoid classification, like the cat in Rudyard Kipling's *Just So Stories*, desiring "to walk by himself when all sorts of people are trying to tie him down to stay with them for always and always and always, and to do their work."[9] Even if it is only partial, this account is helpful because it reveals how the ideologies of science and especially biology have shaped diverse bibliographical practices and identities since the nineteenth century. At the same time, it suggests bibliography's close affinity with what we might call humanist identities, the gendered "man of letters," for example. Helpfully, the debate also provides another figure for the bibliographer, that of a cat associated with the "freedom . . . to walk by itself"[10] so as not to be duped into doing the political or ideological work of others because the ideologies and political desires of others have been built into the descriptive means of describing what is and has been known.

HENRY BRADSHAW AND THE "NATURAL HISTORY METHOD"

Henry Bradshaw is remembered in an obituary that appeared in the February 18, 1886, issue of *Nature* as "a man of letters" whose sympathies were "deeply with the man of science." His

> great intimacy with the late Mr. G[eorge] R[obert] Crotch [1842–1874] had led him to take an extreme interest in the literature of systematic zoology, and particularly in the precision which is required of those who pursue the branch of it relating to the Coleoptera, not that Mr. Bradshaw must be supposed to have had any knowledge of the subject. It was simply the method of accurate work which excited his admiration, and that method, he has more than once told the present writer, had largely influenced his own bibliographical investigations, the high value set upon which must be told by those whom they concern.[11]

His eulogist suggests, "Of his literary ability, his bibliographical accuracy, his mastery of one important period of English poetry, and his knowledge of early printed books, this is not the place to speak,"[12] presumably because the obituary appeared in a scientific publication. But acknowledging an intellectual divide still familiar to us today, we learn "some acknowledgment of" Bradshaw's interest in the natural sciences was necessary because "unfortunately it far too often happens that there seems to be an impassable gulf fixed between the man of letters and the man of science, which hinders the one not only from partaking in, but even from appreciating, the ideas, the objects, and the methods of the other."[13]

Although we need to acknowledge that his eulogists and biographers in the late nineteenth century will have been firmly situated in the intellectual episteme of their day—one that, like our own, firmly divides the humanities from the sciences—it is clear that the intellectual equivalences that Bradshaw drew out between the natural sciences, librarianship, and what we now call "textual scholarship" enthralled them. It is also worth pointing out that, contrary to the division between scientific and humanistic inquiry, bibliography as a mode of what we might now call "textual studies" and bibliography as primarily enumerative and descriptive work were not so divided. Bradshaw is emblematic of a figure who worked in both capacities. George Prothero (1848–1922), a historian and Bradshaw's biographer, reprints a letter that Bradshaw sent to a colleague concerning a Bible that he had bought for the Cambridge University Library. "Books," Bradshaw writes to the Reverend J. T. Fowler (1833–1924), "are to me living organisms, and I can only study them as such; so every particle of light which I can obtain as to their personal history is so much positive gain."[14] Bradshaw's metaphor, that books are "living organisms," enabled him to grant them "personal histories," and indeed, almost histories as people. He is reported to have said, "I want to see the printer at work. . . . I want to understand why he printed this particular book, and what guided the form of his production."[15] As Frederick Edward Warren (1842–1930), another eulogist, described, this attention to the details of a book enabled him to "see the men of the past at their work":[16]

> In books which the mere bibliographer described as reprints, he would find the local colouring, the peculiar prejudice or the special glory of a district, introduced by some slight change. What for us had been at first merely twenty editions of the same book, he would show were all variations. He would trace the development from one prototype, and he would point out the local or temporal value of each phase of growth. As he handled the pages of some early folio, and described how two presses had been employed, one working away at this point, the other at that; how the first stock of paper had been exhausted here, and the second there; how at this point the printer had thought to improve on his original, or had bought somebody else's cuts, or chopped up his own—the auditor felt himself carried back centuries, and saw the men of the past at their work.[17]

Introducing what Bradshaw called his "natural history method," Prothero cites William Blades (1824–1890), a printer and historian of print:

> From an early period he perceived that to understand and master the internal evidences contained in every old book, the special peculiarities of their workmanship must be studied and classified, much in the same way as a botanist treats plants, or an entomologist insects. This he called "the natural-history system." . . . To make his work more effectual and scientific, he did that which many a bibliographer has to his great loss omitted to do—he made acquaintance with the technicalities of book-making. He knew how punches were cut, how matrices were struck, and how types were cast. . . . To this he added a knowledge of how paper-moulds were used and water-marks made.[18]

Prothero continues, explaining what he understood Bradshaw meant by his "natural-history system":

> Mr Blades alludes to what Bradshaw called his natural history method in bibliography. It was a phrase which he was never tired of using. He appears to have meant by it a careful and exhaustive ascertainment of facts, minute observation of characteristics, thoughtful co-ordination of the results, and deductions made without prejudice and untrammelled by preconceived ideas. With regard to early printed books, in particular, it meant the arrangement and classification of them, as natural objects are classified, under families, genera, and species. His published lists are illustrations of this system. I cannot do better than quote his own words respecting the principles on which these lists are based.[19]

We find Bradshaw's own assertions in a work that he published in 1870, *A Classified Index of the Fifteenth Century Books in the Collection of the Late M. J. de Meyer, Which Were Sold at Ghent in November 1869*:

> We do not want the *opinion* or *dictum* of any bibliographer however experienced; we desire that the types and habits of each printer should be made a special subject of study, and those points brought forward which shew changes or advance from year to year, or, where practicable, from month to month. When this is done, we have to say of any dateless or falsely dated book that it contains such and such characteristics, and we therefore place it at such a point of time, the time we name being merely another expression for the characteristics we notice in the book. In fact each press must be looked upon as a *genus*, and each book as a *species*, and our business is to trace the more or less close connexion of the different members of the family according to the characters which they present to our observation. The study of palaeotypography has been hitherto mainly such a *dilettante* matter, that people have shrunk from going into such details, though when once studied as a branch of natural history, it is as fruitful in interesting results as most subjects.[20]

Nearly 150 years later, in his *Bibliographical Analysis: A Historical Introduction*, G. Thomas Tanselle would suggest that Bradshaw, his bibliography, and this passage should be considered "a landmark in intellectual history."[21] "Indeed," he would write, "as far as bibliographical scholarship is concerned, [it is] one of the greatest landmarks—for it contains a passage of major significance emphasizing the importance of systematically examining the physical evidence in printed books."[22] While Tanselle focuses on the attention to physical evidence as key to the passage and the significance of Bradshaw's method, it is clear that Bradshaw was thinking of bibliography as a "branch of natural history" where a press could be considered a "*genus*" and each book a "*species*."

Less emphasized, although acknowledged by Tanselle, is that Bradshaw's landmark of intellectual history appears in what can be called an *enumerative bibliography*, a list of books, as its "unpromising title" suggests, in the collection of M. J. de Meyer. Indeed, Tanselle calls Bradshaw's bibliography "a little pamphlet" rather than a bibliography. Recognizing that Bradshaw's "pamphlet" is an enumerative bibliography that describes a particular group of documents is important for a variety of reasons. The first is that, as Tanselle's chosen descriptive terms suggest, bibliography for bibliographers can be distinct. For Tanselle, Bradshaw's bibliography is less important for how it works as an enumerative bibliography and more important for what it suggests about methods that are important to textual scholarship, a field that, as I have suggested, has had a great variety of names, including *descriptive, analytical, historical,* and *critical bibliography.*

This is not to suggest that Tanselle is insensitive to aspects of Bradshaw's enumerative bibliography that serve his purpose as a textual scholar. He acknowledges the innovative organization of Bradshaw's bibliography around the location of printers, rather than alphabetically according to the title of a text, for example. For Tanselle, this organization helps to articulate the focus of textual scholarship on the material production of books. Indeed, the passage that Tanselle singles out as the most important in Bradshaw's "pamphlet" appears in a note on printing in the Dutch city of Zwolle. Tanselle does not emphasize that this arrangement by location also had an analogy to natural history. As Warren suggests in his remembrance of Bradshaw, the idea of a "watershed" was an important metaphor for him: "'The watershed,' he would say, in his quiet, half-paradoxical way, 'is as important for books as for trade.'"[23] Warren goes on to write, "[Bradshaw's] great hope was that some day the German *incunabula* and the German woodcuts would be worked out by grouping towns together geographically; thus the intellectual life of each district, and its influence upon its neighbours, would become, for the first time, manifest. It was distinctly the modern, the scientific, method which traces growth and evolution at work, as opposed to the old classification by titles."[24]

As biologists and natural historians would investigate the evolution of biological life in specific watersheds and regions, so too would bibliographers study the reproduction of books and their evolution. This equivalence helps to account for the ideas and ideologies that formulate how bibliographers arrive at their judgments and perform their work. Similarly, accounting for the extent that bibliographers such as Tanselle acknowledge enumeration and enumerative bibliographies for how they serve bibliographical description and analysis helps to reveal bibliography's plural identities.

THE AIMS OF BIBLIOGRAPHY: THE 1932 DEBATE IN *THE LIBRARY*

We can further explore this plural identity and the ways that its ambiguous territories are articulated by equivalences drawn among bibliography, natural history, and biology by reviewing an important debate about the aims of bibliography that took place in *The Library* in the 1930s. *The Library* is aptly named for my purpose because it suggests the library as a shared historical locus for bibliographical practice as infrastructure for what we now call "information science." While few information scientists are likely to be readers of *The Library* today because of its focus on what we might call "textual studies," we see that in the 1930s, it is where librarians advocating for the scientific methods like those that now gird information science debated what should be understood as the aims of bibliography. We can account for the contemporary split between what we now call "information science" and the historical pursuits, often undertaken with scientific means, of textual scholars by acknowledging that bibliography was and remains a means by which both communities pursue their aims.

Stephen Gaselee

"I have tried as far as possible . . . to confine myself to facts and avoid theories, for only by working from facts can we help to keep bibliography in the position to which Henry Bradshaw raised it, of a scientific study."[25] Gaselee begins his address to the Bibliographical Society on Monday, October 17, 1932, with an echoing homage to Henry Bradshaw. The address would be published as "The Aims of Bibliography." The citation with which Gaselee begins is from the preface of Gordon Duff's 1893 *Early Printed Books*, which Duff dedicates to Bradshaw. By utilizing a citation that praises Bradshaw from the preface of *Early Printed Books*, Gaselee establishes Bradshaw as an authoritative figure. In the same breath, he establishes the axis around which the debate that he enters will revolve: the idea that the study of and description of books should be scientific. The idea that bibliography should be considered a science, like biology and natural history, was shared with his interlocutor, W. W. Greg, the previous president of the society, who would speak against many of Gaselee's prescriptive assertions about the aims of bibliography at the same Monday meeting in October 1932.

The debate focused on whether enumeration should rightly be considered an aim of bibliography. The arguments on all sides were supported rhetorically by the idea that bibliography should be considered a science akin to biology and the kind of natural history advocated by Bradshaw. Greg, in an address made to the society as its president in March 1932, had argued for understanding bibliography as "the science of the transmission of literary documents."[26] Gaselee did not object strenuously to this, but he would profoundly object to what Greg had to say about what both called "enumerative bibliography." Greg asserted:

> Bibliography . . . is in no way particularly or primarily concerned with the enumeration or description of books—a belief which has done much in the past to reduce it to futility and retard the recognition of its real nature and importance. It ought not to be necessary further to argue, though it may be well to put on record, that bibliography has nothing to do with the subject-matter of books, but only with their formal aspect.[27]

He added in a footnote, "It has been suggested that enumeration is a necessary preliminary to study. This is in fact not true: were it so, every natural science would be primarily enumerative."[28] In passages such as these, Greg can be seen attempting to divest what had been called *bibliography* (and is still often associated with bibliography in information science)—namely, the enumeration and description of books according to their subjects—from what he believed to be the proper focus of bibliography: literary documents and their creation and transmission as physical objects.

It is important to emphasize that Greg, in this context, is associating the description of books with the description of their subjects, which he would wish to exclude from the proper work of bibliography as he conceived it. In chapter 8, we will see how important the description of books as material objects was to Greg and bibliographers who would follow his intellectual lead. For now, we will stay focused on how the debate about the aims of bibliography was formulated by beliefs in science and anchored metaphorically by equivalences drawn between biology and bibliography.

Gaselee responds to Greg's address in March 1932, which would be published in *The Library* as "Bibliography—An Apologia" that September, by writing:

> There are both deductive and inductive sciences: even in the former (e.g. metaphysics, mathematics) there are certain postulates or axioms which have to be described and agreed before we can begin to reason; in the latter the natural sciences with which Dr. Greg compares bibliography (and Bradshaw was always speaking of the 'natural history method' which he followed in the study of early printed books) enumeration and description necessarily precede the general principles deduced by the investigator, and thence applied to cases which do not solve themselves by inspection. [Francis] Jenkinson [1853–1923, University of Cambridge librarian], outside his activities as librarian and bibliographer, devoted himself to *coleoptera* (he was in fact, I think, as much interested in flies as in beetles), and in this branch of science he was a collector and enumerator, leaving to others the deductions to be drawn from his collection and enumeration.[29]

We see Gaselee building his case for the inclusion of enumerative aims in a conception of bibliography, an argument that he pursues rhetorically by aligning bibliography closely with the natural sciences and especially biology, as Greg does. He does not contest Greg's assertion that bibliography is a science of the transmission of literary documents; rather, he disputes the narrowness of Greg's assertion, especially the exclusion of enumeration from what Greg believed to be the proper focus of bibliography. Equating bibliography with biology and Bradshaw, a figure equally admired by Greg, with biologists, Gaselee continues to build his case for the inclusion of enumeration in the scope of bibliography:

> Would the work of Darwin have been possible without that of Linnaeus? I do not propose here to discuss the respective importance of the two branches of study, but merely to state my opinion that both are a part of science, at any rate of that natural science to which bibliography is ordinarily and reasonably compared, and that in order of time ("primarily") collection, enumeration, description must precede the application of the 'natural history method' and the results obtained by it. If I am right in this contention, Bradshaw did not raise bibliography to a science, but developed it by a change of direction almost comparable to the work of Darwin or Mendel.[30]

As this passage makes clear, Gaselee's argument for the inclusion of enumeration in bibliography is facilitated by the equation of bibliography with the natural sciences, and bibliographers with biologists. We also find one of the historical precedents for my assertion in chapter 1 for understanding bibliography as four integrated processes: enumeration, description, analysis, and critique. Gaselee ventures "to suggest that bibliography consists of five different stages, successively (1) collection, (2) enumeration, (3) description, (4) analysis, and (5) conclusion."[31] While there are differences between how Gaselee enumerates his terms, his assertions share broad similarities with the idea that bibliography entails enumeration, description, analysis, and critique.

Gaselee similarly provides a historical precedent for the idea that bibliography, while capable of being an end in itself, is more often a means for pursing other ends. As Gaselee points out, for Greg these ends were literary, but for him, they were more historical, as his presentation to the society had focused on a history of enumerative bibliography as he understood it—a history that he presented to refute Greg's attempt to rearticulate bibliography as the study of the physical characteristics of literary documents, as they might reveal how they had been made and transmitted. "I am far from disparaging the value of discovery in itself," Gaselee writes about the roles that he imagines bibliography playing as a science that supports historical and literary investigation, "as in mathematics and natural science, it is praiseworthy to arrive at new and certain results quite independently of any use to which they may or may not be put."[32] However, he writes, "bibliography is, on the whole, of the nature of an applied science, and more often than not we traverse the stages I have described in order to draw some conclusion, literary or historical."[33] We see again bibliography's association with science in the service of what we might call "humanistic ends."

Gaselee concludes his address to the bibliographical society by hinting at an even wider scope for bibliography, one that extends beyond scientific support for humanistic ends. Describing the rapid expansion of book production and circulation in a way that will be familiar in our current era of expanding access to diverse forms of human knowledge, he suggests that bibliography can help make the learning in books "useful" to "valuable ends" rather than a "mere weariness of the flesh," adding:

> Dr. Greg dealt with the latter in his presidential address last March, when he accepted for bibliography the definition "the grammar of literary investigation" if that phrase could be construed as equivalent to "the science of the transmission of literary documents." If, in this paper, I have laid stress on historical results, it is not to disparage the other, but rather to endeavour to redress the balance in the consideration of the aims which we, as members of the Bibliographical Society, have or should have before us and must direct our future activities: the historian and the critic are two very different people; we and our work, I think, are equally necessary to both. If of making of books there is no end (and so it seems to be in the present state of our civilization) it is we bibliographers, and perhaps we alone, who can prevent the much learning in them from being a mere weariness of the flesh and guide it to useful and valuable ends.[34]

W. W. Greg

Greg's primary objection to Gaselee's categorization of bibliography is that, by including enumeration in the concept, bibliography would not be able to become a proper and respected science. Acknowledging where they agree about bibliography's critical roles of analysis and critique as they support what Greg calls "textual criticism," he writes, "It is, of course, over this question of enumeration that we come into conflict."[35] The idea that enumeration, which Greg associated with cataloging, should be considered the proper work of bibliography incensed him: "On the occasions on which I have addressed you I have spoken of enumeration in terms perhaps dictated by a revulsion from the view so often held that the compilation of subject catalogues is the true and proper function of the bibliographer."[36] Catalogs and the work of cataloging are important, Greg would argue. But cataloging was not to be associated with the term *bibliography*. "I have no quarrel with subject catalogues,"[37] he writes. "After spending thirty-five years enumerating and describing the printed editions of early English plays, I am hardly likely to underestimate the importance of such work, but though bibliography enters very largely into what I have been doing, I cannot regard that work as itself bibliography."[38]

The argument that Greg presses relies heavily on the equivalences that he sees between bibliography and biology. "I undoubtedly regard bibliography as an inductive rather than a deductive science," he writes, "with some analogy to biology."[39] Indeed, it is his interest in establishing bibliography as a natural science akin to biology that motivates his desire to exclude enumeration from work considered "proper" bibliography: "I doubt whether a botanist or a zoologist to-day would admit that enumeration held an outstanding position in his study—let alone a chemist or a physicist."[40] Greg's argument is that enumeration is not itself properly scientific. "While in no way desiring to disparage enumeration,"[41] he writes, "I should be inclined to regard it—in so far as it is essential at all—rather as a prerequisite than as a proper department of the science."[42]

Summarizing and entrenching his position that bibliography should be allowed to develop as its own science, Greg pulls his mentor, Alfred Pollard, into the fray:

> The position I am contesting has never been better expressed than by Mr. Pollard in the words quoted by our President [Gaselee]: "What, then, is the business of the bibliographer? Primarily and essentially, I should say, the enumeration of books. His is the lowly task of finding out what books exist, and thereby helping . . . the specialist with information as to the extent of the subject-matter with which he has to deal." Of course, the sting of this lies in the "Primarily and essentially" and in the suggestion that the justification of bibliography lies in the assistance it can afford to other studies. I do not believe that Mr. Pollard, though he may with his amiable conservatism defend the words he wrote thirty years ago, when I was still one of his younger disciples, would have written them to-day. Mr. Gaselee, however, adopts them with little or no qualification—and he then proceeds very kindly to refute his own position.[43]

The problem, or "sting," of Pollard's position for Greg is that bibliography is to be understood as in service "to other studies." As Greg wished to understand it, bibliography was to have its own authority and not be subservient to other disciplines. If bibliography were not divested from its then (and in some ways still) current association with list making and cataloging, bibliography would never live up to its own potential as an independent science. For Greg, enumeration was clearly a kind of lower art. "The work of enumeration," he writes, "is the task of students and specialists in various departments of knowledge: it is not the task of the bibliographer."[44] Independence as a science was Greg's aim for bibliography. If it were "chained" to the work of enumeration for "all the professors and specialists in various departments who are too lazy or too incompetent to do their own work for themselves," bibliography would never attain its freedom:

> Mr. Gaselee would include the work of general enumeration and description, as "primary," along with various more recondite developments, or what he terms "higher flights," in one science of bibliography. This I am convinced and must contend is a disastrous attitude. Once you have forged chains for bibliography by acknowledging that it is the duty of bibliographers to compile book-lists for all the professors and specialists in various departments who are too lazy or too incompetent to do their own work for themselves, what freedom do you suppose will be left for bibliography to develop its own special interests, whether in the history of typography or the study of textual transmission? If bibliography is to be a science worthy of the attention of serious students it must justify itself through its own special labours and outlook, not as the drudge of every Tom, Dick, and Harry of the faculties. That is why I have said, and still maintain, that the enumeration theory reduces bibliography to futility.[45]

Greg would seem to be directly contradicting the argument that I have been making that bibliography is marginal work in the service of various ends. Rather, both he and his interlocutors provide historical evidence for my position. Indeed, Greg is making a case for bibliography serving as means to a specific end, establishing a scientific discipline devoted to the study of literary documents and their transmission. The debate over the aims of bibliography is about which ends bibliography should be understood to support as means. Gaselee and Pollard, as we shall see momentarily, were arguing for understanding bibliography as scientific means serving diverse ends. Greg was arguing for understanding bibliography as scientific means in the support of literary ends. Collectively, they present a historical precedent for my assertions that bibliography is best understood as marginal work serving other ends, even in debates about the aims of bibliography as they have been undertaken by presidents of bibliographical societies.

A twist in Greg's argument, which would seem to undercut his argument in favor of excluding enumeration from bibliography's proper work, helps to solidify mine. He admits that enumeration can be included in bibliography if it serves the history of early books and, by implication that history serves an ability to know how literary documents were created and transmitted. To make his point, and mine, about bibliography serving ends, he writes:

> It would be foolish of me to argue that the works Mr. Gaselee enumerates are not in the fullest sense bibliographical, just as it would be foolish to seek to exclude the Short Title Catalogue of English Books to 1640—though I might urge that I consult that invaluable work a dozen times for literary information, for once that I turn to it as a bibliographer. But I contend that these works belong to bibliography, not in virtue of their enumeration of books, but of the motive that governs that enumeration—the history of early printing and the output of the press. It is the end that the enumeration is to subserve that determines whether a work is bibliographical or not.[46]

Greg goes on to enumerate the ends that would *not* qualify work as bibliographical: a great deal of what we might associate with contemporary information science, especially as it is practiced in library settings. In keeping with his talent for crafting memorable polemical statements, he writes:

> If [the work of] enumeration is governed by the subject-matter of the books then it is not bibliographical. A bibliographer has no business to know a bible from a Decameron or a sermon from a fabliau. An enumeration of books of patristic theology or on the structure of the atom has no place in bibliographical science, in spite of the fact that it is traditionally and quite reasonably called "a bibliography." . . . I should once more quote Whitehead's remark that as a rule the last thing to be discovered concerning any science is what it is about.[47]

Greg will agree with Gaselee that "the sifting, ordering, and co-ordinating of material necessary 'to prevent the much learning in them from being a mere weariness of the flesh and guide it to useful and valuable ends' is a vast and a noble task."[48] Although the idea of "co-ordinating" materials will be important to his theory of bibliography as a means of studying the transmission of literary documents, Greg argues for "co-ordinating" them so "the making of many books" does not become "a terrifying problem that threatens to entangle all knowledge in a labyrinth of specialization" that would hinder bibliography from becoming the science that he envisioned. He concludes his address by saying, "I have not minced words in endeavouring to make clear the difference that lies between our President's [Gaselee's] attitude and my own[,] the difference . . . between those who seek to justify bibliography through the service it can render to other sciences."[49] Emphasizing his stance, he states, "I . . . most sincerely hope that 'we bibliographers' may never be seduced into so mistaking our function and our powers."[50]

A. W. Pollard

The structure of the debate among Gaselee, Greg, and eventually Pollard, is wonderfully instructive of the bibliographical impulse to recursively assess and reassess accounts, even as these assessments and reassessments can repeatedly inscribe ideological attitudes. Because a passage from an article that he had published roughly thirty years before had become a focal point of Gaselee and Greg's debate, Pollard asked for Gaselee's permission to "add to the official report of the meeting the context in which the sentence quoted occurs."[51] Gaselee agreed, and Pollard began his response by reprinting the larger context of his 1903 assertion that bibliography is "primarily and essentially . . . the enumeration of books."[52] The longer passage begins with Pollard referencing Kipling: "The true bibliographer, like the cat in Mr. Kipling's 'Just So' story, ever bargains to walk by himself."[53] Having put the passage in context, Pollard goes on to refute Greg's assertion that he will have certainly changed his mind, while at the same time suggesting that he had not understood the context of his assertion: "I hope that Dr. Greg will agree that, taking what I wrote as a whole, I was far from forging chains for bibliography, but demanding for it the cat's freedom to walk by itself."[54] Politely asserting his role as the elder bibliographer, Pollard sides with Gaselee before finding a way to accommodate the positions of both:

> Dr. Greg, in what seems to me excessive concern to prove that the study for which he has done so much is worthy of the name of a science, has given, I think, rather undue pre-eminence to an aspect of it which until lately was regarded as a department of "criticism," "textual" or "higher." I have done something myself to claim "criticism" of this kind as a province of bibliography. But, as Mr. Gaselee has kindly noted, the historical import of bibliography in which enumeration plays a special part, greatly attracts me and I should regret the acceptance of any new definition of our study which may tend to ignore,

or depreciate it. Fortunately the question appears to be almost entirely one of definition, and there seems to be no dispute as to what should or should not be done. Dr. Greg during his Presidentship did his utmost to procure help for making a start with a special catalogue of English books from 1641 to 1700, and Mr. Gaselee is far too good a classic to be indifferent to the study of the transmission of texts. We all want the same things: the question at issue is as to whether we want them *as bibliographers*, or in some other capacity. My own preference is for a big umbrella.[55]

Although phrased very differently, Pollard's suggestion is something similar to what I have been proposing—the idea that bibliography can be understood as practices serving as means to various ends, practices that recursively generate accounts and then account for what has been generated. Indeed, the debate among Gaselee, Greg, and Pollard, each agreeing in principle on bibliographical methods, if disagreeing on the ends to which these methods should be devoted, suggests the idea that bibliography is marginal in terms of its mixed identity and how it supports central ends from distinct peripheries. Pollard's desire for a "big umbrella" and that bibliography have a "cat's freedom" is not one that has not been taken up as readily as bibliography as a science equivalent to biology and what Bradshaw called "natural history."

Bibliography as biology. Bibliography as a freedom-seeking cat. Metaphors, at least as they are often formulated in the Western rhetorical tradition, allow transference through equivalences. A description of the biological metaphors that have shaped Anglo-European bibliographical traditions similarly provides access to equivalences that have shaded bibliographical and biological thinking. In their debates about the aims of bibliography, we see Bradshaw, Gaselee, Greg, and Pollard in their ambiguous territories prescribing and inscribing the ideologies of science and biology into their descriptions of bibliography, even as they advocate for different views of what bibliography should be and pursue. Indeed, the formulation of rough ideological equivalences between biological and textual reproduction by bibliographers such as Bradshaw, Gaselee, Greg, and Pollard has ensured that theories of bibliography inform biology, and biology informs conceptions of bibliography. In fact, because they have shared models of creativity, conceptions of bibliographical and biological reproduction have been so thoroughly entangled through metaphorical associations for such a long time that the metaphors themselves can sometimes be difficult to recognize and the equivalences that enable the metaphors appear to be inevitable and natural.

Yii-Jan Lin helps to articulate the tangle when, borrowing from the poet and cultural critic Lewis Hyde, she writes that a manuscript such as those associated with the Christian New Testament can be thought of as "a material thing that symbolizes a biological fact."[56] She adds:

> The New Testament texts may be seen as reproductive in at least two ways: first, copies and copies of copies are produced physically throughout the ancient world; second, the texts themselves, their spiritual content and message, help create converts that grow movements, which in turn creates a greater demand for copies of the text. These phenomena of church life, faith, message, and textual transmission reinforce the idea that "at some level, biological, social, and spiritual life cannot be differentiated."[57]

"Biological, social, and spiritual life" can be differentiated, of course. They have been modes of intellectual analysis, as well as lived experience. But recognizing the shared analogical framework of biology and bibliography begins to account for the conceptual relationship and its reiterative force in information science, as information science intersects with the records that formulate the identities that we inhabit willingly and those that are forcefully ascribed to us. Metaphors that enable conceptual transference, as Judith Butler and others have suggested, can formulate bodies in the world through reiterative descriptive practices.[58] Geneticists now speak of "editing" genes in ways that are made conceptually similar to how bibliographers edit literary works, while genetic critics study the dynamics of writing to trace creative processes.[59] Poet/biologists like Christian Bök translate verse into chemical sequences so they can be implanted into the genomes of bacteria,[60] and deoxyribonucleic acid (DNA) is being actively explored as an alternative to digital devices as a storage medium.[61] Bioartists such as Anna Dumitriu, Sonja Bäumel, and Elaine Whittaker consider biology "contemporary art practice,"[62] exploring infectious diseases and the bacterial biomes that inhabit the surfaces of our bodies as artistic media in order to raise a host of questions about the boundaries between art and science, and the nature of human and other kinds of bodies. The legal institutions that regulate the work of biologists and bioartists also regulate technology. Software is considered a "literary work" in many legal frameworks around the world such that copyright can be used to control how it can be reproduced. Similar legal systems govern how edited organisms can be allowed to reproduce.

Recognizing that biology has helped to formulate equivalences in bibliography facilitates a contemplative pause not unlike the pause enabled by ontography. We see anew that old ambiguous territory. What do literary and user warrant recommend as responsible descriptions of the knowledge being produced? What do our worldviews prescribe? Do we continue to use descriptive mechanisms that rely so heavily on biological equivalences and the ideologies of science as they have been articulated and rearticulated by white men to create modes of measurement that facilitate descriptive control and the organization of knowledge? Do we need to reconsider these measures and means of control for what they afford, and to whom? How should gender and race and other inhabited identities as librarians and scientists and information scientists formulate the descriptive infrastructure that we use and are supported by?

The stakes are high because our own contingent descriptive choices will articulate boundaries and contexts that will afford (which is to say enable and disable) means of knowing what the records of human knowledge document: the deaths of animals, and also the "Stomachion," the Content Standard for Digital Geospatial Data (FGDC-STD-001-1998), and a way to know how we know Archimedes, biomes and art, DNA, and new media for recording our human knowledge. How we draw up equivalences and reiterate them as descriptions will shape how we formulate bodies, and bodies of knowledge. Even if it cannot provide a prescriptive recommendation for how to create descriptions, revitalized bibliography offers accounts that provide the ability to pause reflectively to consider what has been recorded as human knowledge, how it has been accounted for, and how we might create new descriptive accounts.

By providing examples of how bibliographical description works as a kind of carpentry that facilitates the pursuit of various ends, as in the case of the Archimedes Palimpsest, and also works to account for records of human knowledge, as I have suggested with my description of biological metaphors in bibliography, we better appreciate bibliographical description as foundational infrastructure in information science. Juxtaposing recent bibliographical descriptions with historical debates from nearly a century ago, we see bibliography serving many aims, even among those who think of themselves as bibliographers. These same juxtapositions provide a moment to pause and wonder again from a new vantage point how we inhabit our complex identities and how we should formulate the descriptive infrastructure that we build.

Chapter 8 will use the vantage points provided here to begin building a case for understanding big data and AI in their many iterations as forms of bibliographical description. Having established bibliographical description as constructive means to ends that can also provide useful opportunities to reflect on what has been and should be built, the chapters that follow describe the generative power of the bibliographical descriptions that we have called *big data* and *AI* and how they also present opportunities to reflect on and critique what we are building.

8 NEW BIBLIOGRAPHICAL DESCRIPTION

This chapter and those that remain in this book continue my description of bibliographical description and how it matters. I advance my argument about the foundational roles played by bibliography in information science by building a case for understanding artificial intelligence (AI) as a form of bibliographical description. I also make the case that critiques of bibliographical description as an inductive science leveled by bibliographers such as D. F. McKenzie provide a useful framework for assessing and accounting the new forms of bibliographical description that we call "machine learning" (ML). This chapter begins to lay out these arguments by describing bibliographical description as it was pursued by New Bibliographers in the early twentieth century.

The science studying the transmission of literary documents that took shape among Anglo-American bibliophiles in the late nineteenth and early twentieth centuries, which came to be called "New Bibliography," is most closely associated with the work of W. W. Greg, A. W. Pollard, Fredson Bowers, R. B. McKerrow (1872–1940), and Philip Gaskell (1926–2001). In this chapter, I focus on Greg and Bowers since they became the "major apologists for the influence"[1] of New Bibliography. My focus will be on the inductive methods that Greg and Bowers imagined as "instruments of thought and investigation" that could "co-ordinate" facts and enable "constant causes"[2] to be traced. A historical contemporary of Claude Shannon, Greg's intellectual move to divest meaning as it might be formulated by readers receiving a literary message from problems related to literary transmission predates

Shannon's efforts to enumerate messages to exclude what they might mean to those receiving them. Indeed, Greg's suggestions can be considered even more radical than Shannon's when one considers that Greg was proposing that the meaning of literary texts—everything from their subjects to the individual meanings that might be associated with individual elements of historical writing systems—should be bracketed from consideration for bibliography to contribute to literary studies. I have often wondered why Stephen Gaselee and Pollard overlooked this radical assertion to focus their critical attention on the issue of enumeration. But sixteen years before Shannon's 1948 mathematical theory of communication, Greg wrote in his 1932 "Bibliography—An Apologia": "The bibliographer is concerned with pieces of paper or parchment covered with certain written or printed signs. With these signs he is concerned merely as arbitrary marks; their meaning is no business of his."[3]

Isolating arbitrary marks as bibliographical objects distinct from what the marks might signify within linguistic or historical context, Greg believed, would allow ordered data collection and a scientific means for generating more accurate predictions about the past and what caused the bibliographical facts he wished to understand. As I show in the next few chapters, the descriptive methods employed by the New Bibliographers to produce what they believed to be accurate predictions about the past correspond with methods and assumptions of many who are working to make predictions with various forms of ML. Because it is likely to be less familiar, this chapter starts with a brief historical description meant to situate New Bibliography in the context of bibliography as its history has been proffered by Anglo-American textual critics and scholars. This brief contextual description will also help situate McKenzie's useful critique of Greg and the New Bibliographers and how similar critiques of ML can be leveled, issues that we take up in more detail later.

STEMMATICS, IDEAL COPIES, AND MATERIAL EXEMPLARS

Karl Lachmann (1793–1851) is pointed to as a progenitor of a modern philology in the West,[4] and he is a convenient person with whom to begin my brief historical description of the New Bibliographers. Lachmann and his method were especially important to Greg, the New Bibliographers, and bibliography as they practiced it.[5] Lachmann, a German, worked as professor of classical philology at the University of Königsberg and then at Humboldt University. He was particularly important to later bibliographers in the Anglo-American tradition, especially Greg, who used what has come to be called "Lachmannian recension," the idea of tracing the origins of manuscript texts to an archetype. While Lachmann used the technique to make predictions about the nature of extant manuscripts in relation to an idealized historical archetype, Greg used similar methods to describe books of the hand-press period, especially the works of English authors such as Shakespeare. Stemmatics, or the careful study of textual genealogies, was the heart of the so-called Lachmannian method. Relying again on equivalences that can be associated with natural history and what would take shape as biology, the assumptions were that later manuscripts will contain more errors and that errors appearing in two or more manuscripts indicated a common line of textual descent. Exploiting the fact that copies are not what they reproduce, the theory holds that one can trace variations in manuscripts by creating a genealogy of codices, often called a *stemma codicum*, to formulate an archetype. This archetype and the genealogy used to produce it were presumed to be the best means for making critical judgments or additional copies. The aim was the production of a conceptual ideal, a model, produced by careful investigation of material evidence, but not necessarily the revelation of any particular historical text.

Lachmann developed his method as an alternative to simply taking as given what had been received, especially when what had been received was biblical. In the early sixteenth century, the Dutch humanist Desiderius Erasmus (1466–1536) collaborated with the publisher Johann Froben to produce an edition of the Greek New Testament. Despite the fact that the work was done sloppily, at least according to modern scholars,[6] Erasmus's Greek New Testament became the basis of later European editions for the next 400 years.[7] When Lachmann and others rejected the *Textus Receptus* created by Erasmus and the Majority Text, a collection of shared biblical readings that were used by Erasmus to create the *Textus Receptus*, as "inferior to other, more ancient texts . . . , their work was decried not (only) as poor scholarship but as sacrilege."[8] Yet the Lachmann method would take hold as a powerful bibliographical ideology. It held that through careful study of what we would now call empirical evidence, it is possible to posit a model, an archetype, that is useful for organizing diverse phenomena and future investigations.

This idea that a descriptive ideal, a *codex optimus*, provides the best mode for making critical bibliographical judgments and descriptions would be challenged from a variety of perspectives. Perhaps the best known of these is exemplified by a professor of French literature, Joseph Bédier (1864–1938). As David Greetham has suggested, Bédier has come to be seen as a representative of a competing and equally powerful bibliographical ideology among studiers of texts, the idea that concrete historical texts should be established to organize similarly diverse phenomena, future investigations, and "higher criticism." Bédier was interested in establishing a physical artifact as the measure of other artifacts, not an inferred ideal.

Greetham sets these two bibliographical desires in opposition to one another and uses the tension between them to organize the history of textual scholarship. He associates methods such as Lachmannian stemmatics and later the eclectic editing practices of the Anglo-American New Bibliographers with the editorial practices that started to take shape in the Greek city of Alexandria in the third century BCE.[9] He associates this mode of bibliographical practice with *analogy*, the idea that by comparing copies assumed to be similar, it is possible to arrive at a model of an ideal text. As Greetham describes, the belief was that a comparison of multiple copies would enable one "to reach beyond the concrete and the actual into an 'ideal' form not available in any individual state."[10] As Greetham organizes the story, the Alexandrians did not attempt to designate any particular copy as the most authentic, but rather "tried to use the admittedly corrupt *remaniements* (the 'remains' of a text) in the extant documents to reach beyond the concrete and the actual into an 'ideal' form not available in any individual state." Greetham associates this process and its aims with "the (neo)platonism that was to dominate Alexandrian thought in the third to fifth centuries CE, and can still be seen in the textual theories of some modern critics."[11] He suggests that it is ordinarily called "analogy," which, like the word itself, suggests a form of reasoning that utilizes similarity and resemblances among objects.

Greetham contrasts the editorial practices of Alexandria with Alexandria's rival city Pergamum. He also relies on a distinction between Platonic and Stoic philosophies:

> Working against Alexandrian *analogy* and instead promoting the concept of *anomaly* (dependent on a Stoic acceptance of the unavoidable corruption of all worldly phenomena), the linguistically based textual scholars of Pergamum favored a careful analysis of the provenance, philological features, even the paleography and grammar, of each surviving witness. This analysis was then used to select a "best text" (warts and all) that could at least represent an actual historical moment rather than veering off into an idealism for which no concrete demonstration could be made.[12]

In contrast to practices that aim to arrive at an idealized archetype or model that can be used to guide critical judgments, Greetham is describing bibliographical practices that draw out distinctions and equivalences to arrive at a physical document, one that can be used to make critical judgments about other physical documents.

Greethams's physical and rhetorical geography is complex but worth recounting for a variety of reasons. First, Greetham's history provides yet another example of how bibliography, even within histories of bibliography as textual scholarship, can be understood as working in the service of differing ends, in this case the establishment of models of books versus using physical books as models for making critical judgments. Second, these distinctions between (1) the impulse to create an abstract model against which new phenomena can be compared; and (2) the impulse to establish a particular physical object as a measure that can guide judgment will in turn guide our discussion in this and the chapters to come. As I show, ML is a form of bibliographical description akin to the descriptive ideals of the New Bibliographers. Modes of bibliographical critique associated with the sociology of texts, as we will discuss, help to provide useful critiques of the bibliographical descriptions that we call "machine learning" (ML).

Greetham's complex metaphors also provide a means of returning to the important theme of equivalences and how they are drawn. A complex literal and figurative geography support his description. These geographies are expansive spatially and temporally but they also are quite narrow. This is to make an observation and level an obvious but important critique. Greetham's description allows us to observe how equivalences between copies, as well as their distinction, have been used to establish both abstract and physical models to formulate additional forms of measurement. Copies are measured as a function of their equivalence with an ideal copy or specific material manifestation. Critical judgments are made based on the measurements taken.

But it is also important to point out that the metaphorical and rhetorical equivalences that Greetham fashions to create his historical description suggest that bibliography be equated with what has been practiced in Greek cities in northern Africa and the Mediterranean West. He leaves out, as just one of myriad examples, how Chinese Buddhists attempted to establish the texts of their massive canon by establishing if a text had a historically verifiable translator.[13] Rather than attempting to establish the best physical exemplar as a textual model, as Bédier might, or working to establish a textual archetype, as Lachmann might, Chinese Buddhists would work to establish if historical translators could have produced a text that they were considering for inclusion in their canon. Despite the usefulness of his history, one that I will continue to utilize to suggest the ways that ML should be thought of as bibliographical description, this does not allow us to forgo our bibliographical obligation to acknowledge Greetham's limits (and mine) as I continue my rudimentary description of Anglo-European bibliographical description.

COORDINATING FACTS

Since both Greg and Bowers were interested in discerning something akin to a Lachmannian archetype through careful documentation—the empirical collection of data—and its scientific analysis, they provide good examples of the "Alexandrian" ends, as Greetham would call them, pursued by bibliographers attempting to establish the texts of English and American literature. As I have been emphasizing, bibliography in this mode was meant to be a science. Although apparently paradoxical, as with Shannon, what the materials might mean to a reader was not the primary concern of these bibliographers, even though they imagined their scientific bibliographical work to be serving literary ends. Rather than attending to literary meaning, the aim was to document and understand the communication channel from authorial intention (information source) through manuscript, and especially printshop encodings (transduction) (signal-noise-signal) (transduction) to a reader's hand. Issues of meaning were to be left to literary critics as readers who were positioned like the "destination" in Shannon's diagram (see figure 1.1 in chapter 1). Interestingly, we can also discern in the New Bibliographical model hints of the East Asian model of poetry mentioned in chapter 1, where intention is transposed from an internal manifestation to an external one in words. The New Bibliographers assumed that the intentions of authors and printers could be transpositioned and made available to interpretation. Like Shannon,[14] New Bibliographers saw it as their job to model a communication channel. The aim was to reproduce a message present in an information source (i.e., what an author or printer intended) with as much fidelity as possible for literary readers.

Logic and thorough Lachmannian genealogies, this time applied to printed materials and manuscripts when available rather than manuscripts exclusively, formed a bedrock of Greg's practice and the work of the New Bibliographers. This work focused intensely, although not exclusively, on the works of Shakespeare. "Greg's authority was grounded in the application of an all but unrivalled faculty of analytic logic to a rich archival observation and experience. His personal strengths, in turn, were rooted in classical and medievalist methodologies of textual criticism, pivoted on the organicist historicism of stemmatics."[15] Careful examination, documentation, and logic would, Greg suggests, enable facts to be "co-ordinated" and "constant causes" traced. In 1911, he writes in *Transactions of the Bibliographical Society* (which would become *The Library* in 1920):

> If bibliography is to-day a science by which we co-ordinate facts and trace the operation of constant causes, if we are gradually evolving a rigorous method for the investigation and interpretation of fresh evidence, if we are able, within the sphere of our work, in any way adequately to reconstruct the past out of the indications of the present, it is in a large measure due to the patient accumulation and recording of facts.[16]

Greg was attempting to predict the past by making inferences from evidentiary materials available in the present. As in the natural sciences, the patient accumulation of documents that could serve as evidence of facts was central to the endeavor. Of course, as we will discuss in more detail in later chapters, computers—people first, and then machines—have for us become the ever-patient compilers of documents that serve as evidence of facts. They quite literally coordinate the electrical charges that contribute to establishing what we take as given, and how these things taken as given suggest evidence that can inform belief.

Greg held out "instruments of thought and investigation" as a central end for his method of patiently collecting and coordinating facts through systemization. Like Paul Otlet, the Belgian librarian we met in chapter 3, Greg was interested in changing the world and our "relation to knowledge."[17] This was to be done through logic, determination, diligence, and a bit of luck. He writes: "Facts are observed and catalogued by the systematizers, and then suddenly, as if by chance, an idea is born that introduces order and logic into what was a mere chaos, and we are in possession of a guiding principle, of an instrument of thought and investigation, that may transform the whole of our relation to knowledge or alter the face of the physical globe."[18]

In the next sentence, Greg quickly recloaks his grand aspirations in the humility of a bookish scientist, adding: "Perhaps no discoveries that we make in bibliography are likely to have such far-reaching results as these, but they are quite capable of revolutionizing the subject itself and the methods by which it is pursued."[19]

Passages like these reveal Greg's belief that meticulous, inductive investigations of material facts held the power to alter the "face of the globe" and put us in a new position relative to knowledge. For bibliographers such as Greg and Bowers, developing a consistent method of documenting the material particularities of books, as well as their various species, was an important first step toward changing the world and occupying a new position relative to knowledge. As we will discuss in later chapters, especially chapters 10 and 11, a similar aspirational methodology girds big data and AI.

BIBLIOGRAPHICAL DESCRIPTION

As Bowers rightly points out, descriptive bibliography, even if it goes by different names, is fundamental to scholarship. This is not, of course, to suggest that descriptive statements are not fraught morally and politically, as discussed in chapter 7. "Descriptive bibliography is an outgrowth of the catalogue, or handlist," writes Bowers, "a type of compilation which will always exist as one of the basic needs of scholarship."[20] For New Bibliographers like Bowers, the moral, political, and philosophical aims are "Alexandrian," to borrow Greetham's term again. Bibliographical description aims to describe an ideal through the meticulous documentation of individual copies of texts considered similar enough to be put into a descriptive schema where terms such as *edition*, *issue*, and *variant* function like *genus*, *species*, and *specimen* in biology, or *expression*, *manifestation*, and *item* in the Functional Requirements for Bibliographic Records (FRBR). In chapter 10, we will see how these descriptive schema and the methods for creating them are not unlike those of data modelers, ontologists, and creators of knowledge graphs. The method is logical and essentially Lachmannian. Bowers writes:

> The concern of the descriptive bibliographer . . . is to examine every available copy of an edition of a book in order to describe in bibliographical terms the characteristics of an ideal copy of this edition, to distinguish between issues and variants of the edition, to explain and describe the printing and textual history of the edition, and finally to arrange it in a correct and logical relationship to other editions.[21]

The end pursued by Bowers was a particular kind of ideal copy that enabled the generation of descriptive classificatory schema. Bibliographical description, at least for Bowers, was focused quite narrowly on creating an ideal descriptive model that suggested a copy of a text as printers intended them to be, not necessarily as they were printed. Bowers wished to establish texts as printers intended them to be printed.[22] This end distinguishes him from other bibliographers who have been concerned primarily with an ideal representation of authorial intention as a governing model, despite mid-twentieth-century literary theory that considered "intention" to be a "fallacy."[23] Roland Barthes declared the author "dead,"[24] and discussions of authors' intentions were delegated by cultural critics to discussions of "author functions."[25] Bowers writes, "A bibliographer is not concerned with accidental combinations resulting from binding; his business is to describe the ideal copy as the printer intended it to leave his hands."[26] As just one example of the narrowness of Bowers's evidentiary focus, we can note that Henry Bradshaw believed bindings to be an important part of bibliographical investigation. Bradshaw was fascinated by bindings because they frequently were made from leftover parchment, which sometimes contained rare typographical examples that could shed light on printing history.[27]

The purpose of bibliographic description, as Bowers describes and prescribes it, is twofold. First, it is to serve as a basis "for the analysis of the method of publication, which has direct bearing to the relations and transmissions of texts."[28] Second, the description is to "provide sufficient evidence for readers to identify books in their possession as being members of the precise state, issue, impression, and edition of the 'ideal copy' listed, or as being unrecorded variants requiring further bibliographical investigation."[29] In other words, for Bowers, bibliographical description was a means for achieving the end of articulating a classificatory ideal. As he conceived it, bibliographical description was a scientific exercise that required a standard detailed notational practice. The collation formula, which we will discuss in more detail next, becomes a central tool for bibliographers such as Bowers for describing the relationship of texts to each other using a taxonomic system that defined hierarchical differences from an ideal. In this context, collation concerns the comparison of copies. The collation formula, echoing mathematical formulas, is a method for expressing axioms, objects, and relationships. Collation formulas enable a precise description of an abstraction, "an ideally perfect copy," and "not for any individual copy, because an important purpose of the description is to set up a standard of reference whereby imperfections may be detected and properly analyzed when a copy of a book is checked against the bibliographical description."[30]

Collation formulas used in conjunction with transcriptions of title pages and categorical definitions such as "state," "issue," "impression," and "edition" situated copies of books in relation to an "ideal." Although Bowers is not mentioned,[31] we can note that classification systems such as FRBR used by librarians today work on the same principle of descriptively ordering relations between individual physical copies of books by means of bibliographical "ideals,"[32] ideals that similarly formulate and coordinate data when modeled by data modelers, ontologists, and those graphing knowledge. Importantly, for Bowers, bibliographical categorical definitions were based on abstract forms of measurement and what were, through detailed research, logic, and historical imagining, considered norms of printing and publishing during the hand-press period in Europe. An *edition* is a "whole number of copies printed at any time or times from substantially the same setting of type-pages."[33] An *edition* encompasses issues, variant states, and impressions. An *issue* is "the whole number of copies of a form of an edition put on sale at any time or times as a consciously planned printed unit."[34]

As we see, the category requires the bibliographer to imagine what was consciously planned by printers and publishers as a unit and, of course, the assumption that books were to be sold. A *state* suggests variations in typesetting, "including the addition or deletion of material in some copies, caused by alterations executed in the course of the original printing before public sale."[35] "Time and form"[36] govern these categorical relationships, Bowers writes, emphasizing these abstract methods of temporal and morphological measurement rather than historically situated social processes, such as exchange, upon which his categories are also predicated.

The notational system developed and employed by Bowers and Greg, which remains in use among textual critics, aims to be succinct and speed the scientific work of bibliographers. Like mathematical notation, many parts of the descriptive system formulated by Bowers and Greg were not designed to enlighten members of the general public, who could not be expected to understand what was being described. Where they aimed to establish how literary texts should be counted and put in relation to each other as a service to the literary community and lay bibliophiles, their own bibliographical descriptions were meant to support their own scientific work as bibliographers. For Bowers, "the arguments of the nontechnical school cannot, from a scholarly point of view, be maintained in view of the superior qualifications of the technical symbols for bibliographical collation and reference."[37] The result was that descriptions of the 1664 edition of John Evelyn's *Sylva, or*

A Discourse of Forest-Trees and the Propagation of Timber, for example, would include a collation formula such as the following:

$$A - R^4\ \chi^2;\ {}^2A^2\ B - C^4\ \chi\text{I}\ D - E^4\ F^4(F_2 + \chi\text{I})\ G^4\ H^4(—H_\text{I})\ I - L^4\ {}_2\chi\text{I}$$ [38]

This shorthand descriptive notation was much preferred by Bowers to less succinct descriptions such as the following: "$A - R^4\ [*]^2\ A^2\ B - L^4$, one leaf inserted after C_4, one leaf inserted between F_2–F_3, H_1 cancelled, one leaf inserted after L_4 (all in the second alphabet); 114 leaves."[39]

His reasoning was that "a reader unacquainted with the basics of book production and how it is described by bibliographers, is unlikely to know enough about gatherings and their signings to be enlightened"[40] even by more verbose description, such as one that I might reconstruct from Bowers's description: The ideal copy of the 1664 edition of Evelyn's *Sylva* has two sections, each with groups of signed gatherings. The first section contains seventeen gatherings, which are signed A to R. These gatherings are followed by an unsigned gathering with two leaves. The second section has additional gatherings signed A to L. The initial two-leaf gathering of the second section is signed A. This is followed by gatherings signed B to L. A leaf has been inserted after the gathering signed C. A leaf has also been inserted between the second and third leaves of the gathering signed F. The first leaf of the gathering signed H has been canceled, and one unsigned leaf has been inserted after the gathering signed L.

ANALYTICAL BIBLIOGRAPHY

The collation formula and other elements of bibliographical description aimed to enable a trained bibliographer to place a historical copy of a text in relation to an ideal formulated through a careful historical study associated with analysis. Indeed, analytical bibliography has often been used as a synonym for the New Bibliography project. "[Books] are products of a particular manufacturing or technical process, and the study of that process for printed texts is usually called *analytical bibliography*,"[41] as Greetham describes succinctly. For bibliographers considering printed materials, "it involves the consideration of all those stages of printing (from paper, ink, and type manufacture to the habits of the compositor, the press-work, the binding and so on) that might tell us something about how the text reached its present condition."[42]

The biological metaphors discussed previously have continued to govern not only bibliographical description but how bibliography, especially analytical bibliography, is described. Among the ever-shifting boundaries drawn by the studiers of books attempting to describe their work, analytical bibliography is often positioned as an investigatory hybrid serving two ends: historical inquiry into books and their manufacture; and accurate bibliographical description. Bibliographical description in what we might call the "Greg Bowers system" is premised on a deep historical knowledge of textual instantiations and morphologies. To understand how those morphologies came to be, there was a need for *historical bibliography*, a term often used interchangeably with *analytical bibliography*. Historical bibliography, as Greetham describes, was "sometimes referred to as the 'biology of books,' the study of them as part of a Darwinian evolution of a manufacturing process."[43] "The biology of books" assessed the iron and lead of presses and type, as well as the fibers of pulped rags and trees, for what could be discerned about evolving practices for producing texts. In turn, bibliographical description fueled the drive to properly order and account for how books came to be as they are. Descriptive bibliography "uses the information gained in the practice of analytical and historical bibliography to prepare an account of the 'bibliographical nature' of the book."[44]

Tensions between analysis and its relations to description are inherent to both as they were practiced by New Bibliographers and those that have been inspired by them. Which historical elements of books should be enumerated to enable description? Should bookbindings be included (as Bradshaw suggests) or excluded (as Bowers suggests) as enumerated elements in bibliographical descriptions? How should historical knowledge gleaned by studying the "Darwinian evolution of a manufacturing process" inform the work of creating an abstract science based solely on the comparison of material artifacts? This later tension flared into debates about whether "historical bibliography" could even be considered "bibliography."[45] Fascinating as they are, we will not dwell on these debates here.

Rather, I wish to close this chapter by returning our attention to the guiding belief among New Bibliographers in inductive procedures to reveal essential realities, natures, and nature. Implicit in this inductive approach is a deep commitment to the minute material particulars of textual objects and efforts to describe them. The promise held out by a commitment to these documentary procedures was described by Greg. All the meticulous and painstaking work would result, as if by chance, in the revelation of the world's constant causes. Out of chaos, a sense of order would be born. This search for "constant causes" motivated fewer studiers of books later in the twentieth century, but as we will see, a similar search that shares deep conceptual and procedural affinities with the descriptive and analytical bibliography of the Greg Bowers school is underway in intellectual and professional communities associated with data science, AI, and ML.

9 BIBLIOGRAPHICAL DESCRIPTION, "PRINTERS OF THE MIND," AND THE SOCIOLOGY OF TEXTS

By the latter half of the twentieth century, the clout of New Bibliographers had started to fade. Studiers of texts in the Anglo-American tradition began pursing ends distinct from those pursued by the likes of Fredson Bowers and W. W. Greg. They also began to actively reconsider the boundaries that might constitute the objects of bibliographical study as it served ends associated with textual scholarship and literature. This occurred while many of their means (list making, a deep commitment to history and slow, careful interactions with textual objects, as well as detailed description) remained the same. As Greetham suggests, Jerome McGann and D. F. McKenzie have become emblems of the alternative ends pursued by many in Anglo-American bibliography and what has come to be called "social bibliography." McKenzie, McGann, and like-minded scholars questioned many of the underlying methodological assumptions of bibliography, if not its fundamental aim of establishing texts as opportunities for meaningful individual and social engagement. The biological metaphors guiding the discipline remained, but they changed. Deoxyribonucleic acid (DNA), double helixes, and similar objects more often provided metaphorical equivalences to support arguments, along with comparisons with physics. Instead of attempts to discern a singular origin for a text, documents are studied and documented to reveal the multiplicity of a text's states of being and the varied intentions of authors and all those involved in the production, transmission, and reception of texts. The faith of the New Bibliographers in inductive methods was tempered by deductive approaches and what can be deduced from evidence of all kinds, not just what was presented by documents placed in isolation by scientific bibliographical apparatuses. The work of intellectuals like McGann and McKenzie aims to disclose the pluralities that a text could reveal as a record of the interactions of all those involved in creating, transmitting, and receiving it.

Bibliography as sociohistorical investigation can be seen as serving a new end. Rather than attempting to mediate cultural experience and philological inquiry through scientific means focused on the establishment of a single communicative channel from author to critic, it works to establish texts as complex interactions that can reveal a diversity of personal, cultural, and physical forces at play that individuals and communities find differently meaningful. This short chapter presents a close reading of one of McKenzie's best-known essays, "Printers of the Mind," as a way to lay the groundwork for my suggestion that bibliography in these kinds of sociohistorical modes can provide useful critical accounts of the bibliographical descriptions created by data scientists working in ways recognizably similar to the New Bibliographers. "Printers of the Mind" provides a powerful critique of New Bibliographical methods, lays the foundations of McKenzie's theory of bibliography as the sociology of texts, and presents a way to think about how we can better account for the newfound bibliographical powers we call artificial intelligence (AI).

MCKENZIE AND "PRINTERS OF THE MIND"

"The essential task of the bibliographer," McKenzie writes, "is to establish the facts of transmission for a particular text."[1] This is similar, of course, to Greg's proposal. What is different is McKenzie's insistence that a bibliographer "use *all* relevant evidence to determine bibliographical truth."[2] What counted as bibliographical description and what counted as a bibliographical object became infinitely more complex. "Facts" were not simply "observed and catalogued by the systematizers,"[3] but themselves had to be established, including the facts of the bibliographer's own position in relation to evidence.

The most powerful emblems of McKenzie's critique were what he called the "printers of the mind," conjured by New Bibliographical inductive inference. These printers of the mind were phantoms created by what he considered vague assumptions about the normal practices of pressmen and publishers in seventeenth- and eighteenth-century Europe. These assumptions about presswork and how books would be sold into markets are, as we have seen, integral to the bibliography of Greg and Bowers. It is at these assumptions that McKenzie takes aim. McKenzie does not critique the idea that bibliography should be considered a science, but he does impugn practices that he felt were overly reliant on inductive investigation in both science and bibliography. Both bibliography and science needed to be improved: "It is not that bibliographical inquiry differs in any essential respect from 'scientific' inquiry . . . but that the method common to both is itself logically unsound. Bibliography, as it happens, is a convenient area in which to demonstrate its unsoundness."[4]

The logically unsound method common to both science and bibliography, in McKenzie's view, is sociohistorically unsituated inductive inference. He writes, "To limit our knowledge to that which may be derived by inductive inference from direct observations is to invite the obvious objection that no finite number of observations can ever justify a generalization."[5] Citing Bertrand Russell, he writes that induction is "a mere method of making plausible guesses."[6] The logic of induction and the scientific method did not bother McKenzie as much as the fact that available data often did not allow the kinds of inductive inferences being made by bibliographers and others working in the sciences. "Indeed, if I were to give this paper an epigraph," he writes in "Printers of the Mind," "it might well be that quoted by Sir Karl Popper from Black's *Lectures on the Elements of Chemistry* published in 1803: 'A nice adaptation of conditions will make almost any hypothesis agree with the phenomena. This will please the imagination, but does not advance our knowledge.'"[7]

The alternative that McKenzie suggests is to embrace "multiple 'probabilities'" as "hypotheses" when considering how texts came to be and have been transmitted. In this way, he builds a recursive mechanism into his bibliographical practice. His proposal is that the multiple probabilities that formulate what can be surmised about a text be considered multiple hypotheses "to be tested *de*ductively."[8] These hypotheses can be arrived at inductively, and even imaginatively, but they are to be formulated to be disproved with evidence and are not meant to produce "demonstrable proofs."[9] The aim, McKenzie writes, is to expand bibliography's "hospitality to new ideas."[10] The hunt for historical evidence is thus a hunt for evidence in the "service of disproof."[11] Inductive methods play a role but as means for proposing "probabilities"[12] that await disproof: "Inductive process[es] carr[y] a burden of assumed truth waiting to be converted into proven error: knowledge, that is, comes with the act of disproof."[13] Imagined probabilities await similar disproof through recursive attempts to account for knowledge. "And until that moment arrives" when a hypothesis is "converted into proven error," conclusions "lay claim only to some degree of 'reliability' or 'probability.'"[14] This degree of "reliability" or "probability" is based on "assumptions about the comprehensiveness of the evidence used and about the predictability of past or 'normal' examples into the future."[15] Using the work of Greg and Bowers as foils to advance his argument, McKenzie writes:

> If the "scientific" proofs offered in some recent bibliographical analyses of older books were seen philosophically for the conjectures they are, we should I think be nearer the true spirit of scientific inquiry and the humility that always accompanies an awareness of the possibility of fresh evidence and therefore of falsification. The subject would not then be circumscribed by the demand for demonstrable proofs; rather it would be expanded in its hospitality to new ideas and in its search for fresh historical evidence in the service of disproof.[16]

In a headnote to a reprinting of "Printers of the Mind" that appeared after McKenzie's death in *Making Meaning: "Printers of the Mind" and Other Essays*, editors extend the tropes that hold bibliography in analogical orbit with the sciences: "With this, arguably the most influential of his essays, McKenzie established his own 'uncertainty principle,' which was as far-ranging in its consequences for analytical bibliography as Heisenberg's was for quantum physics."[17] Indeed, the consequences have been far-ranging. Moreover, the analogy with quantum physics is apt, given that McKenzie was aiming to find a way to account for the minute particulars of individual texts with a method that recognized that acts of viewing affect what can be known through bibliographical investigation.[18] As Heisenberg and Bohr had with their notions of uncertainty and complementarity, McKenzie made bibliographers part of the observational apparatus of bibliography in a manner that necessitated insistent, recursive accounting for a bibliographer's positionality. He also clearly saw the relationship, already established through observation in any bibliographical inquiry, between meaning and the perception of utility. As in physics, the effect was to entangle human inquiry with the smallest particles of the bibliographical universe so as to recognize the limits that these entanglements impose on human knowledge. McKenzie aligns the ends of bibliography to address epistemological issues similar to those presented by Yi Sang in his aptly named poem, "Publication Laws." Bibliographical tools are to diagnose the foundations of bibliographical systems. McKenzie, like Yi Sang, is suggesting that "at the very center of things carried out against" us, we can't know and, while coming to know things, we can't help but know new things again.[19]

McKenzie's attention to how bibliographers are entangled with the evidence that they observe, as well as his emphasis on hypothesis falsification, will help to formulate the useful critique of the bibliographical descriptions produced by machine learning (ML) that we will entertain in the chapters to come. Akin to the bibliographical descriptions of the New Bibliographers, descriptive statements produced by data modelers, ontologists, those graphing knowledge, and those using ML can be reconsidered and usefully accounted for as bibliographical hypotheses proposed by individuals and communities entangled with their evidence. While it is commonplace to acknowledge that the data and procedures of data science are always "biased" and to imply that those working with data are entangled with what they have taken as given, bibliography as McKenzie pursues it provides a mechanism for insistent critique that goes beyond acknowledging inevitable biases. The mechanism is persistent critique, enabled by the idea that any account is a hypothesis that needs to be accounted for. As McKenzie writes of Greg-style analytical bibliography, and I will suggest when discussing the descriptive force of ML models, "bibliography might grow the more securely if we retained a stronger assurance of its hypothetical nature."[20]

McKenzie provides "a final paradox"[21] in his essay that usefully summarizes his critique of New Bibliography and provides a means of bringing this brief chapter to a close. "Bibliography has nothing to do with bibliographies,"[22] writes McKenzie, echoing Greg. The distinction that McKenzie aims to draw with this rhetorical flourish concerns the ends pursued by bibliography. I have been accentuating their differences, but there were a great many things upon which Greg and McKenzie agreed. Although he critiques Greg's reliance on inductive methods and the narrowness of how he defines what can count as bibliographical evidence, McKenzie fundamentally agrees with Greg that bibliography is the study of texts as they have been made, circulated, and received, even if he would later radically expand bibliographical investigation to include much more than literary texts. He also agrees with Greg when Greg suggests that bibliography concerns the rigorous investigation of texts, even if he would understand rigor as a commitment to what we might describe as the rigorous hypotheses testing of bibliographical facts though an investigation of *all* relevant evidence, where *all* and *relevant* are paradoxically already functions of selection and position (a root meaning of *hypothesis*).

Echoing Greg's position in the debate with Gaselee and Pollard, or so it would seem, McKenzie writes that "author and subject bibliographies have a completely different function and it would be preposterous now to demand of them any great bibliographical sophistication."[23] His point is that author and subject bibliographies do not attempt to rigorously establish the facts of textual transmission. However, in a twist emblematic of McKenzie's attempt to make his case for bibliography as a rigorous attempt to establish the facts of texts and their transmission, he directly contradicts Greg's position that enumerative bibliographers should be exiled from bibliography's republic. In fact, McKenzie reemphasizes the importance of enumeration to testing hypotheses and assumptions. He understands enumerative bibliography as an essential service for those who wish to have useful records of what has been recorded as human knowledge: "If our basic premise is that bibliography should serve literature or the criticism of literature, it may be thought to do this best, not by disappearing into its own minutiae, but by pursuing the study of printing history to the point where analysis can usefully begin, or by returning—and this is the paradox—to the more directly useful, if less sophisticated, activity of enumerative 'bibliography.'"[24] Pointing to the collective work of Pollard, Gilbert Redgrave (1844–1941), and Donald Wing, which resulted in enumerative bibliographies such as the *Short-Title Catalogue of Books Printed in England, Scotland, Ireland, Wales, and British America and of the English Books Printed in Other Countries, 1641–1700*, he writes that enumerative bibliography has "been of inestimable service to the study of history, life, thought—and bibliography—in the 16th and 17th centuries."[25] He continues, "It will be a pity if history, life, thought—and bibliography—in the 18th century are long deprived of a comparable service."[26]

For both Greg and McKenzie, bibliographies were, paradoxically, not bibliographical, although for different reasons. For Greg, enumerative bibliographies were not bibliographical because they were not scientific. For McKenzie, bibliographies were not bibliographical if they were not serious, self-reflective considerations of texts and their transmission. Enumerative bibliography is bibliography, as far as McKenzie is concerned, if it is used to generate hypotheses and test what has been hypothesized by bibliographical enumeration and description.

To overextend the physics analogy employed in this chapter, we might say that McKenzie was to New Bibliography what Niels Bohr and Werner Heisenberg were to Newtonian physics. Bibliography was as much a science for McKenzie as it was for Greg and Bowers: "In recent years we have all come to recognize the need for what might be called 'scientific' investigation in bibliography, a phrase which at its best implies, as Professor Bowers has succinctly put it, a strict regard for certain fixed bounds of physical fact and logical probability."[27] Where Greg and Bowers were concerned with formulating bibliographical descriptions inductively from arbitrary marks on parchment or paper to formulate knowledge about the transmission of literary texts, McKenzie was concerned with how the "arbitrary" marks were formulated as meaningful in the first place as a means of hypothesizing bibliographers' own positions in bibliographical processes.

While "Printers of the Mind" was formulated to critique a Greg Bowers–style analytical bibliography, and consequently largely constrains its scope to literary concerns, McKenzie would ultimately be concerned with the transmission of anything that can be taken as meaningful: a stone, a story, a book, a CD, or indeed any kind of electronic text. "Texts" for him, as we remember from chapter 1, "include verbal, visual, oral, and numeric *data*, in the form of maps, prints, and music, of archives of recorded sound, of films, videos, and any computer-stored information."[28] Familiarity with these earlier arguments in "Printers of the Mind" will be particularly helpful for considering how bibliographical critiques such as McKenzie's can be usefully employed to consider increasingly ubiquitous bibliographical descriptions produced by various kinds of AI as they are enabled and enacted by data models, ontologies, and knowledge graphs.

10 MODELS, MODELING, AND THE SOCIALIZATION OF DATA

In previous chapters, we met "Alexandrian" New Bibliographers intent on using the powers of bibliographical description to track and clarify the ways that public documents (printed books, for the most part) facilitate or obstruct the transmission of what was intended by authors and printers. Here, I describe how "Pergamene" bibliographers such as Jerome McGann are interested in the "thick" and "noisy" textures of literary art.[1] For literary bibliographers such as McGann, these textures provide means for taking the measure of the diverse and multiple intentions that have helped to formulate a literary text. Juxtaposing theories of textual editing formulated by McGann to celebrate the "extreme concrete particularity"[2] of literary texts with the theory and practice of data modeling, ontology building, and building knowledge graphs, I suggest that the enumerative and descriptive practices of data scientists confer the ability to infer personal intentions from private, nonliterary texts with the kind of extreme, concrete particularity that McGann associates with literary art. Borrowing and reiterating language from the discourse associated with bibliographical control, I show how bibliographical descriptions developed by information and data scientists facilitate the ability to line up data so that they march to one's command (descriptive control) in order to achieve desired ends (exploitative control).[3]

As we have seen, bibliographical control is a phrase most commonly associated with the ability to retrieve appropriate textual resources in a library. Here, I suggest that the term can be rethought in broader frameworks of power articulated by powerful bibliographical descriptions that serve as diverse forms of artificial intelligence (AI). I propose that information and data scientists gain their newfound bibliographical powers from enumerative and descriptive practices that socialize data in manners analogous to how textual editors socialize literary documents. Both recast what they have taken as given in new social formations. They place what has been taken under special kinds of aesthetic "horizons," as McGann calls them, by which he means specific material formulations. Chapter 9 described McKenzie's critique of the New Bibliographers; this one suggests that the work of model building by data modelers, ontologists, and those graphing knowledge stands in synonymic relation with the work of New Bibliographers. It also suggests that the bibliographical descriptions crafted by contemporary modelers shape the horizons of our material experience by socializing data in manners similar to how literary bibliographers take what literary texts offer as given in order to craft new critical editions. This similarity, I propose, provides an opportunity to consider how we might provide more critical accounts of the bibliographical descriptions produced by those modeling our data.

MODELS AND MODELING

In previous chapters, I used the term *model* to describe the descriptive practices of Anglo-American studiers of texts. Bibliographical description concerned establishing texts, both physical objects and inferred ideals, as models that could enable comparison, measurement, and categorization, as well as be exemplars for further copying. The debates among W. W. Greg, Stephen Gaselee, A. W. Pollard, and McKenzie concerned what kinds of models should be crafted and whether data collection as enumeration should be called *bibliography*. Gaselee and Pollard, along with McKenzie, argued for "big umbrella" approaches to bibliography where data collection as the enumerative work of identifying and listing texts, as well as describing them, were considered proper aims for bibliography. McKenzie, as we have seen, would include deductive frameworks for considering what might count as bibliographical evidence in support of bibliographical descriptions put forward as hypotheses. For Greg and Fredson Bowers, bibliography was a narrower science that enabled, through logic and empirical methods of data collection, the ability to make inductive inferences about the nature of individual texts. Their aim was to use evidence provided by the sociotechnological processes of textual production to create productive abstractions that could serve as descriptive ideals. If no perfect exemplar of a text existed, for example, an ideal text could be created. We can call these descriptive ideals "models."

In information and data science, the terms *model* and *modeling* are ubiquitous but infrequently defined. No entries for "model" or "modeling" appear in the fourth edition of the *Encyclopedia of Library and Information Sciences*, with the exception of "Modeling Documents in Their Context" by Airi Salminen, which describes "methods for analyzing and modeling [i.e., describing] documents in an organizational context" associated with the Finnish Parliament and ministries.[4] The International Society for Knowledge Organization's *Encyclopedia of Knowledge Organization* similarly has no entry for "model" or "modeling," although it presents descriptions of specific models such the International Federation of Library Association's Library Reference Model.[5]

In data science more specifically, the situation is similar. Models and modeling are so ubiquitous that the terms can appear hundreds of times in books about data science without any definition of a model or modeling. Specific models and modeling techniques will be defined and described, of course, but general assertions about what models are or might be, or how practices and ideas associated with modeling serve as infrastructure for the field, are infrequent. Indeed, primers on data science such as John Kelleher and Brendan Tierney's otherwise very useful *Data Science* do not include "model" or "modeling" in its index even though, according to the search function in my Kindle reader, the term "model" appears 376 times in the 267 pages of that book.

A similar lacuna represents efforts to conceptualize models and modeling in recent primers and textbooks about knowledge representation. Mayank Kejriwal, Craig A. Knoblock, and Pedro Szekely's *Knowledge Graphs: Fundamentals, Techniques, and Applications* and Robert Arp, Barry Smith, and Andrew D. Spear's *Building Ontologies with Basic Formal Ontology* are useful examples of recent and widely cited publications that do not attempt to conceptualize models and modeling even though descriptive modeling is a central concern.[6] The meaning and force of the words are taken to be self-evident, a clear sign that they have become part of the conceptual infrastructure supporting the discourses with which they engage.

This is not to say that debates about conceptions of models and modeling have been entirely absent from the data modeling literature and literature about ontologies and knowledge graphs, even if they tend to focus on the practical work of building specific models or formulating an argument in favor of what an ontology ought to describe. For example, in *Data Modeling: Theory and Practice* (2007) and a somewhat more recent journal article published in 2012, Graeme Simsion has argued that tension between conceptions of modeling as description and modeling as design animates debates among academic and practicing database specialists. Although his work is somewhat dated and cannot be viewed as all-encompassing, it provides a useful entry into some of the evolving beliefs about models and modeling held by those that enumerate and establish what will be taken as given by diverse communities. It provides an opportunity to describe a central intellectual tension that still animates the field, a version of realist/nominalist debates that view models as being descriptive of reality or in some nominal relation to an undisclosed reality. Simsion's work also helps to show how beliefs and definitions of data modeling overlap with concepts of bibliographical description as we have discussed it here, while suggesting again how bibliography, with its recursive urge to account for accounts, can document and assess the descriptive bibliographical accounts of data modelers, ontologists, and creators of knowledge graphs.

For Simsion's purposes, data modeling as descriptive activity is directed toward "document[ing] some aspect of the real world,"[7] where the model as document stands in unproblematized relation to what is being documented. Design activity aims to "create data structures to meet a set of requirements"[8] that acknowledge both the domain being modeled and also how models will be instantiated in relation to what they document. In broad terms, modeling as a descriptive practice describes a real world, while modeling as a design practice creates data structures according to a set of contingent human requirements as they are perceived and formulated through specific implementations. He confines the scope of his discussion "to the use of data models for purposes . . . [of] designing databases," where databases are "conventional, record-based databases, in particular databases to be built using relational or object-relational database management systems."[9] Simsion suggests that data modeling is commonly characterized "as description," but there are "dissenting views" (notably his) that use "common metaphors which align better with the design characterization."[10] Dominant views about data modeling, as Simsion describes them, are "in line with . . . 'reality mapping',"[11] in which "reality mapping," as Kalle Lyytinen describes, "supposes a mapping process from the 'real world' into a formal model—the conceptual."[12]

Although knowledge graphs are distinct from the traditional relational databases that concern Simsion, a similar tension between design and reality mapping animates the thinking among those building knowledge graphs and the ontologies that structure them. As Kejriwal, Knoblock, and Szekely write, "A K[knowledge] G[raph] is a practical and machine-readable way of representing information about the world, including entities, relationships, attributes, facts, beliefs, and even provenance, including justifications and uncertainty."[13] Ontologies, the structures that support knowledge graphs more or less perfectly, are themselves "representational artifacts,"[14] according to Robert Arp, Barry Smith, and Andrew D. Spear. Ontologies as "representational artifacts" are "some combination of universals [types], defined classes, and certain relations between them."[15] Arp, Smith, and Spear emphasize the artificiality of ontologies by calling them "artifacts," things that are "deliberately designed (or, in certain borderline cases, selected) by human beings to address a particular purpose."[16] In addition to the ontologies that they describe, "representational artifacts include things such as signs, books, diagrams, drawings, maps, and databases."[17]

Echoing what I have been suggesting about bibliography as the art and science of crafting accounts, the word *artifact,* as Arp, Smith, and Spear note, "comes from the Latin *ars,* meaning 'human skill' or 'product.'"[18] "A representational artifact," they write, "is an artifact that has been designed and made to be *about* something (some portion of reality) and using some public form or format."[19] Arp, Smith, and Spear use design in a way similar to Simsion. The distinction is that for Arp, Smith, and Spear, ontologies as "representational artifacts" are meant to represent "some portion of reality," while for Simsion, data modeling is more often a practice of modeling data for a set of technical constraints and human requirements as they are perceived. Their differences of opinion are, in part, surely a function of the communities with which they have more often worked (Arp, Smith, and Spear with scientists and Simsion with business practitioners).

The larger bibliographical point is that the data models of databases and the ontologies that structure and enable tools such as knowledge graphs, whether they are in the service of describing some portion of reality or being designed to human specifications, are built and understood to re-present information about the world. This is true if the world is understood to be a construction of human minds or a reality distinct from human formulation. In other words, knowledge graphs and traditional relational databases are bibliographical accounts of data, things taken as given, however those things are taken. They are texts in the sense that they weave what has been taken as given into, as Arp, Smith, and Spear suggest, "some public form or format." In turn, these bibliographical accounts establish what will be taken by others as given.

As mentioned previously, the practices of data modelers, ontologists, and those creating knowledge graphs are recognizably bibliographical and remarkably similar to the enumerative and descriptive practices of the New Bibliographers. "The concern of the descriptive bibliographer," according to Bowers, "is to examine every available copy of an edition of a book in order to describe in bibliographical terms the characteristics of an ideal copy of this edition, to distinguish between issues and variants of the edition, to explain and describe the printing and textual history of the edition, and finally to arrange it in a correct and logical relationship to other editions."[20] Copies of books are organized by enumerated categorical terms such as *state*, *issue*, *impression*, and *edition* in relation to an *ideal*. Data modelers similarly examine the domains that they model—the Universe of Discourse; that is, the "part of the real world that is to be modeled"[21]—and enumerate terms that facilitate a descriptive "representation of the things of significance to an enterprise and the relationships among those things,"[22] an "abstract representation of the data about entities, events, activities, and their associations,"[23] and "a data model . . . for describing entities and their relationships."[24] Both create "abstract representations" of "essential" qualities that "describe entities and their relationships." The domains of concern are distinct, but both enumerate categorical abstractions to formulate useful descriptions that have data from "universes of discourse" line up and march to their command.

The craft of New Bibliographical description can also be juxtaposed with the enumerative craft of formulating the shared vocabularies and relations of ontologies. Echoing a widely held sentiment, Arp, Smith, and Spear suggest that the structured lists of ontologies serve science by enabling interoperability. Indeed, their book is largely about "the obstacles to interoperability"[25] and their attempts to show how, in the service of science, "ontology can help overcome them."[26] They add:

> Think of a doctor specializing in a certain rare disease with immediate access to the most current information about all the patients suffering from this disease and about novel treatment outcomes. Imagine, still more ambitiously, a single, integrated biomedical knowledge base, a kind of Great Biomedical Encyclopedia, comprehending all biomedical knowledge within one constantly evolving system. Such possibilities are not beyond our reach. Experiments are currently being made under headings such as "semantically enhanced publishing" or "Big Data to Knowledge" (BD2K), and the potential benefits of success of such ventures are easy to appreciate. These benefits can be achieved, however, only through radical improvements in the degree to which the information systems involved are capable of interoperation.[27]

Like Arp, Smith, and Spear, Bowers and New Bibliographers built their models to serve their science. Indeed, New Bibliographers were keenly interested in enabling interoperability, even if that is not what they would have called it. Recall that a central aim of bibliographical description for Bowers was to "provide sufficient evidence for readers to identify books in their possession as being members of the precise state, issue, impression, and edition of the 'ideal copy' listed, or as being unrecorded variants requiring further bibliographical investigation."[28] Just as Arp, Smith, and Spear imagine a system that affords the right medical information at the right time to doctors, and understand that such a system will rely on a carefully crafted descriptive infrastructure that they associate with ontology to coordinate the interactions of such a system, the New Bibliographers imagined a similar system for literary scholars and understood that it would similarly require a well-crafted descriptive infrastructure. The ontologies (to use the term anachronistically to suggest the similarities of intention and practice, even if in the service of different ends) created by Bowers and Greg made it possible to know that the *Hamlet* discussed by scholar A is the same *Hamlet* discussed by scholar B. Indeed, the descriptive infrastructures created by Greg and Bowers still allow doctors of philosophy specializing in certain rare texts immediate access to the most current information about all the copies of a text, what distinguishes each from the others and an ideal copy, as well as how they might be treated by editorial intervention. It is a power facilitated by the descriptive infrastructure that they built to organize literary documents into enumerated categories such as "edition" and "issue," what Arp, Smith, and Spear and other proponents of the "Basic Formal Ontology" (BFO) might associate with different kinds of "continuants."[29]

Knowledge graphs and those that build them similarly create descriptive models that both rely on and enable interoperability. They rely on the structures of ontologies and the data that they represent. As the term *knowledge graph* implies, knowledge graphs also rely on graphs and their mathematical properties as useful organizing abstractions to formulate, for example, how historical web pages will be described by their relationships to one another. As Google has most famously demonstrated with the sidebars that appear in its search interface, data can be modeled and organized by graphs such that descriptions of people, products, and concepts are usefully similar enough to be shared as knowledge. The technologies that formulate these descriptions are enabled by measurement, comparison, and categorization, in this case by means of the shared descriptive models and the mathematics of graphs.

Literary bibliographers like Greg and Bowers, data modelers, ontologists, and those graphing knowledge will differ in their intentionalities (e.g., to map reality or to design useful databases to fit with human conceptions of reality) and the ends that they pursue (literary and humanistic, biological and scientific, to organize the world's knowledge and to make a profit), but through their work they create descriptive representations that are offered to others as what can be taken as given. They establish texts and data by "coordinating facts," however they have been formulated. Through social forms of re-presentation that use enumeration's descriptive powers, they establish representational frameworks that line up books and data so that they might march to one's command and facilitate what Patrick Wilson calls "exploitative control": books and data in the service of literary understanding, scientific knowledge, or the bottom line of a large multinational company. The force and power of enumeration and description as they serve these various communities becomes apparent when we recognize the infrastructural role that they play in so much of our work as information scientists, but also as infrastructure for our daily lives.

THE SOCIALIZATION OF DATA

By lending social form to what has been taken as given through the lists and descriptions that they formulate, ontologists, data modelers, and those graphing knowledge socialize data in a manner analogous to how the models of New Bibliographers socialize literary texts by putting them into categorical relation for studiers of texts. My use of *socialize* is indebted to a seminal essay in late twentieth-century Anglo-American bibliographical theory by McGann, "The Socialization of Texts." In this essay, McGann positions himself between and betwixt long-running debates in textual editing that concern how best to take given texts and make them available again through new representations. A central dilemma for textual editors is how to copy what has been enumerated and described. Should a particular literary object be copied again to represent the diversity of a textual work's instantiations? If so, which object? Or, if a single literary object is not going to be made to stand for a work's many instantiations, how might different elements of its many incarnations be conjoined into a representation that suggests the work as it should be? McGann's central point is that new critical editions of literary texts should be thought of like galleries displaying paintings. Critical editions force engagements with literary works under special kinds of aesthetic "horizons"[30] that recast what has been taken as given by situating it in a new social formulation. As new copies, these new social formations, like the social formations taken as given, never entirely reveal "earlier frame[s] of reference."[31]

For McGann, "original documents are fictions we practice in order to manage their losses and our limits."[32] Whatever may have been original will have been layered over by continual processes of socialization. For him, the aim of a critical edition is to create a horizon that enables one to see, as fully as possible, the diversity of human intentions that have helped to formulate a literary work and the aesthetic horizons that have situated it—the author's and printer's intentions as they may have changed or remained insistent, of course, but also the intentions of all those who may have contributed to shaping a literary work's many historical formulations.

The debate and McGann's stance are important because they help us to consider the data formulated by the models, ontologies, and graphs of data scientists as objects that force engagements under special kinds of horizons. They enable us to consider intentionality and distinctions between public and private data in ways that helpfully reveal data-scientific practices to be bibliographical and the import of attending thoughtfully to the infrastructures that support our new bibliographical powers.

To articulate his position, McGann pits the opinions of G. Thomas Tanselle against those of Hershel Parker (b. 1935). Tanselle argues in an important essay that McGann uses as a foil that, as far as descriptive and editorial practice are concerned, no distinction should be drawn between literary and historical documents. Tanselle's essay is a critique of what he believed to be the less-than-careful attention paid by historical editors to the materialities of historical documents, especially when compared to the meticulous attention paid to texts' material instantiations by literary bibliographers. Tanselle's main argument is that distinctions between private and public documents provide better editorial heuristics than genre categories such as "literary" and "historical." The debates over categories and their powers will be familiar to data modelers and ontologists of all kinds, even if the particular categories being debated are, in this case, specific to debates about textual editing.

Parker's argument is that a distinction between literary and other kinds of texts *should* be maintained. Moreover, he argues, it is important to focus descriptive and editorial attention on manuscripts as they would have been created by authors since such manuscripts were most likely to represent authors' intentions. By unearthing and carefully rearticulating authorial manuscripts, an editor enables access to a description of an author's intentions before those intentions are remediated by the work of typesetters, printers, and publishers. In Simsion's language, Parker is suggesting that the representational activities of bibliographical practice associated with establishing and reproducing texts be designed to represent what was on an author's mind when a text was created.

McGann stands "with Parker (and against Tanselle) in maintaining the distinction between historical and literary work, and . . . support[s] Tanselle (as against Parker) in Tanselle's view of the distinction between private and public documents."[33] He understands texts as ongoing social processes made manifest by intersecting intentions and a diversity of personal, industrial, technological, and institutional forces. He is concerned with literary knowledge and, making use of a newer biological metaphor, suggests literary works are structured like deoxyribonucleic acid (DNA):

> I have been taking the word "text" to signify . . . linguistic text, the verbal outcome at every level (from the most elementary forms of single letters and punctuation marks up to the most complex rhetorical structures that comprise the particular linguistic event). And even if we agree, for practical purposes, to restrict the term "text" to this linguistic signification, we cannot fail to see that literary works typically secure their effects by other than purely linguistic means. Every literary work that descends to us operates through the deployment of a double helix of perceptual codes: the linguistic codes, on one hand, and the bibliographical codes on the other.[34]

Original authorial intentions, like original material manifestations, are let go of as guiding bibliographical ideals. "Texts" in McGann's model are dynamic interactions of linguistic and material codes. They come into being through social processes that, like the double helix of DNA, braid materials and material processes with linguistic formations and other modes of sense making.

McGann emphasizes that bibliographical description and editorial practice should attend to the braid of a text's instantiations because the particulars of a text's material and linguistic formulation provide access, if never completely, to the intentions of those that have had a hand in making it. He defends the distinction that he draws between literary and historical documents by arguing that "history and literature differ . . . along the line of their intentionalities."[35] By this, he means that historical documents and what he considers informational texts have different presentational intentions. For McGann, "literary texts differ from informational texts by being polyvocal. Whereas 'noise' is always a form of corruption for a channel of information, it can be exploited in literary texts for positive results. The thicker the description, so far as an artist is concerned, the better."[36] A literary text is "thick," "noisy," and "polyvocal."[37] Claude Shannon might quip that noise is just another variable, but that would miss McGann's point. Indeed, the noise, rather than mathematically defined communication, is the point for McGann, who sees it as a means of gaining access to whoever or whatever created it, and by creating it, contributed to how a text might be formulated as a meaningful object. McGann points to the intentions of authors and the profound role that authorial intention has played in literary scholarship, but, like McKenzie, he also recognizes that many intentions beyond those of authors articulate texts as private or public documents.

At essentially the same historical moment that McKenzie levies his critique of the New Bibliographers' inductive approaches, McGann independently critiques intellectual models in bibliography that formulate a single "authorial" intention or, as Bowers describes it, the intention of a particular printer. McGann's essential point, one analogous to McKenzie's concerning the positionality of bibliographers, is that the intentions of all those who have contributed to fashioning a text contribute to shaping it as a social object. Each provides a position from which to consider a text and, when reproducing a text as part of some editorial process, an opportunity to consider how to represent it.

At issue for us as information scientists is how diverse intentions contribute to the authoring of representational models that socialize data in the service of diverse ends. McGann's model of textuality provides a useful critical tool by suggesting that the intentions of those doing the work of building data models, ontologies, and knowledge graphs are articulating data as social objects. Their work and their intentions shape data as social forms and affect how we can interact with what has been taken as given and made known again under alternative material horizons. A final juxtaposition will suggest how and provide a prologue to chapter 11, on ML as a new bibliographical description.

"Literary works are distinct from other linguistic forms in their pursuit of extreme concrete particularity,"[38] McGann suggests. Arp, Smith, and Spear suggest the opposite about ontology: "Ontology is concerned with representing the results of science at the level of general theory (the generalizations and laws of science), not of particular facts. More precisely: it is directed at encoding certain sorts of information about the general features of things in reality, rather than information about particular individuals, times, or places."[39] The "extreme concrete particularity" of literary works has two consequences, according to McGann:

> First, literary works tend toward textual and bibliographical dispersion (signalled at the earliest phases of the work by authorial changes of direction and revision, which may continue for protracted periods). Second, they are committed to work via the dimension of *aesthesis* (i.e., via the materiality of experience that [William] Blake called "the doors of perception" and that [William] Morris named "resistance"). In each case, literary works tend to multiply themselves through their means and modes of production. These processes of generation are executed in the most concrete and particular ways. *Oliver Twist* is produced during Dickens's lifetime in several important creative forms. But then there are equally important versions of that work—equally significant from an aesthetic point of view—that are produced later. Kathleen Tillotson's is a splendid edition of a great literary work, but perhaps we should want to argue that her edition is not the work of Charles Dickens. And perhaps we should be right in doing so.[40]

Comparing and contrasting McGann's statements about literary documents with Arp, Smith, and Spear's about ontology, I wish to suggest how a concern for "encoding certain sorts of information about the general features of things in reality, rather than information about particular individuals, times, or places," can socialize data in ways that approach the kinds of "extreme concrete particularity" that McGann associates with literary texts. Indeed, new forms of bibliographical description provide data scientists with the ability to infer intentions from private, nonliterary texts with kinds of extreme concrete particularity that warrant attention and new contextualizing bibliographical accounts.

Arp, Smith, and Spear are primarily discussing ontologies for biomedical applications, but similar ontologies deployed as knowledge graphs will have, many times during any ordinary day, taken as given the data associated with my emails and purchases, what I have searched for online, global positioning system (GPS) locations provided by my phone and the Internet Protocol (IP) address associated with my desktop, information about my age, and how I have answered questions about my sex in the many apps that I have signed up for and forgotten about. They will have gathered similar data from others and modeled it to have ready artificially intelligent answers for which I need to formulate questions. Although AI is often only associated with techniques like deep learning (addressed in the next couple of chapters), knowledge graphs and the ontologies that help to formulate them are forms of AI that can provide tremendous inferential powers. From my home north of Seoul, I might be considering a pizza for dinner. When I type "nearest pizza" into the search window, it's hardly *Oliver Twist*. Nor am I attempting to focus anyone's attention on the materiality or modality of the phrase autocompleted by Google to read "nearest Pizza Hut" as an opportunity for aesthesis. Like the contestant slow to the buzzer on *Jeopardy!*, I have not even formulated a question before it has been reformulated and a variety of new answers are enumerated as a contextualizing list:

A. Pizza Hut, Samsong-dong 74-1
B. Dominos 174-1 Goyang-dong
C. Pizza Hut Bulgwang[41]

Included with my list, like toppings for my pizza, are hours of operation, website links, maps, and directions for the various restaurants.

The twist here is that my text will have been taken as given in the models that data scientists have fashioned to support the production of private, descriptive statements of such extreme concrete particularity that I can know that the trip from my home to the nearest Pizza Hut will take fifty-one minutes if I ride the 033 bus from the stop nearest my house and thirty-two minutes if I am willing to transfer buses a few times. Where particular novels or poems have been established by literary bibliographers to facilitate an understanding of the intentions of a particular author or the diversity of intentions associated with a particular literary work, the descriptive bibliographical models built by data scientists now edit and socialize our decidedly nonliterary texts to provide us with highly personalized statements about our likely intentions—predictive statements that have the power to reshape and even formulate our intentions.

Data science bibliographers, like the literary bibliographer Kathleen Tillotson (1906–2001), are collecting everything that we write to make statements about us, as well as those like us. We can argue that what is created by these data scientists is not what we have written; and we would be correct. But that would overlook the power exerted on literary interpretation by literary bibliographers such as Tillotson when they make statements about Dickens, as well as the power of data scientists when they make statements about us. One power of recognizing the work of data modelers, ontologists, those creating knowledge graphs, and data scientists more generally as producers of bibliographical descriptions is the opportunity to consider how we might wish to create bibliographical accounts of these descriptions and the material horizons that they formulate for us.

By contemplating the idea that their descriptive accounts are akin to what is provided by the critical editions of literary works, we can consider how we might be more critically attentive to the aesthetic horizons that they articulate. We can ponder how we might account materially for the powers of control and exploitation that they provide, and the ways that data are socialized in extremely concrete and particular ways by diverse intentionalities, our own but also those of other data science bibliographers. Even if how we are to fashion new bibliographical descriptions of our increasingly complex bibliographical accounts is not entirely clear, what is clear is that enumerative and descriptive bibliographical practices have formulated information systems that matter materially by shaping what has been taken as given and what we might take from our engagements with them. It is also clear that thinking from diverse modes of bibliographical practice can help us to reflect on how we might go about creating our next accounts.

11 DATA SCIENCE AND MACHINE LEARNING AS NEW BIBLIOGRAPHICAL DESCRIPTION

As I hope is becoming clearer, *data science* is a new term that can be used to describe the reproduction and transformation of things taken as given. These reproductions and transformations are frequently useful in their similarity to what has been taken as and can be considered copies. This is to say that a class of people loosely described by the term *data scientist* are socializing the data that we and our multiplicity of sensing devices create through the copies of data that they create. Scholars suggest that data science is an amalgam of skills and experience. One "skills-set desideratum for a data scientist"[1] includes communication, domain expertise, data ethics and regulation, data wrangling and databases, computer science and high performance computing, data visualization, statistics and probability, and machine learning (ML).[2] As a mixture of specific technologies (high-performance computing and databases), academic disciplines (statistics and computer science), general ideas (domain expertise), the directives of authorities (regulation), design and representation (data visualization), genres of practice (data wrangling and ML), modes of sharing and making things common to many (communication), and new compound-concepts (data ethics), this list compares favorably with those created by Ian Bogost and other speculative realists if we use categorical diversity as a measure. The logic of these relations is not defined by the history of academic disciplines, or even the needs of industry, but rather by the helter-skelter ends pursued by people working to use the extraordinary volume of what we are gathering as givens and copying through experimental procedures aimed to enable knowing. A brief history of data science's brief history and its relationship with big data and artificial intelligence (AI) as these relate to ML will help to reveal some of the ways that ML can be thought of as bibliographical description. It also will situate my contention that, like the descriptive models formulated by ontologists, data modelers, and those who graph knowledge, the inductive approaches of those creating machine-learned models are homologous with the approaches of literary bibliographers such as W. W. Greg and Fredson Bowers.

DATA SCIENCE

In 2012, the *Harvard Business Review* famously called "data scientist" the "sexiest job of the 21st century."[3] In 2015, *Fortune* magazine suggested that the job market for data scientists was "white hot."[4] In 2017, *Data Science Community* reported that, globally, there were approximately 550 programs devoted to training students in data science[5]—this only two decades after the term *data science* began to appear with any regularity in the late 1990s.[6] Despite the short history of the term, many of the practices and methods that constitute what have been described as data science's salient features have much longer histories, as Kelleher and Tierney describe in *Data Science*: "One thread in this longer history is the history of data collection; another is the history of data analysis."[7]

Data Collection

Kelleher and Tierney associate data collecting with the earliest forms of writing and recordkeeping, which, somewhat hyperbolically, associates data science with "the earliest methods for recording data . . . , notches on sticks to mark the passing of the days or poles stuck in the ground to mark sunrise on the solstices . . . , and the earliest form of writing developed in Mesopotamia around 3200 BC."[8] Translating these inscriptional methods into a language familiar to data science, he suggests that these types of recordkeeping capture "what is known as transactional data," which "include event information such as the sale of an item, the issuing of an invoice, the delivery of goods, credit card payment, insurance claims, and so on."[9] Kelleher and Tierney continue their translation project by associating the earliest-known censuses by Amasis in Egypt (dating to about 3000 BCE) with nontransactional data.[10] If we wished to make similarly hyperbolic claims, we could suggest that bibliography shares this history with data science.

If we do not wish to trace bibliography back quite so far in history, we could point to Liu Xiang and Liu Xin and the work that they did to list books for the Han imperial library during the first century BCE.[11] Or we could describe the tangled relationship between the cataloging of people and the cataloging of books using standardized descriptions of both and their locations during the Enlightenment in Europe. As Markus Krajewski has shown, Enlightenment efforts to describe populations to facilitate the conscription of men into military service by numbering houses and creating a named grid of streets share a logic with library cataloging methods that enable librarians to call up books by demarcating locations and standard descriptive grids that included entities such as titles and subjects.[12] Even more finely lined grids gird bibliographical practices that enable data scientists to index our locations to deliver advertisements, movies, and whatever else they and their models infer we desire.

The opportunities to model made possible by bibliographical practices of copying records that index what we do and where have only increased since the Enlightenment, the Han dynasty, and the time of Amasis. Zooming through the interceding millennia, scholars such as Kelleher and Tierney point out that "in the past 150 years, the development of the electronic sensor, the digitization of data, and the invention of the computer have contributed to a massive increase in the amount of data that are collected and stored."[13] "Massive" in this case is scholarly understatement. Despite the scale of what is being recorded, it is important not to lose sight of the fact that the basic procedures of recording—creating a representation (a copy, a document) and transforming that representation through additional copies (facsimiles of various kinds, summaries, indexes, digital documents as vector spaces, etc.) to facilitate some desired end—remain the same even if important social, material, and technological changes alter how these creative, representational, and reproductive processes are conducted. A sketch of these changes as Kelleher and Tierney enumerate them helps make the point that data science is one of bibliography's many identities—a specific identity articulated by the ends pursued by data scientists and the specifics of the technologies used.

Related to our discussion in the last few chapters as they have concerned data modeling, Kelleher and Tierney suggest that data collection concerns indexicality within an organizing framework. Kelleher and Tierney single out Edgar F. Codd's seminal 1970 paper, "A Relational Model of Data for Large Shared Data Banks," as "a milestone in data collection and storage."[14] It was "revolutionary," Kelleher and Tierney write, "in terms of setting out how data were (at the time) stored, indexed, and retrieved from databases."[15] The core problem that Codd wished to solve concerned representation. His essential insight was that a large corpus of data required an equivalently detailed knowledge of that data and how they were organized in order to gain access to them. His solution was to split how the records would be organized internally in a system and externally for users. Indeed, he essentially split data representation as stored on media from representations that allowed users to access that data. He then put these systems in relation to each other by mapping what is represented to users (not users as we might think of them today, but programmers building database systems) to internal machine representations. The first line of his canonical paper reads: "Future users of large data banks must be protected from having to know how the data is organized in the machine (internal representation)."[16] This new "relational data" model "enabled users to extract data from a database using simple queries that defined what data the user wanted without requiring the user to worry about the underlying structure of the data or where they were physically stored."[17]

Codd's paper is emblematic of important shifts in bibliographical description—namely, a need and desire to "protect users" from knowing the representational methods and mechanisms at work in information systems or, for that matter, the mechanisms that put these representational methods and mechanisms in relation to what a user can learn by engaging these systems. Procedures for copying texts and organizing them have historically often been opaque for a variety of reasons—to hide how records were created or statements were generated, or simply because no one was interested—but with the development of the relational database, this obfuscation became a central enabling feature of documentary and information systems. Codd believed, like many since, that opacity enabled tremendous efficiencies. These efficiencies and those like them continue to fuel our ability to experiment with different ways to model and represent our ever-larger stores of data. The cost, at least for "users" (of all kinds now), is transparency. The representational processes of copying, indexing, and organizing data within systems that affect what can be taken as given from systems become less transparent.

Big Data

Big data is the term most frequently associated with newer methods of making and storing records in relational and newer forms of databases. Emblematic of the close relationship between data science and big data, the term *big data* began circulating in the mid-1990s,[18] at about the same time that the term *data science* came into use. In 2001, Doug Laney, an analyst for the consulting company Meta Group (which was later acquired by Gartner), produced a report that aimed to predict business trends. In this now frequently invoked report, Laney suggests that big data are characterized by "3Vs"—volume, velocity, and variety. What is frequently left out of discussions by those representing the report is any discussion of the report itself, the context of its composition, or how definitions of the 3Vs proffered now only approximately align with Laney's initial suggestions.

A quick comparison of the discourse about big data now and how Laney describes "controlling data volume, velocity, and variety"[19] is useful for revealing data science as one of bibliography's many identities. As the title and contents of Laney's short report suggests, he was primarily concerned with what Patrick Wilson would call "bibliographical control." Although volume is now often defined by researchers as "consisting of enormous quantities of data,"[20] velocity as data "created in real-time,"[21] and variety as being "structured, semi-structured and unstructured,"[22] Laney was not addressing the data landscape in general, but rather the specific data management challenges presented by e-commerce: "E-commerce, in particular, has exploded data management challenges along three dimensions: volumes, velocity, and variety."[23] This statement was made as part of a recommendation: "In 2001/02, [information technology (IT)] organizations must compile various approaches to have at their disposal for dealing with each."[24]

Data volume as Laney discusses it in February 2001 concerns the "lower cost of e-channels," which allows "up to 10x the quantity of data about individual transactions to be collected—thereby increasing the overall data to be managed."[25] Data volume for Laney does indeed concern large quantities of data, but largely in business contexts associated with the emergence of e-commerce. He notes that "as enterprises come to see information as a tangible asset, they become reluctant to discard it."[26] He cautions against the impulse to store all the data because of what he believed to be diminished returns for each "data point."[27] He adds, "Typically, increases in data volume are handled by purchasing additional online storage. However, as data volume increases, the relative value of each data point decreases proportionally—resulting in poor financial justification for merely incrementing online storage."[28]

To maximize the value of data, he recommends several ways to assess their relative value. What Wilson proposed about bibliographical power as a trade-off between descriptive control and exploitative control in the late 1960s was being formulated in the early 2000s by Laney as a means for identifying the marginal value of data as more became available to businesses with the emergence of e-commerce. This trade-off affected the bibliographical decisions of businesspeople as they considered how to copy and organize data for their purposes. The "thingness" of information[29] was already deeply engrained in corporate culture by the time of Laney's report. Beliefs about data as assets affected calculations about the value of the descriptive control enabled by these assets in relation to the value of the exploitative control that they might enable.

Although data "velocity" in the literature on big data tends to suggest data created in real time, data velocity as Laney describes it in 2001 concerned the speed at which individuals could interact with documents such as web pages, especially as they related to e-commerce: "E-commerce has also increased point-of-interaction (POI) speed and, consequently, the pace of data used to support interactions and generated by interactions."[30] This issue is also related to bibliographical control as it is articulated in business environments—namely, with making the appropriate documents available at the appropriate times. Laney continues, "As POI performance is increasingly perceived as a competitive differentiator (e.g., Web site response, inventory availability analysis, transaction execution, order tracking update, product/service delivery), so too is an organization's ability to manage data velocity."[31] Moreover, in line with the idea that data, documents, and texts depend for their definitions upon the interactions of which they are a part, we see that website responses to those interacting with them can be considered *texts* if we are concerned with the weave of the sociotechnical systems facilitating them, *data* if they are taken as given by some party involved in the interaction, and *documents* if they are evidence of some fact, such as the location of a product. McKenzie would associate the swirl of these interactions with the sociology of texts. McGann would understand them as the socialization of texts, and we have called them the *socialization of data*. Again, we see how people interacting with documents, data, and text is informed and evaluated in terms of issues deeply related to bibliographical control and what other kinds of documents/data/text are made available to control and exploit.

Laney begins his short discussion of data variety as follows: "Through 2003/04, no greater barrier to effective data management will exist than the variety of incompatible data formats, non-aligned data structures, and inconsistent data semantics."[32] Again, the issue that Laney identifies is deeply bibliographical: how to copy documents. Data variety concerns how to transform many kinds of documents into a standard format that can be stored and queried by available systems, which he associates with "interchange/translation."[33] Arp, Smith, and Spear would call this a problem of interoperability, one that Greg and Bowers would solve by standardizing bibliographical description and what can be taken as given. Indicative of the perceived need of businesses to find efficient means of coping with more and more diverse kinds of documents that guided the work of Codd, Laney suggests that by 2003–2004, "interchange/translation mechanism will be built into most [database management systems]."[34] It is a need that Bernhard Rieder has described in one of his insightful blog posts as a need for "automated production of knowledge."[35]

Laney's initial report suggests how in 2001, spurred by increasingly diverse kinds of data, there was a need to formulate more sophisticated ways to copy and transform documents within ever-larger database management systems. The "bottom line," as Laney sees it in 2001, is that "IT organizations must look beyond traditional direct brute-force physical approaches to data management. Through 2003/04, practices for resolving e-commerce accelerated data volume, velocity, and variety issues will become more formalized/diverse. Increasingly, these techniques will involve tradeoffs and architectural solutions that involve/impact application portfolios and business strategy decisions."[36] In other words, data volume, velocity, and variety will become more important to consider since they define economic utility as trade-offs between the descriptive and exploitative bibliographical control of data as they are automatically copied into alternative formats and made to interact with additional data, documents, and texts. It is worth noting that, although Laney's report is frequently cited as the first attempt to categorize big data, he never uses that term. The word *big* does not appear anywhere in his short report.

In addition to appending the adjective *big* and altering Laney's initial definitions of *data volume, velocity,* and *variety* to characterize big data, scholarship about big data in recent years has often increased the number of characteristics used to enumerate the essence of big data. Rob Kitchin and Gavin McArdle provide a snapshot from 2016. In addition to the 3Vs, they describe how scholars have added many other categories: exhaustivity (Mayer-Schönberger and Cukier), fine-grained and uniquely indexical (Dodge and Kitchin), relationality (boyd and Crawford), extensionality (Marz and Warren), veracity and value (Marr), and variability.[37] As yet another example of the quirky power of lists to organize our interpretive horizons, the letter *V* has shaped attempts to categorize and describe big data, so much so that Deborah Lupton in 2015 was prompted to argue for the adoption of "Thirteen Ps" to describe big data in order "to draw attention to the sociocultural dimensions of big data that the 'Vs' lists have thus far failed to acknowledge, and to challenge the taken-for-granted attributes of the big data phenomenon."[38] These thirteen Ps are "portentous, perverse, personal, productive, partial, practices, predictive, political, provocative, privacy, polyvalent, polymorphous and playful,"[39] and they complement and enhance the 3Rs (relation, recognition, and rot).[40] So far as I can tell, even these critical data researchers, despite their crucial critiques of the discourse about big data, have failed to notice how the mnemonic power of lists controlled by the simple repetition of phonemes has influence over the discourse about big data.

Despite these alliterative lists (or perhaps because of them), an evolving consensus about the definition of big data seems to have coalesced around reiterative assertions provided by scholars such as Christine Borgman. "Big data," writes Borgman, citing the *Oxford English Dictionary (OED)*, are "data of a very large size, typically to the extent that . . . [their] manipulation and management present significant logistical challenges; [also] the branch of computing involving such data."[41] This definition is premised on the adoption of the enumerative categories that Laney suggested for controlling data and the changing limits of available computational systems. Big data's definition is also a relative calculation, one based upon the relationship between a community and the data being used. Borgman says: "Data are big or little in terms of what can be done with them, what insights they can reveal, and the scale of analysis required relative to the phenomenon of interest."[42] Communities of practice are implicit in this definition of *big data*. Data are big when their size, speed, and heterogeneity are difficult for communities and their systems to manipulate. Data that are easy to manipulate are considered "small" in this framework.

Data Analysis

The few short histories of data science that have been written suggest "data analysis" can be associated with summaries of and statements about data (i.e., descriptions). The field of statistics has been central to creating summaries and statements about data. As Kelleher and Tierney describe, "The simplest form of statistical analysis of data is the summarization of a data set in terms of *summary* (*descriptive*) statistics (including measures of a central tendency, such as *the arithmetic mean*, or measures of variation, such as the *range*)."[43] Work in the eighteenth and nineteenth centuries by mathematicians such as Pierre Simon de Laplace (1749–1827), Carl Gauss (1777–1855), Thomas Bayes (1701?–1761), and others formulated methods for mathematical descriptions that would eventually produce what we now call "Bayes's theorem," "statistical learning," and "machine learning" (ML).

Beyes's theorem helps predict the probability of an event based on prior knowledge (statements), while methods like least squares allow us to assess how well statements describe data. Visual methods for summarizing data and documents were being developed at about the same time by people such as William Playfair (1759–1823), who suggested the power of "presenting to the eye a figure, the proportions of which correspond with the amount of the sums intended to be expressed,"[44] long before charts like Playfair's and similar graphical representations gained their ubiquity as meaningful descriptive summaries that we now call "data visualizations."

The larger point is that these statistical and graphical forms of analysis re-present data in social forms as descriptive summaries. Other landmarks in data analysis as it is understood by data scientists, such as the mathematical model for a neural network presented in 1943 by McCulloch and Pitts, Shannon's 1948 mathematical theory of communication (which we have discussed in detail already in this book), and the model for solving pattern-recognition problems developed in 1951 by Fix and Hodges,[45] are similarly descriptive. Indeed, where data science concerns statistics, we find another recursive bibliographical loop if we understand statistics to be "the science of collecting, displaying, and analysing data,"[46] as Graham Upton and Ian Cook recommend in *A Dictionary of Statistics*.

Artificial Intelligence and Machine Learning

The terms *artificial intelligence (AI), machine learning (ML),* and *data science* are often used interchangeably. This is not a problem, so long as we are clear about the connotations of each and the relationships among the terms. In the popular press, AI can mean "almost any kind of computerized analysis or automation."[47] But AI experts make a distinction between "general AI" (sometimes called "strong AI") and "narrow AI" (sometimes called "weak AI"). "General AI is the Hollywood kind of AI,"[48] writes Meredith Broussard. It does not exist yet. It "is anything to do with sentient robots (who may or may not want to take over the world), consciousness inside computers, eternal life, or machines that 'think like humans.'"[49] Narrow AI does exist, but it is not nearly so humanlike or intelligent. It is simply a "mathematical method for prediction"[50] that is enabled, as I will describe in a moment, by some fancy bibliographic recordkeeping. For my purposes in this chapter and the next, AI refers to narrow or weak AI and forms of AI associated with ML.

The relationship between AI and ML has been an intimate one since AI was formulated as a field. As Kelleher and Tierney suggest, the term *machine learning* was being used in the early stages of AI's development to "describe programs that gave a computer the ability to learn from data."[51] Machines "learn" by comparing data and keeping a record of their comparisons. A machine has "learned" something when it has created a record of comparisons that usefully describes the relationship between categories of data. As we have been discussing, data scientists often call the descriptions they create "models." The difference between models as representational ideals that we have discussed in the last few chapters and those that machines "learn" is that an algorithmic process, rather than human modelers, will create the descriptive models that machines learn.

More simply and somewhat more formally, as Kelleher and his colleagues write, "Machine learning algorithms automate the process of learning a model that captures the relationship between the descriptive features and the target feature in a dataset."[52] These "descriptive" and "target" features can be anything. For example, we can teach computers to "read" Chinese, Korean, and other writing systems, which is to say "learn" to associate images of elements in these writing systems with numbers known as "code points" that are used to display elements of writing systems in computer systems. "Read" and "learn" must be put is scare quotes. A great deal more research needs to be done before the computational procedures that enable machines to create models capable of predicting associations between images and code points can be compared with what we know about the sociology and neurobiology of reading and learning in humans.

This said, we can say something about what we mean by *machine learning* by describing how data and documents are organized and described to enable machines to learn an association between images of *a*, for example, and a number used in an encoding standard such as 97, which is the code point for "Latin small letter *a*" in the Unicode Standard.[53] For a machine to learn the association between a picture of an *a* and the number 97 (which would allow the display of *a* on a monitor), we would need a data set that includes pictures of *a*'s. We would also need the images to be paired with labels, "targets"—in this case the number 97 for "Latin small letter *a*." Machines "learn" by comparing the features that can be discerned in the images with the targets with which the images have been associated. We will discuss how this "learning" is done in more detail shortly.

For our purposes here, there are a few important things to remember and notice. The first and most obvious is that my simple example of an image and a label, one that I will continue to use, is just one of many that could have been chosen. Descriptive and target features can be anything, not just images and numbers in encoding systems such as Unicode. More profoundly, it is worth noticing how ML operates by coordinating contexts and equivalences. ML procedures create closed-world contexts in which equivalences are prescribed between descriptive features and targets. These worlds are increasingly expansive, but they are still constrained by the nature of what has been taken as given. The constrained nature of the context enables machines to create a summary of which features are useful for explaining equivalences as they have been organized by people collecting, organizing, and labeling images.[54]

REPRESENTATION AND DEEP LEARNING: COPY/TRANSFORM, COMPARE/CRITIQUE . . . REPEAT . . .

Within the field of data science as it engages AI and ML, there are two subfields that are particularly useful for making the case that ML is a form of bibliographical description, which is known as *representational learning*, and the particularly active subfield known as *deep learning*. Ian Goodfellow, Yoshua Bengio, and Aaron Courville provide a convenient schematic for how to think about the relationship between these variously nested and overlapping fields. As they summarize, deep learning "is an approach to AI. Specifically, it is a type of machine learning . . . that achieves great power and flexibility by representing the world as a nested hierarchy of concepts, with each concept defined in relation to simpler concepts, and more abstract representations computed in terms of less abstract ones."[55] The fact that deep learning gains its power through nested representations defined in relation to simpler ones is key to understanding that deep learning is a form of bibliographical description homologous with the literary bibliography of Greg and Bowers described in chapter 8.

As we have seen, studiers of texts such as Greg and Bowers based their descriptions on similar nested and connected representations. They were specific about what features of a text could be enumerated, which is to say represented. These were most often physical marks on sheets of paper and elements of writing systems (primarily English), but also other elements such as *signatures*, alphanumeric notations produced by printers of the European hand-press period to order printed sheets. The narrowness of the evidence collected and the equivalences drawn meant that it could be controlled and, within certain narrow frameworks, "instruments of thought" could be inferred. D. F. McKenzie would worry about the nature of inferences that could be made using such limited amounts of data (see chapter 9). The description of representation learning and deep learning that follows suggests their shared affinities with the inductive analytical approaches of the New Bibliographers described in chapters 8 and 9.

Representation Learning

The advance of representation learning was its algorithms' ability to learn features in data that could be used to infer more extensive patterns. Humans can identify a cat even if most of it is obscured by a bush. We can identify a dog contorted in a blue sky as it jumps to catch a Frisbee. Before representation learning came into its own, this was a difficult computer vision problem because it was not possible for ML processes to identify which features in an image of a cat or dog contribute to formulating an equivalence with a target label such as "cat" or "dog." If associations between targets such as a "cat" (in the bushes) and a (jumping) "dog" were to be learned, images with cats slinking through the bushes and dogs jumping would need to be included in the data that a machine used to summarize the equivalencies between an image with its features and a target like "cat" or "dog." This is because ML algorithms were not yet able to learn for themselves what elements in an image should be consistently associated with the target label "cat."

Colloquially, the essential elements of "catness" and "dogness" could not be identified algorithmically. Less colloquially, and suggestive of the descriptive nature of representation learning, the essential elements useful for equating images of cats with a target label "cat" could not be enumerated and thus described as a pattern. The representation learning solution to this problem, as its name suggests, is to have the machines learn not only the map from descriptive features (inputs) to targets (outputs), but what representations (features) lead most productively to the equation of certain inputs to certain outputs. In other words, rather than just using ML to map the patterns in pictures of cats and dogs to the labels "cat" and "dog," you also use it to map the representations themselves. Representational learning enables machines to enumerate for themselves the key features in data that describe the equivalence between features and a target.

Deep Learning

If ML enables computers to automatically find patterns that map inputs to outputs, and representational learning enables machines to learn not only patterns that enable inputs and outputs to be equated but also discern which patterns in the inputs (representations) enable the mapping, then deep learning enables machines to determine what patterns in the representations discern the representations. The process is called *deep learning* because each representation can be recursively represented by simpler representations. Although the analogy is not perfect, deep learning automates the process of nesting increasingly simpler representations inside more complex representations, a little bit like Russian dolls, where small dolls are nested inside larger ones. Deep learning enables computers to build complex descriptions that can be associated with "dog" and "cat" out of many simpler representations that are nested and interconnected in a representational hierarchy. Again, it is important to remember that here, "learning" is not equivalent to human learning but rather the recorded results of mathematical operations. As Goodfellow, Bengio, and Courville suggest while describing a simple deep learning model, it is "just a mathematical function mapping some set of input values to output values. The function is formed by composing many simpler functions. We can think of each application of a different mathematical function as providing a new representation of the input."[56]

It is also important to point out that these mathematical representations are summaries and copies of documents that have been taken as givens, as data. Indeed, they are highly abstract representations created through complex mathematical transformations, but they are usefully similar for their given purposes. They are learned by machines with the goal of making a statement, such as "Latin small letter '*a*' (decimal value 97)" is equivalent to an image of an *a*, or that what appears in an image is a person, a car, or an animal. Understanding how ML and deep learning work, it is easier to see how each can be considered "description," "a statement or account which describes something or someone by listing characteristic features, significant details."[57] ML and deep learning are systems that automate enumerative procedures for creating statements and accounts. They do this by listing characteristic features and significant details, where "characteristic features" and "significant details" are representations articulated by mathematical functions performed and recorded by machines.

When we remember that data in these contexts are documents taken as given, we recognize the processes of ML and deep learning as fundamentally bibliographical processes. Documents are taken and copied in ways that enable the identification of the documents' characteristic features. In turn, these features can be used to articulate a descriptive statement about the documents as they have been put into relation through equivalences with each other and articulated targets.

New Bibliography and Deep Learning

Understanding that deep learning is an automated method for enumerating representations that can be used to produce descriptive statements, it becomes easier to understand the homologous relationship between deep learning and bibliographical description as it was practiced by New Bibliographers such as Greg and Bowers. This relationship is one where the conceptual processes and procedures are isomorphic but articulated by alternative actors and technologies—data scientists and high-performance computing systems on the one hand, and New Bibliographers at their Hinman collators on the other.

As we recall, for Bowers, the purpose of bibliographic description is twofold. It provides a basis for assessing how texts have been created and transmitted. Description is also meant to organize evidence that can help literary bibliographers categorize books in their possession "as being members of the precise state, issue, impression, and edition" through comparisons with descriptions of "ideal copies" presented in descriptive bibliographies. As Bowers recognizes, and apropos of our earlier discussion of models (see chapters 8, 9, and 10), the bibliographical ideals presented by bibliographies as models also enable discovery since they enable literary bibliographers to discern what has not yet been categorized—"unrecorded variants requiring further bibliographical investigation."[58]

To produce descriptive models of what could be considered ideal copies of a work, Bowers and bibliographers like him would collect and collate every extant version of works such as John Evelyn's *Sylva, or A Discourse of Forest-Trees and the Propagation of Timber*. Each copy of *Sylva* would be measured against all the others using elements in the documents that would enable an individual text to be labeled a state, an issue, or an impression of an edition of *Sylva*. For example, signatures, alphanumeric marks included by printers to help binders properly fold and gather a book's printed sheets, were determined to be a useful descriptive feature for creating descriptions of ideal copies. For the New Bibliographers (and many textual scholars still), the signature is what Susan Leigh Star would call a "boundary object" (see chapter 1), a representational measure adopted by the community. We can also recognize signatures as "technical objects" (see chapter 1) in the sense that the technical need to sign sheets during the hand-press period was used by bibliographers such as Bowers for their own purposes of measurement.

Deep learning is also designed to identify and use the technical objects that articulate digital documentation, such as the data structures of images, for example, where numerical values associated with pixel values can be exploited through controlled transformations that enable representations that are useful for creating descriptive statements to be discerned. Using images as an example again, we can note that a digital image such as the one presented in figure 11.1 is a collection of numerical values associated with colors (red, green, or blue)[59] organized in a grid.

Convolutional neural networks (CNNs), a common form of deep learning, take advantage of these technical elements to enumerate descriptive

Red channel

255	255	255	255	255	255	255	255	255
255	255	255	255	255	255	255	255	255
255	255	255	255	255	255	255	255	255
0	0	0	0	0	0	0	0	0
0	0	0	0	0	0	0	0	0
0	0	0	0	0	0	0	0	0
0	0	0	0	0	0	0	0	0
0	0	0	0	0	0	0	0	0
0	0	0	0	0	0	0	0	0

Green channel

0	0	0	0	0	0	0	0	0
0	0	0	0	0	0	0	0	0
0	0	0	0	0	0	0	0	0
255	255	255	255	255	255	255	255	255
255	255	255	255	255	255	255	255	255
255	255	255	255	255	255	255	255	255
0	0	0	0	0	0	0	0	0
0	0	0	0	0	0	0	0	0
0	0	0	0	0	0	0	0	0

Blue channel

0	0	0	0	0	0	0	0	0
0	0	0	0	0	0	0	0	0
0	0	0	0	0	0	0	0	0
0	0	0	0	0	0	0	0	0
0	0	0	0	0	0	0	0	0
0	0	0	0	0	0	0	0	0
255	255	255	255	255	255	255	255	255
255	255	255	255	255	255	255	255	255
255	255	255	255	255	255	255	255	255

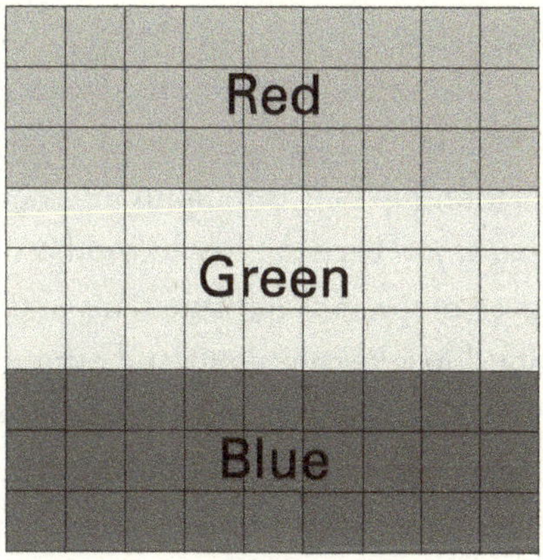

Figure 11.1
Simple representation of image data.

statements. To produce such statements, CNNs and their human operators orchestrate processes that produce and compare copies. A convolution can be thought of as functions describing how to make particular kinds of copies—that is, usefully similar but distinct representations. For example, a convolution might reproduce (i.e., copy) the image in figure 11.1 by using a grid of values, which is sometimes called a *kernel.* Pixel values in the image, which computer scientists would call "vectors" and include values for red, green, and blue, would be multiplied by the values in the kernel in a sequential manner to create a new copy of the original image. Depending on the values in the kernel (i.e., the grid), the original image, as well copies of the original image, can be reproduced in a variety of controlled ways. Intuitively, if not always in practice, values computed by such convolutions reproduce an image so that its edges are sharper or blurrier. Each layer of the network convolves or copies what came before somewhat differently. The copies are then compared to assess if they helpfully predict that a certain portion of an image is useful for describing the relationship between the image and its label. The comparison of these copies is facilitated through a mathematical process known as *backpropagation*. The power of this approach is that the many copies produced can be automatically compared in networked, nested hierarchies.

The results of these processes are stored as computer files that describe which learned features helped to create the most useful description of the relationship between inputs and outputs. These files are sometimes called *weight files* because they record how much importance (weight) should be given to specific representations in the descriptive statement about the relationship between inputs and outputs. Importantly, these descriptions can be used predictively when a new image is compared to them. The weight file can be used to assess if the features in a new image are sufficiently similar to features recorded in the weight file, thereby predicting whether a particular label associated with a target in the data used to create the weight file is appropriate.

Bowers and others performed similar convolutions, albeit using different technologies. Without overlooking these technological differences, we can notice how deep learning and bibliographical description rely on abstracted forms of measurement, comparison, and representation. Like data organized for deep learning frameworks such as CNNs, New Bibliographers such as Bowers gathered every available copy of a text and then organized equivalences between the features of the texts and targets to facilitate the generation of a descriptive ideal through various modes of copying and comparison. The features of texts were enabled by technical objects such as signatures, title pages, and other textual particulars biased by informed historical beliefs about the norms of printing and publishing during the hand-press period in Europe. The targets were categorical assertions, such as "edition," "issue," and "state." The convolutions were various methods for creating standardized, reductive representations—transcriptions of title pages, collation formulas, and standardized descriptions of content.

The descriptions are "deep" in the sense that the reductive representations are many-layered and networked in the sense that standard descriptive transformations enabled any enumerated feature to be compared and evaluated for how well it contributed to describing equivalences with others and an articulated target. The resulting summary description was not any particular copy of a text, but rather an idealized representation that both summarized the historical data and provided an ability to make predictions about any new historical data with which the idealized description might be compared. A newly found copy of Evelyn's *Sylva*, for example, could be compared to the descriptive ideal to determine how it should be categorized.

Like all descriptions, the one I present in this long chapter is incomplete, but it does suggest, I hope, a means to understand how the inductive approaches of ML and deep learning are homologous with the approaches of literary bibliographers such as Greg and Bowers.

12 BIBLIOGRAPHY AND THE SOCIOLOGY OF DATA

To recognize machine learning (ML) and deep learning as forms of bibliographical description, akin to what is practiced by bibliographers in the tradition of New Bibliography, and acknowledge that data modelers, ontologists, and builders of knowledge graphs socialize data with bibliographical methods synonymic with those who follow a Greg Bowers style of bibliographic attention, is to realize that the critiques leveled against the descriptive methods of New Bibliography by bibliographers such as D. F. McKenzie can be leveled against ML methodologies. These critiques can be leveled even though it is safe to assume that even McKenzie would have been impressed by the descriptive power asserted by the inductive approaches of deep learning in our world. Part of his surprise no doubt would have been that his proposal to collect and use "*all* relevant evidence" to make predictions about complex material interactions and human intentions has proved to be so astoundingly prescient. He understood the power of collecting and investigating data as texts of all kinds for the variety of information and knowledge that those collections can reveal, something that we as data scientists, consumers, businesspeople, users, and authors of media in our current era have all come to discover. "In the ubiquity and variety of its evidence," he wrote, "bibliography as a sociology of texts has an unrivalled power to resurrect authors in their own time, and their readers at any time. It enables what Michel Foucault called 'an insurrection of subjugated knowledges.'"[1]

Although McKenzie may have been pleased about being so prophetic, he, like Foucault, would have been concerned about who gets to exploit our new bibliographical powers and newly freed "knowledges." He would also have been anxious about how wrong our new bibliographical descriptions can be since they are so dependent on inductive methods. Indeed, as we have been discussing, data scientists have already gained an unrivaled power to resurrect us, which is to say make accurate guesses about our needs and desires. Reports of large businesses anticipating a young woman's impending need for baby diapers before anyone besides her knows that she might need them[2] multiply and suggest the diverse ways that knowledges subjugated for complex and deeply personal reasons can be exploited. As important, reports about how wrong the predictive descriptions of ML can be, such as when facial recognition fails to recognize women and people of color,[3] are appearing with more regularity. These are known problems that lack good solutions.

This short final chapter suggests bibliography and the sociology of data as a framework for approaching these problems, not so much as ones that can be solved immediately or permanently, but as a method of producing recursively thoughtful accounts of what we produce with our enumerative and descriptive powers. It does so by proposing that the critiques of bibliography as an inductive science leveled by scholars such as McKenzie are isomorphic with critiques that can be leveled against current ML methods. Juxtapose his assertions about bibliography with the work of Judea Pearl, a computer scientist who is best known for his work on artificial intelligence (AI), I suggest that, despite their obvious differences, Pearl and McKenzie approach the problem of making statements about complex phenomena in remarkably similar ways. Both recommend the enumeration of what can be taken as given. But they also recommend the enumeration of counterfactual statements about what might be taken as given to illuminate how things have been taken and why. Together, this is essentially a reformulation of the fundamental bibliographical desire to record what is and then account for what has been recorded. Importantly, both recognize the significance of the imagination in producing hypothetical statements as a means of accounting for how things have come to be as they are. In short, the chapter presents a description of creative, counterfactual imagining as a means of assessing, critiquing, and perhaps more fairly wielding the exploitative powers of bibliographical description in its newer technological forms.

COUNTERFACTUALS, IMAGINATION, AND MAPMAKING

For McKenzie, counterfactuals present a means of assessing bibliographical statements about bibliographical events that can inform human judgment. For Pearl, counterfactual reasoning is a mechanism that enables human intelligence, which he associates with the ability to make decisions about why events occur. Pearl places his hope for AI in the promise of mathematical descriptions of counterfactual reasoning. In this way, Pearl and McKenzie land on a similar mechanism—counterfactual methods of testing hypotheses and making judgments about why events may have occurred.

As part of his attack on the purely inductive methods of New Bibliographers, McKenzie points to imaginative speculation as a method for gaining an understanding of the complexities of textual production during the hand-press period in Europe and why books from that period came to be the way they are. It worked for McKenzie as part of a recursive practice of identifying and testing what might count as the context of a book and its production. By expanding what might count as evidence, bibliography as the sociology of texts would productively expand bibliography, according to McKenzie, by presenting a means of identifying and testing what might be counted as context in relation to a bibliographical object. It would do this in three ways.

McKenzie says, "Released from the straitjacket of induction," bibliography would first gain a "a new imaginative life . . . [and] speculative range."[4] This imaginative life would in turn draw bibliographers into ever-broader historical contexts and closer to the myriad small details of bibliographical objects: "In seeking to recover the complex conditions by which texts and their multiple meanings came to be made,"[5] bibliographical inquiry would, by expanding what counted as evidence, expand "into ever widening circles of historical context."[6] Third, it would direct critical attention toward "other forms of visual evidence in the books themselves as determinants of meaning."[7] Pearl goes even further, suggesting that imagination and the ability to reason counterfactually form a prerequisite for "every philosophical theory, scientific discovery, and technological innovation, from microscopes to airplanes to computers. Every one of these had to take shape in someone's imagination before it was realized in the physical world."[8]

For both McKenzie and Pearl, imaginatively hypothesizing about how complex phenomena came to be is the core of what each pursues as a scholarly ideal. For McKenzie, the end of such pursuits is the recovery of human experience through the careful examination and description of objects and their myriad contexts. For Pearl, the end is a mathematical description that can provide humanlike answers to why something has come to pass. For McKenzie, the central question of why is asked recursively because "a book is never simply a remarkable object."[9] Establishing our standing in relation to a book is a matter of imagining how it came to be by collecting as much data about it as its concentric circles of context enable, while simultaneously attempting to account for how it and its contexts could have been otherwise. As McKenzie writes, "We can acknowledge the intricacies of such a textual world and the almost insuperable problems of describing it adequately—and yet still travel imaginatively and responsibly within it. For ultimately what gives the highest significance to the history of all such forms and their making is their far from silent witness to a wealth of human experience whose recovery is the principal end of our scholarship."[10] For Pearl, somewhat less lyrically, "the main point is this: while probabilities encode our beliefs about a static world, causality tells us whether and how probabilities change when the world changes, be it by intervention or by act of imagination."[11]

Imaginative counterfactual procedures require models, as both Pearl and McKenzie suggest. McKenzie, although he doggedly pursues them, is not sure whether a descriptive model can be produced to explain why any particular text came to be as it is. "The recognition that those forms of record and communication are not disparate but interdependent, whether at any one time or successively down through the years, implies such a complex structure of relationships that no model is likely to embrace them all,"[12] he writes. Whether or not a model could ever be complete, imaginative model making procedures are crucial for "responsible travel" with textual objects for McKenzie because they provide means of testing and tempering inductive inferences that are made possible by collecting ever-greater contextual information. Bibliographical descriptions as models are to remain hypotheses until all possible counterfactual descriptions can be adequately proved false.

In many ways, this is Pearl's essential argument as well. He proposes leveraging the memory and powers possessed by computational systems to systematize the generation of imaginative counterfactual statements describing what might have caused a phenomenon. Pearl's basic idea is one that we have seen before—a recursive procedure similar to those used in deep learning that enables a map to be drawn describing what has been taken as given and a label that has been assigned to it. The difference is that rather than only descriptively mapping what is taken as given, Pearl suggests methods for mapping how what has been taken as given came to be taken. His thinking is Bayesian, as I will explain momentarily, but it is also deeply bibliographical in its aim to graph descriptions of how things have come to be. To produce what he calls a "causal calculus," he creates a symbolic system and a logic for its operations. "The calculus of causation consists of two languages," Pearl writes, "causal diagrams, to express what we know, and a symbolic language, resembling algebra, to express what we want to know."[13] Formalizing this system provides an "arena where imagination takes place," one that "enables us to experiment with different scenarios by making local alterations to the model. . . . This modularity is a key feature of causal models."[14] Like McKenzie, Pearl is describing a model in which descriptive accounts are offered as hypotheses to be tested.

THE IMPORTANCE OF THOROUGHLY DOCUMENTING HOW DATA HAS BEEN TAKEN AS GIVEN—THE MONTY HALL PROBLEM

Pearl offers his "calculus of causation" as a critique of contemporary deep learning and its limits—one that McKenzie would have been found intuitive. To proffer his criticism, Pearl describes a "ladder of causation," with three rungs that correspond with observation, intervention, and counterfactuals. Each rung up the ladder represents a step toward more humanlike abilities to answer "why" questions. Observation enables associations, but not an ability to explain why such associations are possible. Intervention enables experimentation and the ability to learn from the results. Counterfactuals enable the ability to "imagine worlds that do not exist and infer reasons for observed phenomena."[15] Current ML/deep learning procedures, Pearl asserts, sit on the first rung of the ladder. Learning occurs from closed-world observations and processes that essentially fit a function to a data set. In a manner reminiscent of McKenzie's critique of the New Bibliographers, Pearl suggests that deep learning systems are limited by the simple worlds that they can entertain, such as those laid out by games and relatively constrained tasks. Observation alone does not allow for what could be; it only provides a representation of what is assumed to be. "This limitation does not hinder the performance of AlphaGo in the narrow world of go games," Pearl writes, "since the board description together with the rules of the game constitutes an adequate causal model of the go-world. Yet it hinders learning systems that operate in environments governed by rich webs of causal forces, while having access merely to surface manifestations of those forces."[16] As powerful as they have become, even the models created by OpenAI are similarly constrained. For Pearl, as for McKenzie, investigating how things operate in the world beyond the combinatorics of Go or what can be organized as training data by OpenAI is to investigate the deeper complexity of these forces. For McKenzie, as for Pearl, investigating the complexity of these forces means collecting more and more varied data to enable more opportunities to hypothesize about how events have come to pass. Importantly, it also means imaginatively considering what has shaped particular observations and what has not been recorded.

Neither Pearl or McKenzie had faith in more observational data alone—just the opposite, in fact. Both are interested in the opportunities to hypothesize that new data provide. McKenzie would have recognized his critique of the New Bibliographers in Pearl's critique of big data enthusiasts' belief in data alone. Pearl writes:

> A data-centric history still haunts us today. We live in an era that presumes Big Data to be the solution to all our problems. . . . Data can tell you that the people who took a medicine recovered faster than those who did not take it, but they can't tell you why. . . . Most big-data enthusiasts, while somewhat aware of these limitations, continue the chase after data-centric intelligence, as if we were still in the Prohibition era.[17]

Pearl's objection is also McKenzie's. Observed facts alone, even if they are cataloged by ever more diligent systemizers, will not lead, "as if by chance" or some other way, to a description of "constant causes." The reason, Pearl and McKenzie assert, is that a reliance on observational data alone excludes descriptions of context, which provide information about the rules by which the data has been formulated. A discussion of what is called the *Monty Hall problem* will help us to position Pearl's critique of big data and McKenzie's critique of New Bibliography in a way that enables us to better see the limits of deep learning as it is practiced currently. It will also enable me to present one last example of how bibliographical methods and practices provide a sturdy infrastructure for investigations underway in information science.

A typical version of the Monty Hall problem is presented like this: You are a contestant on a game show looking at three doors. Behind one door is a car, and goats are behind the other two. (Why goats and cars is an interesting bibliographical question that I will leave for another time.) Choose the door that hides the car, and you win the car. It is assumed that you would rather win a car than a goat.

The game starts. You choose a door (say, door 1). The game show host opens door 3, behind which there is a goat. The question becomes: Should you stay with your first choice, door 1, or change to door 2? Intuition might suggest that it does not matter, that there is a 50-50 chance of picking the car no matter what. Bayesian statistics, however, suggests that you are twice as likely to win the car if you change your choice of doors and pick door 2 (a two in three chance as opposed to one in three). As standard definitions of the problem suggest and Pearl explains, the key to resolving this problem is to change the assumptions of the model that helped to create it. Our intuitive belief that there is a 50-50 chance of picking the car is based on what we might call the "raw" data of the scenario. It ignores the context situating the data and the rules by which the data have been formulated. The context and the rules provide additional information because they enable an estimation of how the data could have been other than what they are. The rules tell us that the game show host will not open the door behind which the car sits, and the game show host *could* have opened door 2. Given that the host did open door 3, we can reassess our initial guess (hypothesis) based on the rules of data collection and the new information provided by the test of our initial guess provided by the host. If we have taken a statistics class recently and wish to have a better chance of winning the car, we change our choice and pick door 2.

From this example, we learn a general theme of Bayesian analysis: "Any hypothesis that has survived some test that threatens its validity becomes more likely. The greater the threat, the more likely it becomes after surviving."[18] We also find a mathematical reason to support McKenzie's assertion that ever-greater data collection, coupled with data about the bibliographical rules of the game for collecting data and counterfactual hypothesizing, will enable bibliographical description to "prove itself adequate to conditions of far greater complexity"[19] than the New Bibliographers had entertained. It also suggests how, as a practical matter, the kind of bibliographical rigor demonstrated by scholars such as McKenzie, and even W. W. Greg and Fredson Bowers, can be a model for data scientists when documenting how data have come to be taken as given. The systems and rules for how data have attained their givenness profoundly affect the kinds of documentary statements that we can create to describe likelihoods in the world that we inhabit. Recognizing as much, we see how closely McKenzie's critique of the New Bibliographers aligns with Pearl's critique of AI in its current forms. Bibliography as a sociology of data suggests attempts to recursively and imaginatively account for what has been taken as given and how it was taken, along with recursive and imaginative attempts to account for how what was taken might have been taken differently and what has not been taken. It positions those producing its recursive accounts in closer proximity to answers for why something has occurred, even if uncertainty always remains. It provides standing in relation to the people who have made something happen, even if they can never be known completely. It insists on questions such as who or what has been left out of the most recent account so the next account can be made more inclusive and equitable, and just as a representation.

CODA: OUR "AGE OF ALGORITHMS"

This coda takes us back to where we began. The recursive nature of bibliography allows us to begin again in the middle of things. Having revealed bibliography to be an integral infrastructure supporting information science, as well as a recursive means for accounting for its bibliographical infrastructure, we can conclude by returning to the list of questions with which we began. How, as a bibliographical imperative and large unanswered question, do we build systems that can better account for the great variety and complexity of our rapidly expanding bibliographical universe? How do we descriptively record this universe with all its documents and data, as well as the many ways that both are socialized by data models and modeled data are employed to suggest the books that we might read, the movies that we might see, the fastest way home from work, whom we might date, how judges determine our sentences, how human intelligence agencies do their dance with social media companies to assess threats to voting machines and the idea of democracy, how climate scientists describe the health of our planet, how oncologists diagnose cancers, and how epidemiologists predict the spread of viruses like the one that causes COVID-19? Nervous quips about global catastrophe continue to float off the tongue like sheets of ice into the Arctic Ocean. But by presenting a copy of these questions again, we see them at a distance provided by roughly 80,000 words, as well as a new perspective provided by bibliography and its diversity. Coming to know them again from this new perspective, we know something new again, as the quirky, mathematically gifted Korean poet Yi Sang suggests. Or at least we know that our questions are different, even if they have not changed.

The urgency of our need to revitalize bibliography is not new, even if why things have become urgent is. In fact, the bibliographic infrastructure that we overlook but use anyway suggests an ongoing and ever-present urgency to build bibliographical systems capable of accounting for our ever-expanding and increasingly complex bibliographical productions. The urgency of the accounting challenge is a function of the opportunities that our new bibliographical systems present. Shelves were only fashioned as bookshelves when there were enough books to require them. Otlet's and Dewey's systems of accounting were crafted only after there were too many books on too many bookshelves. We inhabit a similarly urgent moment when it is time to consider again how our biobibliographical infrastructures serve our new bibliographical realities.

Although we have astonishing new bibliographical powers made possible by the ever-expanding abilities to capture, copy, model, and socialize data, we do not yet have robust means of accounting for them. From which proverbial shelf in the library can we pull the Google Maps models that are meant to help guide us home, the Tinder models that are meant to help arrange our dates, the models used in the US justice system that are meant to help ensure the safety of the streets we walk with our dates and protect the rights of those who have been accused? How are we going to build these shelves? Who will assign call numbers to the models used by the Central Intelligence Agency to model Facebook's models to ensure democracy, free speech, and privacy? The fraught absurdity of these questions is a function of the fact that the our current systems for organizing, representing, processing, distributing, communicating, and using information are in need of retooling for data as they are socialized by the generative and increasingly powerful bibliographical tools that we ourselves created.

If literature "is an institutional system of cultural memory" and the "Critical Edition" is analogous to a Turing machine, as Jerome McGann suggests,[1] what might constitute a critical edition of the internet as a form of global memory in 2024 and beyond? How might we begin to enumerate what we would take as given? As vital as they are, organizations such as the Internet Archive or Common Crawl that build and maintain repositories of web crawl data[2] do not document the personalized, real-time rearticulations of the internet as it is experienced in similarly different ways by all who use it around the world. How might we formulate descriptive comparisons of what we have taken as the internet when we can be certain that a diversity of data, evolving models, and algorithmic processes will have already formulated it differently for us and everyone else once we have taken it? If we could formulate it, how would we analyze the diversity of people and historical technologies that will have created our bibliographical object? Which special kinds of "horizons" would we wish to create by recasting what we will have had to take so hesitatingly? How would we conceive of the new social formulation, our new "critical edition," into which we would cast what we have taken? Which institutional systems of cultural memory would it serve? What kind of reference room might it sit in and be accessed from? Who would be allowed access?

Even if we were not so ambitious but only wished to provide critical standing in relation to something that we might imagine to be less complex, like the results of deep learning processes that helped to summarize data associated with our own reading habits, they would, as someone else's intellectual property, likely be inaccessible. Should we be able to gain access, the models themselves would present a variety of enumerative and descriptive dilemmas. The so-called black boxes produced by deep neural networks (DNNs) have become a focus of investigation, but it is still often difficult to "fully understand the solutions that DNNs learn, despite having full experimental access in DNNs."[3] Of course, the hypothetical model of our reading habits minus the data that it summarizes and how it has been deployed would lack coordinating context for formulating hypotheses about how it came to be, has been circulated, and the ways that we may have received it. Researchers in industry and academia are making the case that "datasheets" enumerating the data sets used in ML and "model cards" describing "trained machine learning models, including metrics that capture bias, fairness and inclusion considerations"[4] are needed and "have the potential to increase transparency and accountability within the machine learning community,"[5] as well as to "mitigate unwanted societal biases in machine learning models."[6]

These initial calls for documentation suggest that additional bibliographical accounts can begin to address some of the many ethical issues related to ML and could, by offering context, begin to provide an account of how our reading habits have been described. They hint at means to know through additional bibliographical description how we have been presented to ourselves again by the systems that recommend choices to us, and thus create material contexts for the decisions that we make. However, absent more substantial bibliographical apparatuses and sustained modes of attention that bibliographical practice in the service of a diversity of ends has revealed and makes available, they only hint at this.

Our current bibliographical challenges are shared with the future, and, as Clifford Lynch has argued, the scale and diversity of our new bibliographical condition in "the age of algorithms" bend traditional approaches to stewardship and cultural heritage to the point of breaking.[7] How do we think about heritage and stewardship when so many weight files and complex systems are orchestrating such personalized experiences with descriptive summaries of such heterogenous data? The answer is not clear. What is clear, however, is that by recognizing bibliography as foundational infrastructure that facilitates and disables so many aspects of our lives now, we are better positioned to consider this infrastructure and how it might support what from our experience can be presented again in the future. We can better consider our new problems from the diverse, marginal, and plural perspectives that bibliography provides. Our "age of algorithms" is only another age of complex bibliographical challenges and opportunities.

Notes

PREFACE

1. See Jonathan Furner, "Information Science Is Neither," *Library Trends* 63, no. 3 (2015): 362–377.
2. Furner, "Information Science Is Neither," 365–366.

INTRODUCTION

1. A. M. Turing, "On Computable Numbers, with an Application to the Entscheidungsproblem," *London Mathematical Society* s2–42, no. 1 (1937): 230, https://londmathsoc.onlinelibrary.wiley.com/doi/epdf/10.1112/plms/s2-42.1.230.
2. Tefko Saracevic, "Information Science," in *Encyclopedia of Library and Information Sciences*, 4th ed., ed. John McDonald and Michael Levine-Clark (Boca Raton, FL: CRC Press, 2018), 2216. Here, Saracevic is referencing Marcia J. Bates, "The Invisible Substrate of Information Science," *Journal of the American Society for Information Science* 50, no. 12 (1999): 1043–1050.
3. Saracevic, "Information Science," 2216.
4. Yi Sang, "Publication Law," *Chōsen to kenchiku* (July 1932): 26 (my translation).
5. There is debate about how to classify paradoxes. Some argue that paradoxes like the ones we have been discussing can be categorized as semantic, set-theoretic, and epistemic. Others will say that such distinctions are "far from absolute." See Hiam Gaifman, "Naming and Diagonalization, from Cantor to Gödel to Kleene," *Logic Journal of the IGLP* 14, no. 5 (2006): 711. Yi Sang's "Diagnosis 0:1," "Publication Law," and other works suggest how distinctions between "epistemic," "set-theoretic," and "semantic" can be blurred.
6. Saracevic, "Information Science," 2216.
7. Jonathan Furner, "Philosophy and Information Studies," *Annual Review of Information Science and Technology* 44, no. 1 (2010): 166.
8. Furner, "Philosophy and Information Studies," 166.

9. Furner, "Philosophy and Information Studies," 167.

10. Furner, "Philosophy and Information Studies," 167.

11. Furner, "Philosophy and Information Studies," 166.

12. Geoffrey Bowker and Susan Leigh Star, *Sorting Things Out: Classification and Its Consequences* (Cambridge, MA, and London: MIT Press, 1999), loc. 563 of 4690, Kindle.

13. W. W. Greg, "What Is Bibliography?" *Transactions of the Bibliographical Society* 12, no. 1 (1913): 41, https://doi.org/10.1093/libraj/TBS-12.1.39.

14. W. W. Greg, "Bibliography—An Apologia," *The Library* 13, no. 2 (1932): 121–122, https://doi.org/10.1093/library/s4-XIII.2.113.

15. See D. F. McKenzie, *Bibliography and the Sociology of Texts* (Cambridge: Cambridge University Press, 1999).

16. Jerome McGann, "The Socialization of Texts," in *The Textual Condition* (Princeton, NJ: Princeton University Press, 1991), 82.

17. See Patrick Wilson, *Two Kinds of Power: An Essay on Bibliographical Control* (Berkeley and Los Angeles: University of California Press, 1968).

18. D. F. McKenzie, "Printers of the Mind: Some Notes on Bibliographical Theories and Printing-House Practices," *Studies in Bibliography* 22 (1969): 3, https://www.jstor.org/stable/40371475. The fact that Kurt Gödel would show Russell's system to be incomplete does not diminish the power of McKenzie's truth claim.

19. Wilson, *Two Kinds of Power*, 25.

CHAPTER 1

1. D. F. McKenzie, *Bibliography and the Sociology of Texts* (Cambridge: Cambridge University Press, 1999), loc. 136 of 1568, Kindle.

2. *Oxford English Dictionary Online*, s.v. "record" and "recording," accessed December 30, 2019.

3. *Oxford English Dictionary Online*, "record" and "recording."

4. McKenzie, *Bibliography and the Sociology of Texts*, loc. 158 of 1568.

5. McKenzie, *Bibliography and the Sociology of Texts*, loc. 146 of 1568 (emphasis added).

6. *Oxford English Dictionary Online*, s.v. "copy," accessed December 30, 2019.

7. *Oxford English Dictionary Online*, "copy." The *OED* attributes the citation to John Barbour's *Troy Book*. II. 774. (ca. 1375).

8. *Oxford English Dictionary Online*, "copy."

9. Walter Benjamin, *Illuminations*, trans. Harry Zohn (New York: Schocken Books, 2007), loc. 3220 of 4271, Kindle.

10. Benjamin, *Illuminations*, loc. 3251 of 4271.

11. Benjamin, *Illuminations*, loc. 3281 of 4271.

12. Benjamin, *Illuminations*, loc. 3251 of 4271.

13. *Oxford English Dictionary Online*, s.v. "recursive," accessed December 30, 2019.

14. See Fredson Bowers's *Principles of Bibliographical Description* (Winchester, UK, and New Castle, DE: St. Paul's Bibliographies and Oak Knoll Press, 1994), especially chapter 1, and Philip Gaskell's *A New Introduction to Bibliography* (New Castle, DE: Oak Knolls Press, 1995), especially the section "Bibliographical Applications." Also see David Greetham's *Textual Scholarship: An Introduction* (New York and London: Garland Publishing, 1994), which is organized around these four primary modes of bibliography.

15. Greetham, *Textual Scholarship*, loc. 404 of 13371.

16. *Oxford English Dictionary Online*, s.v. "description," accessed December 30, 2019.

17. Greetham, *Textual Scholarship*, loc. 442 of 13371.

18. Greetham, *Textual Scholarship*, loc. 442 of 13371 (emphasis in original).

19. *Oxford English Dictionary Online*, s.v. "analysis," accessed December 30, 2019.

20. *Oxford English Dictionary Online*, "analysis."

21. Greetham, *Textual Scholarship*, loc. 423 of 13371.

22. Greetham, *Textual Scholarship*, loc. 423 of 13371.

23. Greetham, *Textual Scholarship*, loc. 423 of 13371.

24. Raymond Williams, *Keywords: A Vocabulary of Culture and Society* (New York and Oxford: Oxford University Press, 2015), 36, Kindle.

25. Williams, *Keywords*, 36.

26. Williams, *Keywords*, 36.

27. Claude E. Shannon, "A Mathematical Theory of Communication," *Bell System Technical Journal* 27 (July 1948): 379, https://archive.org/details/bellsystemtechni27amerrich/page/n9.

28. Shannon, "A Mathematical Theory of Communication," 379 (emphasis in original).

29. *Oxford English Dictionary Online*, s.v. "mean," accessed December 30, 2019.

30. Shannon, "A Mathematical Theory of Communication," 379.

31. "It is desirable therefore to eliminate the psychological factors involved and to establish a measure of information in terms of purely physical quantities." R. V. L. Hartley, "Transmission of Information," *Bell System Technical Journal* 7 (July 1928): 536, https://archive.org/details/bstj7-3-535.

32. See Wayne de Fremery and Michael Buckland, "Copy Theory," *Journal of the Association for Information Science and Technology* 73, no. 3 (2022): 407–418.

33. Shannon, "A Mathematical Theory of Communication," 399.

34. Roland Greene, Stephen Cushman, Clare Cavanagh, et al., eds., *Princeton Encyclopedia of Poetry and Poetics*, 4th ed., s.v. "Chiasmus" (Princeton, NJ: Princeton University Press, 2012), Kindle.

35. Shannon, "A Mathematical Theory of Communication," 646.

36. *Oxford English Dictionary Online*, s.v. "understand," accessed October 4, 2018.

37. Google, s.v. "Understand," www.google.co.kr/search?q=understand, accessed October 4, 2018.

38. Google, "Understand."

39. Roland Greene et al., eds., *Princeton Encyclopedia of Poetry and Poetics*, s.v. "Defamiliarization."

40. See Tefko Saracevic, "Information Science," in *Encyclopedia of Library and Information Sciences*, 4th ed., eds. John McDonald and Michael Levine-Clark (Boca Raton, FL: CRC Press, 2018), 2216.

41. *Oxford English Dictionary Online*, s.v. "hypothesis," accessed July 31, 2023.

42. Donna Haraway, *Simians, Cyborgs, and Women: The Reinvention of Nature* (New York and Milton Park, UK: Routledge, 1991), loc. 3966–3967 of 7091, Kindle.

43. Williams, *Keywords*, s.v. "science," "art," and "technology."

44. Madeleine Akrich, "The De-scripting of Technical Objects," in *Shaping Technology/Building Society: Studies in Sociotechnological Change*, ed. Wiebe E. Bijker and John Law (Cambridge, MA, and London: MIT Press, 1992), loc. 2633 of 4465, Kindle.

45. Akrich, "The De-scripting of Technical Objects," loc. 2623 of 4465.

46. Akrich, "The De-scripting of Technical Objects," loc. 2849 of 4465.

47. Akrich, "The De-scripting of Technical Objects," loc. 2852 of 4465.

48. Akrich, "The De-scripting of Technical Objects," loc. 2855 of 4465.

49. Akrich, "The De-scripting of Technical Objects," loc. 2869 of 4465.

50. Williams, *Keywords*, s.v. "culture."

51. Williams, *Keywords*, "culture."

52. Williams, *Keywords*, "culture."

53. James J. Y. Liu, *Chinese Theories of Literature* (Chicago: University of Chicago Press, 1975), 7.

54. Liu, *Chinese Theories of Literature*, 7.

55. See James Gibson's many works, especially *The Ecological Approach to Visual Perception* (Boston: Houghton Mifflin, 1979). As I describe in chapter 4, Jakob von Uexküll suggests ideas similar to Gibson's notion of affordance.

56. *Oxford English Dictionary Online*, s.v. "afford," accessed December 30, 2019.

57. *Oxford English Dictionary Online*, s.v. "affordance," accessed December 30, 2019.

58. *Oxford English Dictionary Online*, "affordance."

59. Leah A. Lievrouw, "Materiality and Media in Communication and Technology Studies: An Unfinished Project," in *Media Technologies: Essays on Communication, Materiality, and Society*, ed. Tarleton Gillespie, Pablo J. Boczkowski, and Kirsten A. Foot (Cambridge, MA, and London: MIT Press, 2014), loc. 1166 of 7947, Kindle.

60. Rom Harré and Jean-Pierre Llored, "Procedures, Products and Pictures," *Philosophy* 93, no. 2 (2018): 171. Thank you to Michael Buckland for making me aware of this article.

61. Harré and Llored, "Procedures, Products and Pictures," 171.

62. Johanna Drucker, *The Visible Word: Experimental Typography and Modern Art, 1909–1923* (Chicago and London: University of Chicago Press, 1994), 43.

63. Drucker, *The Visible Word*, 43.

64. Drucker, *The Visible Word*, 43–44.

65. Drucker, *The Visible Word*, 45.

66. Drucker, *The Visible Word*, 45.

67. In this sense, although the topic is not explored deeply in the pages to follow, bibliography can be understood to gird genres of social action in recurrent rhetorical situations as they have been described by Carolyn Miller and others. See Carolyn R. Miller, "Genre as Social Action," *Quarterly Journal of Speech* 70, no. 2 (1984): 151–167; and, more recently, Jack Andersen, ed., *Genre Theory in Information Studies* (Bingley, UK: Emerald Group Publishing, 2015).

68. Jonathan Furner, "'Data': The Data," in *Information Cultures in the Digital Age: A Festschrift in Honor of Rafael Capurro*, ed. M. Kelly and J. Bielby (Wiesbaden, Germany: Springer VS, 2016), 290.

69. Furner, "'Data': The Data," 289.

70. Furner, "'Data': The Data," 289.

71. Furner, "'Data': The Data," 303.

72. Michael K. Buckland, "Information as Thing," *Journal of the American Society for Information Science* 42, no. 5 (1991): 354.

73. Johanna Drucker, "Excerpts and Entanglement," unpublished talk at the Document Academy meeting held at the University of California, Berkeley, School of Information Management Systems (SIMS), August 13, 2003.

74. Niels Bohr, "Quantum Physics and Philosophy: Causality and Complementarity," in *The Philosophical Writings of Niels Bohr*, ed. J. Faye and H. J. Folse, vol. 3 (Woodbridge, CT: Ox Bow Press, 1987), 3.

75. Michel Foucault, *The Archaeology of Knowledge and Discourse on Language*, trans. A. M. Sheridan Smith (New York: Vintage Books, 2010), loc. 123 of 4222, Kindle.

76. Foucault, *The Archaeology of Knowledge*, loc. 112 of 4222.

77. Karen Barad would call these "intra-actions" in order to emphasize "that distinct agencies do not precede, but rather emerge through their intra-action." Karen Barad, *Meeting the Universe Halfway: Quantum Physics and the Entanglement of Matter and Meaning* (Durham, NC, and London: Duke University Press, 2007), 33, Kindle. Barad fashions her neologism to help make her ontological point that "'distinct' agencies are only distinct in a relational, not an absolute, sense; that is, *agencies are only distinct in relation to their mutual entanglement.*" Barad, *Meeting the Universe Halfway*, 33 (emphasis in original). I am sympathetic to the case that Barad makes for understanding "*phenomena . . . [as] differential patterns of mattering* ('diffraction patterns') produced through complex agential intra-actions of multiple material-discursive practices or apparatuses of bodily production, where apparatuses are not mere observing instruments but boundary-drawing practices—*specific material (re) configurings of the world*—which come to matter." Barad, *Meeting the Universe Halfway*, 140 (emphasis in original). Indeed, as will be clear if it is not already, her perspectives have deeply informed mine. The case that I am building, however, is not for any particular ontological formulation but for how, to borrow from Barad's language, bibliographical practices and modes of thought associated with enumeration, description, analysis, and critique gird practices in information science as means that matter to a diversity of ends not only as modes of observation, but also as "boundary-drawing practices" and "specific material (re)configurations of the world."

78. *Oxford English Dictionary Online*, s.v. "information," accessed July 31, 2023.

79. Michael Buckland, *Information and Information Systems* (New York: Greenwood Press, 1991), loc. 89–95 of 2810, Kindle.

80. As James Gleick describes, for Claude Shannon and others involved in the foundation and development of information theory, information is a function of "Choice, Uncertainty and Entropy," to quote a section heading in Shannon's landmark 1948 paper "A Mathematical Theory of Communication." James Gleick, *The Information: A History, a Theory, a Flood* (New York and Toronto: Random House, 2011), 219, passim. Buckland writes in *Information and Information Systems*, "Knowledge is based on belief. A change of knowledge is a change of belief. The information imparted in the process of information is a change of knowledge, a change in belief." Buckland, *Information and Information Systems*, loc. 534–536 of 2810. The Consultative Committee for Space Data Systems, in its *Reference Model for an Open Archival Information System*, defines information as "a type of knowledge that can be exchanged." No definition of "knowledge" is provided, but a "knowledge base" is a "set of information, incorporated by a person or system, that allows a person or system to understand received information." Consultative Committee for Space Data Systems, *Reference Model for an Open Archival Information System* (Washington, DC: Consultative Committee for Space Data Secretariat, 2012), 1–12, http://public.ccsds.org/publications/archive/650x0m2.pdf. "Understanding" in this context does not necessarily mean human understanding.

81. *Oxford Learner's Dictionaries*, s.v. "evidence," accessed July 31, 2023, https://www.oxfordlearnersdictionaries.com/definition/english/evidence_2. See also *Oxford English Dictionary Online*, s.v. "evidence," which provides a more detailed etymology.

82. Classical Latin, *factum*, "deed, action, . . . result of doing, something done"; post-classical Latin, "use as noun of neuter past participle of *facere* to make, do." *Oxford English Dictionary Online*, s.v. "fact," accessed July 31, 2023.

83. Old French, *document*, "lesson, written evidence"; Latin, *documentum*, "lesson, proof." *Oxford English Dictionary Online*, s.v. "document," accessed December 30, 2019.

84. "Therefore we retain the simpler view of information-as-thing as being tantamount to physical evidence: whatever thing one might learn from." Buckland, *Information and Information Systems*, loc. 642–643 of 2810.

85. G. Thomas Tanselle, *Bibliographical Analysis: A Historical Introduction* (Cambridge: Cambridge University Press, 2009), loc. 69 of 4944, Kindle.

86. Drucker, "Excerpts and Entanglements."

87. McKenzie, *Bibliography and the Sociology of Texts*, loc. 154–155 of 1568.

88. McKenzie, *Bibliography and the Sociology of Texts*.

89. Haraway, *Simians, Cyborgs, and Women*, loc. 4119 of 7091.

90. Jonathan Furner, "Information Science Is Neither," *Library Trends* 63, no. 3 (2015): 362–377.

91. Association for Information Science and Technology (ASIS&T) website, "What Is Information Science?" accessed February 3, 2022, https://www.ASIS&T.org/about/what-is-information-science/.

92. Furner, "Information Science Is Neither," 364.

93. See Jonathan Furner, "Philosophy and Information Studies," *Annual Review of Information Science and Technology* 44, no. 1 (2010), 159–200; and Furner, "Information Science Is Neither," for descriptions of some of the activities associated with information science.

94. Furner, "Information Science Is Neither," 368.

95. ASIS&T website, "Bibliography of the History of ASIS&T," accessed February 3, 2022, https://www.ASIS&T.org/history-of-ASIS&T/bibliography-of-the-history-of-ASIS&T/.

96. Greene et al., eds., *Princeton Encyclopedia of Poetry and Poetics*, s.v. "Book."

97. William Butler Yeats, "Among School Children," in *The Yeats Reader*, ed. Richard J. Finneran (New York: Scribner Poetry, 2002), 103.

98. Yeats, "Among School Children," 105.

99. Yeats, "Among School Children," 105.

100. Yeats, "Among School Children," 105.

101. D. F. McKenzie, "Printers of the Mind: Some Notes on Bibliographical Theories and Printing-House Practices," *Studies in Bibliography* 22 (1969): 3–4.

102. Patrick Wilson, *Two Kinds of Power: An Essay on Bibliographical Control* (Berkeley and Los Angeles: University of California Press, 1968), 1.

103. Wilson, *Two Kinds of Power*, 4.

104. Wilson, *Two Kinds of Power*, 25.

105. Wilson, *Two Kinds of Power*, 26.

106. Wilson, *Two Kinds of Power*, 26.

107. Jerome McGann, *A New Republic of Letters: Memory and Scholarship in the Age of Digital Reproduction* (Cambridge, MA, and London: Harvard University Press, 2014), 4, Kindle.

108. Wilson, *Two Kinds of Power*, 3–4.

109. Wilson, *Two Kinds of Power*, 4.

110. McKenzie, "Printers of the Mind," 61.

111. Wilson, *Two Kinds of Power*, 40 (emphasis in original).

CHAPTER 2

1. Geoffrey Bowker and Susan Leigh Star, *Sorting Things Out: Classification and Its Consequences* (Cambridge, MA, and London: MIT Press, 1999), loc. 563 of 4690, Kindle.

2. Bowker and Star, *Sorting Things Out: Classification and Its Consequences* loc. 563 of 4690.

3. Robert Belknap, *The List: The Uses and Pleasures of Cataloguing* (New Haven, CT, and London: Yale University Press, 2004), 34, Kindle. Belknap is citing Stephen Barney, "Chaucer's Lists," in *The Wisdom of Poetry: Essays in Early English Literature in Honor of Morton W. Bloomfield*, ed. Larry Dean Benson and Siegfried Wenzel (Kalamazoo: Western Michigan University Press, Medieval Institute, 1982), 193–194.

4. Belknap, *The List*, citing Thomas Rosenmeyer, *Green Cabinet* (Berkeley: University of California Press, 1969), 258.

5. Belknap, *The List*, 2.

6. "'Marginality' as a technical term in sociology refers to human membership in more than one community of practice." Susan Leigh Star, "Misplaced Concretism and Concrete Situations: Feminism, Method, and Information Technology," in *Boundary Objects and Beyond: Working with Leigh Star*, ed. Geoffrey C. Bowker, Stefan Timmermans, Adele E. Clark, and Ellen Balka (Cambridge, MA, and London: MIT Press, 2015), 155, Kindle.

7. Georg Schneider, *Theory and History of Bibliography*, trans. Ralph Robert Shaw (New York: Columbia University Press, 1934), 14.

8. Like Star, "I am not using *marginality* here in the sense of center/margin or center/periphery (e.g., not 'in the margins'), but rather in the old-fashioned sense of Robert Park's 'marginal man,' the one who has a double vision by virtue of having more than one identity to negotiate (Park 1952; Stonequist 1961; Simmel [1908] 1950; Schutz 1944). Strangers are those who 'come and stay a while,' long enough so that membership becomes a troublesome issue—they are not just nomads passing through, but people who sort of belong and sort of don't." Star, "Misplaced Concretism and Concrete Situations," 155.

9. Michelle C. Wang, "Thousand-Armed and Thousand-Eyed Avalokiteshvara," Object Narrative, in *Conversations: An Online Journal of the Center for the Study of Material and Visual Cultures of Religion* (2014), doi:10.22332/con.obj.2014.32.

10. David Greetham, *Textual Scholarship: An Introduction* (New York and London: Garland Publishing, 1994), loc. 321 of 13371, Kindle.

11. Barbara Hale, *The Subject Bibliography of the Social Sciences and Humanities* (Oxford, New York, Toronto, Sydney, and Braunschweig, Germany: Pergamon Press, 1970), 4, Kindle.

12. Schneider, *Theory and History of Bibliography*, 16.

13. Schneider, *Theory and History of Bibliography*, 39.

14. Schneider, *Theory and History of Bibliography*, 39.

15. Schneider, *Theory and History of Bibliography*, 13.

16. Schneider, *Theory and History of Bibliography*, 13.

17. Schneider, *Theory and History of Bibliography*, 13.

18. Schneider, *Theory and History of Bibliography*, 13.

19. Schneider, *Theory and History of Bibliography*, 13–14.

20. Schneider, *Theory and History of Bibliography*, 14.

21. Matthew Kirschenbaum and Sarah Werner, "Digital Scholarship and Digital Studies: The State of the Discipline," *Book History* 17 (2014): 408.

22. Kirschenbaum and Werner, "Digital Scholarship and Digital Studies," 408.

23. Kirschenbaum and Werner, "Digital Scholarship and Digital Studies," 409.

24. See Fritz Machlup and Una Mansfield, eds., *The Study of Information: Interdisciplinary Messages* (New York, Chichester, Brisbane, Toronto, and Singapore: John Wiley and Sons, 1983).

25. Ch'ŏn Hye-bong, *Han'guk sŏjihak* (Korean bibliography) (Seoul: Minŭmsa, 2006), 23.

26. *Tonga ilbo*, February 14, 1933, 6.

27. Ch'ŏn Hye-bong, *Han'guk sŏjihak*, 33.

28. Ch'ŏn Hye-bong, *Han'guk sŏjihak*, 27.

29. Geoffrey Bowker and Susan Leigh Star, *Sorting Things Out: Classification and Its Consequences* (Cambridge, MA, and London: MIT Press, 1999), loc. 572 of 4690, Kindle, citing Susan Leigh Star and Karen Ruhleder, "Steps toward an Ecology of Infrastructure: Design and Access for Large Information Spaces," *Information Systems Research* 7 (1996): 111–134.

30. Bowker and Star, *Sorting Things Out*, loc. 572 of 4690, citing Star and Ruhleder, "Steps toward an Ecology of Infrastructure."

31. See Belknap, *The List,* and also Rebecca Laemmle, Cédric Scheidegger Laemmle, and Katharina Wesselmann, eds., *Lists and Catalogues in Ancient Literature and Beyond: Towards a Poetics of Enumeration* (Berlin: Walter de Gruyter GmbH, 2021).

32. Harold Borko, "Information Science: What Is It?" *American Documentation* 19, no. 1 (1968): 3.

33. Martha E. Williams, "Defining Information Science and the Role of ASIS," *Bulletin of the American Society for Information Science* 14, no. 2 (1988): 17–18.

34. Tefko Saracevic, "Information Science," in *Encyclopedia of Library and Information Sciences,* 4th ed., ed. John McDonald and Michael Levine-Clark (Boca Raton, FL: CRC Press, 2018), 2216.

35. Bowker and Star, *Sorting Things Out,* loc. 572 of 4690, citing Star and Ruhleder, "Steps toward an Ecology of Infrastructure."

36. Jonathan Furner, "Information Science Is Neither," *Library Trends* 63, no. 3 (2015): 362–377.

37. Bowker and Star, *Sorting Things Out,* loc. 572 of 4690, citing Star and Ruhleder, "Steps toward an Ecology of Infrastructure."

38. Bowker and Star, *Sorting Things Out,* loc. 572 of 4690, citing Star and Ruhleder, "Steps toward an Ecology of Infrastructure."

39. Bowker and Star, *Sorting Things Out,* loc. 572 of 4690, citing Star and Ruhleder, "Steps toward an Ecology of Infrastructure."

40. Harold Borko, "Information Science: What Is It?" 3.

41. Robert Taylor, "Professional Aspects of Information Science and Technology," in *Annual Review of Information Science and Technology,* ed. C. A. Cuadra (New York: John Wiley & Sons, 1966), 19, https://archive.org/details/annualreviewofin00cuad, accessed July 26, 2020.

42. Taylor, "Professional Aspects of Information Science and Technology," 19.

43. Taylor, "Professional Aspects of Information Science and Technology," 28.

44. Borko, "Information Science: What Is It?" 3 (emphasis in the original).

45. Association for Information Science and Technology (ASIS&T), "What Is Information Science?" https://www.ASIS&T.org/about/what-is-information-science/, accessed July 26, 2020.

46. Taylor, "Professional Aspects of Information Science and Technology," 36, cites the following in its bibliography: Harold Borko, *The Conceptual Foundations of Information Systems,* Systems Development Corporation, Santa Monica, CA, May 6, 1965 (Report No. SP-2507) (AD-615 718).

47. Bowker and Star, *Sorting Things Out,* loc. 561 of 4690.

48. Bowker and Star, *Sorting Things Out,* loc. 3655 of 4690.

49. Bowker and Star, *Sorting Things Out,* loc. 561 of 4690.

CHAPTER 3

1. *Oxford English Dictionary Online*, s.v. "co-ordinate," accessed July 31, 2023.

2. Michel Foucault, *The Order of Things* (New York: Vintage Books, 1994), loc. 20 of 8030, Kindle. Foucault is referring to a short essay by Jorge Luis Borges titled "El idioma analítico de John Wilkins" (The analytical language of John Wilkins), published in *Otras inquisiciones 1937–1952* (Buenos Aires: Sur, 1952). It is worth noting that Borges includes a discussion of the "Bibliográfico de Bruselas" (Bibliographical Institute of Brussels), which would seem to be a reference to the Institut International de Bibliographie (International Institute of Bibliography) of Henri La Fontaine and Paul Otlet or one of their other organizations. Jorge Luis Borges, *Other Inquisitions, 1937–1952*, trans. Ruth L. C. Simms (Austin: University of Texas Press, 1964), 103, 104.

3. *Oxford English Dictionary Online*, s.v. "List," accessed July 31, 2023.

4. Google, s.v. "List."

5. *Oxford English Dictionary Online*, "List."

6. Patrick Wilson, *Two Kinds of Power: An Essay on Bibliographical Control* (Berkeley and Los Angeles: University of California Press, 1968), 3–4.

7. See W. W. Greg, "What Is Bibliography?" *Transactions of the Bibliographical Society* 12, no. 1 (1913): 39–53, which was first delivered as a speech in February 1912 to the Bibliographical Society (of England).

8. Alex Wright, *Cataloging the World: Paul Otlet and the Birth of the Information Age* (New York and Oxford: Oxford University Press, 2014), 102, Kindle.

9. Michael Buckland, "What Is a 'Document'?" *Journal of the American Society for Information Science* 48, no. 9 (1997): 805 (emphasis in the original).

10. Buckland, "What Is a 'Document'?" 805.

11. See Michael K. Buckland, "Information as Thing," *Journal of the American Society for Information Science* 42, no. 5 (1991): 351–360.

12. Cited in Wright, *Cataloging the World*, 31.

13. Wright, *Cataloging the World*, 84–85.

14. Buckland, "Information as Thing," 351.

15. G. Thomas Tanselle, "The Work of D. F. McKenzie," *The Papers of the Bibliographical Society of America* 98 (2004): 514.

16. WorldCat, s.v. "Butler, An Introduction to Library Science 1933," https://www.worldcat.org/title/introduction-to-library-science/oclc/731694673&referer=brief_results, accessed July 27, 2020.

17. WorldCat, s.v. "McKenzie, Bibliography and the Sociology of Texts," https://www.worldcat.org/title/bibliography-and-the-sociology-of-texts/oclc/1171369284&referer=brief_results, accessed July 27, 2020.

18. Pierce Butler, *An Introduction to Library Science* (Chicago: University of Chicago Press, 1933), 31–33.

19. D. F. McKenzie, *Bibliography and the Sociology of Texts* (Cambridge: Cambridge University Press, 1999), loc. 166–169 of 1568, Kindle.

20. McKenzie, *Bibliography and the Sociology of Texts*, loc. 169–170 of 1568.

CHAPTER 4

1. See Leah A. Lievrouw, "Materiality and Media in Communication and Technology Studies: An Unfinished Project," in *Media Technologies: Essays on Communication, Materiality, and Society*, ed. Tarleton Gillespie, Pablo J. Boczkowski, and Kirsten A. Foot (Cambridge, MA, and London: MIT Press, 2014), loc. 573–1208 of 7947, Kindle.

2. Jakob von Uexküll, *A Foray into the Worlds of Animals and Humans: With a Theory of Meaning*, trans. Joseph D. O'Neil. (Minneapolis and London: University of Minnesota Press, 2010), loc. 465 of 2765, Kindle.

3. Madeleine Akrich, "The De-scripting of Technical Objects," in *Shaping Technology/Building Society: Studies in Sociotechnological Change*, ed. Wiebe E. Bijker and John Law (Cambridge, MA, and London: MIT Press, 1992), loc. 2628 of 4465, Kindle.

4. Akrich, "The De-scripting of Technical Objects," loc. 2847 of 4465.

5. Uexküll, *Foray*, loc. 560–562 of 2765.

6. Uexküll, *Foray*, loc. 1179–1183 of 2765.

7. Uexküll, *Foray*, loc. 1419 of 2765.

8. Uexküll, *Foray*, loc. 1270 of 2765.

9. Uexküll, *Foray*, loc. 1270 of 2765.

10. Uexküll, *Foray*, loc. 1224 of 2765.

11. Uexküll, *Foray*, loc. 1225 of 2765 (emphasis added).

12. Marcia J. Bates, "The Invisible Substrate of Information Science," *Journal of the American Society for Information Science* 50, no. 12 (1999): 1043.

13. Uexküll, *Foray*, loc. 1419 of 2765.

14. Uexküll, *Foray*, loc. 1270 of 2765.

15. Ian Bogost, *Alien Phenomenology, or What It's Like to Be a Thing* (Minneapolis and London: University of Minnesota Press, 2012), loc. 771 of 4016, Kindle.

16. Bogost, *Alien Phenomenology*, loc. 1140 of 4016.

17. Graham Harman, *The Quadruple Object* (Winchester, UK: Zero Books, 2011), 124, quoted in Bogost, *Alien Phenomenology*, loc. 1145 of 4016.

18. Bogost, *Alien Phenomenology*, loc. 919–920 of 4016.

19. Bogost, *Alien Phenomenology*, loc. 884 of 4016.

20. *Oxford English Dictionary Online*, s.v. "Semicolon," accessed July 31, 2023.

21. Whymarrh, "Reading \r (Carriage Return) vs \n (Newline) from Console with getc?" updated April 7, 2012, https://stackoverflow.com/questions/10059142/reading-r-carriage-return-vs-n-newline-from-console-with-getc#:~:text=4%20Answers&text=%5Cn%20is%20the%20newline%20character,the%20enter%20key%20was%20pressed.

22. Bogost, *Alien Phenomenology*, loc. 1969 of 4016.

23. Bogost, *Alien Phenomenology*, loc. 1969 of 4016.

24. Bates, "The Invisible Substrate of Information Science," 1043.

25. Bogost, *Alien Phenomenology*, loc. 1969–1976 of 4016.

26. Bogost, *Alien Phenomenology*, loc. 1958 of 4016.

27. Bogost, *Alien Phenomenology*, loc. 1956–1964 of 4016.

28. Richard Parry, "Episteme and Techne," in *Stanford Encyclopedia of Philosophy*, winter ed., ed. Edward N. Zalta (Stanford, CA: Metaphysics Research Lab, Philosophy Department, Stanford University, 2021), https://plato.stanford.edu/archives/win2021/entries/episteme-techne.

CHAPTER 5

1. Johanna Drucker, *Visualization and Interpretation: Humanistic Approaches to Display* (Cambridge, MA, and London: MIT Press, 2020), 22.

2. Drucker, *Visualization and Interpretation*, 22.

3. James Turner, *Philology: The Forgotten Origins of the Modern Humanities* (Princeton, NJ: Princeton University Press, 2014), loc. 10023 of 19247, Kindle.

4. *Oxford English Dictionary Online*, s.v. "Description," accessed July 31, 2023.

5. *Oxford English Dictionary Online*, "Description."

6. *Oxford English Dictionary Online*, "Description."

7. See Markus Krajewski, *Paper Machines: About Cards & Catalogs, 1548–1929* (Cambridge, MA, and London: MIT Press, 2011).

8. *Oxford English Dictionary Online*, s.v. "Describe," accessed July 31, 2023.

9. Georg Schneider, *Theory and History of Bibliography*, trans. Ralph Robert Shaw (New York: Columbia University Press, 1934), 20.

10. Schneider, *Theory and History of Bibliography*, 24.

11. Richard Sennett, *The Craftsman* (New Haven, CT, and London: Yale University Press, 2008), loc. 114–115 of 3540, Kindle.

CHAPTER 6

1. Reviel Netz and William Noel, *The Archimedes Codex: How a Medieval Prayer Book Is Revealing the True Genius of Antiquity's Greatest Scientist* (New York: Da Capo Press, 2007), 110, Kindle.

   > The Palimpsest is an important piece of evidence not only for the year 225 BC but also for the year AD 975. The scribe who copied the works of Archimedes perhaps did not do much to advance the concepts of mathematics. He was no Archimedes. In fact, I am sure the scribe knew no mathematics at all. But he did make a contribution to the history of the interfaces of mathematics. His choices in the manner of writing down the words, arranging them on the page, and putting the works together all made a contribution to the way Archimedes would be read by later mathematicians. This is true throughout history, all the way from Archimedes in Syracuse down to the present day. Scribes, typesetters, and publishers make a silent contribution to the history of science, sometimes as important as that of the scientists themselves.
   >
   > Netz and Noel, *The Archimedes Codex*, 110.

2. Spelling modernized. Robert Recorde, *The whetstone of witte, whiche is the seconde parte of Arithmetike: containyng thextraction of Rootes: The Cossike practise, with the rule of Equation: and the woorkes of Surde Nombers* (London: J Kyngstone, 1557), https://archive.org/details/b30333179/page/n9/mode/2up?q=. The book is not foliated in a modern sense. This passage appears on page 248 of the PDF.
3. Recorde, *The whetstone of witte.*
4. Florian Cajori, *A History of Mathematical Notation*, Dover ed. (Mineola, NY, and New York: Dover Publications, 2012), 388.
5. Netz and Noel, *The Archimedes Codex*, 215.
6. Netz and Noel, *The Archimedes Codex*, 222.
7. Netz and Noel, *The Archimedes Codex*, 222.
8. Netz and Noel, *The Archimedes Codex*, 222.
9. LinkedIn, s.v. Doug Emery, https://www.linkedin.com/in/doug-emery-8642372/, accessed February 9, 2022.
10. Cait Coker and Kate Ozment, eds., "A Bibliography: Women in Book History," http://www.womensbookhistory.org/.
11. See Jacqueline Goldsby and Meredith McGill, eds., *"Black Bibliography Project,"* https://blackbibliog.org.
12. Michael Toth and Doug Emery, "From Decayed Parchment to 'Bit Rot'—Challenges in Digitizing Archimedes," January 22, 2009, Library of Congress, video recording, https://tile.loc.gov/storage-services/media/webcasts/2009/090122prv1300_640x480_800.mp4.
13. Toth and Emery, "From Decayed Parchment to 'Bit Rot'."
14. Toth and Emery, "From Decayed Parchment to 'Bit Rot'."

15. See Doug Emery "The Galen Palimpsest and the Modest Ambitions of the Digital Data Set," *Manuscript Studies* 3, no. 1 (2019): 83–109.

16. Cited in Netz and Noel, *The Archimedes Codex*, 291–292.

CHAPTER 7

1. For scholarly descriptions of how biological analogy has shaped cataloging, see, for example, Melissa Adler, "Classification along the Color Line: Excavating Racism in the Stacks," *Journal of Critical Library and Information Studies* 1, no. 1 (2017): 1–32, https://doi.org/10.24242/jclis.v1i1.1; and Thomas M. Dousa, "Evolutionary Order in the Classification Theories of CA Cutter and EC Richardson: Its Nature and Limits," *North American Symposium on Knowledge Organization* 2, no. 1 (2011): 76–90. For an annotated bibliography of related scholarship, see Jeremy Berg et al., "Social Justice in Cataloging Annotated Bibliography," *Faculty and Staff Publications–Milner Library* 141 (2021), https://ir.library.illinoisstate.edu/fpml/141. See also Decolonising through Critical Librarianship, "Bibliography for Cataloguing and Classification," https://decolonisingthroughcriticallibrarianship.wordpress.com/2019/09/09/bibliography-for-cataloguing-and-classification/; and Robert D. Montoya, *Power of Position: Classification and the Biodiversity Sciences* (Cambridge, MA, and London: MIT Press, 2022).

2. See Michelle R. Warren, "The Politics of Textual Scholarship," in *The Cambridge Companion to Textual Scholarship*, ed. Neil Fraistat and Julia Flanders (Cambridge: Cambridge University Press, 2013), 119–133, Kindle.

3. Kari Kraus, "Conjectural Criticism: Computing Past and Future Texts," *Digital Humanities Quarterly* 3, no. 4 (2009), http://www.digitalhumanities.org/dhq/vol/3/4/000069/000069.html.

4. Katlyn Turner, Danielle Wood, and Catherine D'Ignazio, "The Abuse and Misogynoir Playbook," in *The State of AI Ethics* (Montreal: Montreal AI Ethics Institute, 2021), 15, https://montrealethics.ai/jan2021/.

5. Jonathan Furner, "Dewey Deracialized: A Critical Race-Theoretic Perspective," *Knowledge Organization* 34, no. 3 (2007): 165.

6. Library of Congress, "Structural Overview of LCHS," Library of Congress Subject Headings: Online Training, Library of Congress, updated March 23, 2020, https://www.loc.gov/catworkshop/lcsh/PDF%20scripts/2-1-Structural Overview.pdf (emphasis in original).

7. Library of Congress, "Structural Overview of LCHS."

8. Library of Congress, "Structural Overview of LCHS."

9. A. W. Pollard, "Note by A. W. Pollard," in Stephen Gaselee, "The Aims of Bibliography," *The Library* 13, no. 3 (1932): 256.

10. Pollard, "Note by A. W. Pollard," 257.

11. A. N., "Henry Bradshaw," *Nature* 33 (February 18, 1886): 366, https://doi.org/10.1038/033366d0.

12. A. N., "Henry Bradshaw."

13. A. N., "Henry Bradshaw."

14. George Walter Prothero, *A Memoir of Henry Bradshaw: Fellow of King's College, Cambridge, and University Library* (London: Kegan Paul, Trench & Co., 1888), 327.

15. Frederick Edward Warren, "In Memoriam, Henry Bradshaw," *The Academy* 30, no. 721 (February 27, 1886): 147.

16. Warren, "In Memoriam, Henry Bradshaw," 147.

17. Warren, "In Memoriam, Henry Bradshaw," 147.

18. William Blades, *Printers' Register* (March 6, 1886), cited in Prothero, *A Memoir of Henry Bradshaw*, 363–364.

19. Prothero, *A Memoir of Henry Bradshaw*, 364–365.

20. Henry Bradshaw, *A Classified Index of the Fifteenth Century Books in the Collection of the Late M. J. de Meyer, which were sold at Ghent in November 1869* (London: Macmillan and Co., 1870), 15–16 (emphasis in original).

21. G. Thomas Tanselle, *Bibliographical Analysis: A Historical Introduction* (Cambridge: Cambridge University Press, 2009), loc. 69 of 4944, Kindle, 6.

22. Tanselle, *Bibliographical Analysis*, 6.

23. Warren, "In Memoriam, Henry Bradshaw," 147.

24. Warren, "In Memoriam, Henry Bradshaw," 147.

25. Stephen Gaselee, "The Aims of Bibliography," *The Library* 13, no. 3 (December 1932): 225.

26. W. W. Greg, "Bibliography—An Apologia," *The Library* 13, no. 2 (1932): 114, 115, https://doi.org/10.1093/library/s4-XIII.2.113.

27. Greg, "Bibliography—An Apologia," 114.

28. Greg, "Bibliography—An Apologia," 114.

29. Gaselee, "The Aims of Bibliography," 227.

30. Gaselee, "The Aims of Bibliography," 227–228.

31. Gaselee, "The Aims of Bibliography," 247.

32. Gaselee, "The Aims of Bibliography," 249–250.

33. Gaselee, "The Aims of Bibliography," 249–250.

34. Gaselee, "The Aims of Bibliography," 250.

35. W. W. Greg, "Dr. W. W. Greg," in Gaselee, "The Aims of Bibliography," 251–252.

36. Greg, "Dr. W. W. Greg," in Gaselee, "The Aims of Bibliography," 251–252.

37. Greg, "Dr. W. W. Greg," in Gaselee, "The Aims of Bibliography," 251–252.

38. Greg, "Dr. W. W. Greg," in Gaselee, "The Aims of Bibliography," 251–252.

39. Greg, "Dr. W. W. Greg," in Gaselee, "The Aims of Bibliography," 252.

40. Greg, "Dr. W. W. Greg," in Gaselee, "The Aims of Bibliography," 252.

41. Greg, "Dr. W. W. Greg," in Gaselee, "The Aims of Bibliography," 252.

42. Greg, "Dr. W. W. Greg," in Gaselee, "The Aims of Bibliography," 252.

43. Greg, "Dr. W. W. Greg," in Gaselee, "The Aims of Bibliography," 253–254.

44. Greg, "Dr. W. W. Greg," in Gaselee, "The Aims of Bibliography," 254.

45. Greg, "Dr. W. W. Greg," in Gaselee, "The Aims of Bibliography," 253.

46. Greg, "Dr. W. W. Greg," in Gaselee, "The Aims of Bibliography," 253.

47. Greg, "Dr. W. W. Greg," in Gaselee, "The Aims of Bibliography," 253.

48. Greg, "Dr. W. W. Greg," in Gaselee, "The Aims of Bibliography," 255.

49. Greg, "Dr. W. W. Greg," in Gaselee, "The Aims of Bibliography," 255.

50. Greg, "Dr. W. W. Greg," in Gaselee, "The Aims of Bibliography," 255.

51. Pollard, "Note by A. W. Pollard," in Gaselee, "The Aims of Bibliography," 255.

52. Pollard, "Note by A. W. Pollard," in Gaselee, "The Aims of Bibliography," 257.

53. Pollard, "Note by A.W. Pollard," in Gaselee, "The Aims of Bibliography," 256. Pollard is citing his response to James Duff Brown in "Practical Bibliography," *The Library* s2–4, 14 (1903): 156–159; A. W. Pollard, "By Alfred W. Pollard," in James Duff Brown, "Practical Bibliography," *The Library* s2–4, 14 (1903): 151–162.

54. Pollard, "Note by A.W. Pollard," 257.

55. Pollard, "Note by A.W. Pollard," 257–258.

56. Yii-Jan Lin, *The Erotic Life of Manuscripts: New Testament Textual Criticism and the Biological Sciences* (New York: Oxford University Press, 2016), 3, Kindle.

57. Lin, *The Erotic Life of Manuscripts*, 3.

58. See Judith Butler, *Bodies That Matter: On the Discursive Limits of Sex* (New York: Routledge, 1993).

59. See Dirk Van Hulle, *Genetic Criticism: Tracing Creativity in Literature* (Oxford: Oxford University Press, 2022), and William Kinderman and Joseph E. Jones, eds., *Genetic Criticism and the Creative Process: Essays from Music, Literature, and Theater* (Rochester, NY: University of Rochester Press, 2009).

60. See Christian Bök, *The Xenotext: Book 1* (Toronto: Coach House Books, 2015).

61. See the Molecular Information Storage (MIST) program carried out under the US Office of the Director of National Intelligence through the Intelligence Advanced Research Projects Activity program, https://www.iarpa.gov/research-programs/mist.

62. Elaine Whittaker, "Artist Statement," https://www.elainewhittaker.ca/artist-statement.

CHAPTER 8

1. David Greetham, *Textual Scholarship: An Introduction* (New York and London: Garland Publishing, 1994), loc. 5354 of 13371, Kindle.
2. W. W. Greg, "What Is Bibliography?" *Transactions of the Bibliographical Society* 12, no. 1 (1913): 41, https://doi.org/10.1093/libraj/TBS-12.1.39.
3. W. W. Greg, "Bibliography—An Apologia," *The Library* 13, no. 2 (1932): 122, https://doi.org/10.1093/library/s4-XIII.2.113.
4. David Greetham, "A History of Textual Scholarship," in *The Cambridge Companion to Textual Scholarship*, ed. Neil Fraistat and Julia Flanders (Cambridge: Cambridge University Press, 2013), 32–33, Kindle.
5. Hans Walter Gabler, "Late Twentieth-Century Shakespeares," in *The Cambridge Companion to Textual Scholarship*, ed. Neil Fraistat and Julia Flanders (Cambridge: Cambridge University Press, 2013), 79, Kindle.
6. Yii-Jan Lin, *The Erotic Life of Manuscripts: New Testament Textual Criticism and the Biological Sciences* (New York: Oxford University Press, 2016), 43.
7. Lin, *The Erotic Life of Manuscripts*, 43.
8. Lin, *The Erotic Life of Manuscripts*, 44. Lin points to John William Burgon, *The Revision Revised* (London: Clowes, 1883).
9. Greetham, "A History of Textual Scholarship," 20.
10. Greetham, "A History of Textual Scholarship," 21.
11. Greetham, "A History of Textual Scholarship," 21.
12. Greetham, "A History of Textual Scholarship," 22 (emphasis in the original).
13. See Jiang Wu and Lucille Chia, "Introduction," in *Spreading Buddha's Word in East Asia*, ed. Jiang Wu and Lucille Chia (New York: Columbia University Press, 2016), 1–14.
14. Shannon does not appear to have read the New Bibliographers. And, of course, Greg, at least initially, could not have read Shannon when he was initially proposing his bibliographical project.
15. Hans Walter Gabler, "Late Twentieth-Century Shakespeares," 79.
16. Greg, "What Is Bibliography?" 39.
17. Greg, "What is Bibliography?" 41.
18. Greg, "What Is Bibliography?" 41.
19. Greg, "What Is Bibliography?" 41.
20. Fredson Bowers, *Principles of Bibliographical Description* (Winchester, UK, and New Castle, DE: St. Paul's Bibliographies and Oak Knoll Press, 1994), 3.
21. Bowers, *Principles of Bibliographical Description*, 6.

22. "A bibliographer cannot be expected to inquire minutely into a publisher's or author's intention and to decide on literary grounds whether an alteration is a correction or an attempt at a re-issue. He can be concerned with a publisher's intention only when manifested on the title-page." Bowers, *Principles of Bibliographical Description*, 79.

23. See W. K. Wimsatt and M. C. Beardsley, "The Intentional Fallacy," *The Sewanee Review* 54, no. 3 (1946): 468–488.

24. See Roland Barthes, "The Death of the Author (*La mort de l'auteur*)," 1967. Barthes's essay appeared first as a translation by Richard Howard in the avant-garde journal *Aspen* 5 + 6, and then in French in *Mantéia* 5 in 1968. It has been widely anthologized since. For a useful bibliography, see Thierry Leguay, "Roland Barthes: Bibliographie Générale (Textes et Voix), 1942–1981," *Communications* 36 (1982): 131–171, https://doi.org/10.3406/comm.1982.1545.

25. See Michel Foucault, "What Is an Author? (*Qu'est-ce qu'un auteur?*)," 1969. For a helpful history of the transmission of what was initially a lecture delivered in February 1969, see Stuart Elden, "The Textual Issues around Foucault's 'What Is an Author?'" *Progressive Geographies*, April 11, 2017, and updated November 2021, https://progressivegeographies.com/2017/04/11/the-textual-issues-around-foucaults-what-is-an-author/.

26. Bowers, *Principles of Bibliographical Description*, 8.

27. George Walter Prothero, *A Memoir of Henry Bradshaw: Fellow of King's College, Cambridge, and University Library* (London: Kegan Paul, Trench & Co., 1888), 362.

28. Bowers, *Principles of Bibliographical Description*, 23

29. Bowers, *Principles of Bibliographical Description*, 23.

30. Bowers, *Principles of Bibliographical Description*, 113

31. International Federation of Library Associations and Institutions, "Functional Requirements for Bibliographic Records: Final Report," 2009, https://repository.ifla.org/bitstream/123456789/811/2/ifla-functional-requirements-for-bibliographic-records-frbr.pdf.

32. See Wayne de Fremery and Michael Buckland, "Copy Theory," *Journal of the Association for Information Science and Technology* 73, no. 3 (2022): 407–418.

33. Bowers, *Principles of Bibliographical Description*, 39.

34. Bowers, *Principles of Bibliographical Description*, 40.

35. Bowers, *Principles of Bibliographical Description*, 41–42.

36. Bowers, *Principles of Bibliographical Description*, 40.

37. Bowers, *Principles of Bibliographical Description*, 27.

38. Bowers, *Principles of Bibliographical Description*, 28.

39. Bowers, *Principles of Bibliographical Description*, 27.

40. Bowers, *Principles of Bibliographical Description*, 27.

41. Greetham, *Textual Scholarship*, loc. 438 of 13371 (emphasis in original).

42. Greetham, *Textual Scholarship*, loc. 444 of 13371.

43. Greetham, *Textual Scholarship*, loc. 444 of 13371.

44. Greetham, *Textual Scholarship*, loc. 444 of 13371.

45. See McKenzie's discussion in "The Book as an Expressive Form" in D. F. McKenzie, *Bibliography and the Sociology of Texts* (Cambridge: Cambridge University Press, 1999), Kindle.

CHAPTER 9

1. D. F. McKenzie, "Printers of the Mind: Some Notes on Bibliographical Theories and Printing-House Practices," *Studies in Bibliography* 22 (1969): 61.

2. McKenzie, "Printers of the Mind," 61 (emphasis in original).

3. W. W. Greg, "What Is Bibliography?" *Transactions of the Bibliographical Society* 12, no. 1 (1913): 41, https://doi.org/10.1093/libraj/TBS-12.1.39.

4. McKenzie, "Printers of the Mind," 3.

5. McKenzie, "Printers of the Mind," 3.

6. McKenzie, "Printers of the Mind," 3.

7. McKenzie, "Printers of the Mind," 3.

8. McKenzie, "Printers of the Mind," 3 (emphasis in original).

9. McKenzie, "Printers of the Mind," 6.

10. McKenzie, "Printers of the Mind," 6.

11. McKenzie, "Printers of the Mind," 6.

12. McKenzie, "Printers of the Mind," 5.

13. McKenzie, "Printers of the Mind," 4.

14. McKenzie, "Printers of the Mind," 4.

15. McKenzie, "Printers of the Mind," 4.

16. McKenzie, "Printers of the Mind," 6.

17. Headnote in D. F. McKenzie, *Making Meaning: "'Printers of the Mind"' and Other Essays*, ed. Peter D. McDonald and Michael F. Suarez, S.J. (Amherst and Boston: University of Massachusetts Press, 2002), 13.

18. "To observe at all is to bestow meaning of some kind on the thing observed; to gather particular pieces of evidence is to seek those relevant to some preconceived notion of their utility." McKenzie, "Printers of the Mind," 3–4.

19. This is a paraphrase of a line from Yi Sang, "Publication Law," *Chōsen to kenchiku* (July 1932): 26.

20. McKenzie, "Printers of the Mind," 61.
21. McKenzie, "Printers of the Mind," 61.
22. McKenzie, "Printers of the Mind," 61.
23. McKenzie, "Printers of the Mind," 61.
24. McKenzie, "Printers of the Mind," 61.
25. McKenzie, "Printers of the Mind," 61.
26. McKenzie, "Printers of the Mind," 61.
27. McKenzie, "Printers of the Mind," 1.
28. D. F. McKenzie, *Bibliography and the Sociology of Texts* (Cambridge: Cambridge University Press, 1999), loc. 146 of 1568 (emphasis added).

CHAPTER 10

1. Jerome McGann, "The Socialization of Texts," in *The Textual Condition* (Princeton, NJ: Princeton University Press, 1991), 75.
2. McGann, "The Socialization of Texts," 82.
3. See Patrick Wilson, *Two Kinds of Power: An Essay on Bibliographical Control* (Berkeley and Los Angeles: University of California Press, 1968).
4. Airi Salminen, "Modeling Documents in Their Contexts," in *Encyclopedia of Library and Information Sciences*, 4th ed., ed. John McDonald and Michael Levine-Clark (Boca Raton, FL: CRC Press, 2018), 3105–3116.
5. *ISKO Encyclopedia of Knowledge Organization*, https://www.isko.org/cyclo/.
6. "Model complexity," "modeling dependencies between mentions," and "modeling KG [knowledge graphs]" appear in the index of *Knowledge Graphs: Fundamentals, Techniques, and Applications*, but not "model." "Modeling KG" points to chapter 2, which opens with the following statement: "KG representational models that have become dominant in KG-centric communities such as the Semantic Web. Chief among these models is the Resource Description Framework (RDF) model, as well as models that have been built on top of it, such as RDF Schema (RDFS). We also detail the Wikidata model and provide a brief primer on property-centric models such as the property graph and the property table." Mayank Kejriwal, Craig A. Knoblock, and Pedro Szekely, *Knowledge Graphs: Fundamentals, Techniques, and Applications* (Cambridge, MA, and London: MIT Press, 2021), 21. A search of the book using my Kindle reader suggests that the word appears 500 times in the 530 pages of the book, almost once a page on average. Similarly, only "Model for Clinical Information (MCI)" appears in the index of Robert Arp, Barry Smith, and Andrew D. Spear's *Building Ontologies with Basic Formal Ontology* (Cambridge, MA, and London: MIT Press, 2015).
7. Graeme Simsion, *Data Modeling: Theory and Practice* (Denville, NJ: Technics Publications, 2007), loc. 229–233 of 9427, Kindle.

8. Simsion, *Data Modeling*, loc. 229–233 of 9427.

9. Simsion, *Data Modeling*, loc. 489–491 of 9427.

10. Simsion, *Data Modeling*, loc. 780–781 of 9427.

11. Simsion, *Data Modeling*, loc. 1338–1340 of 9427.

12. Kalle Lyytinen, "Two Views of Information Modeling," *Information & Management* 12, no. 1 (1987): 9.

13. Mayank Kejriwal, Craig A. Knoblock, and Pedro Szekely, *Knowledge Graphs: Fundamentals, Techniques, and Applications* (Cambridge, MA, and London: MIT Press, 2021), 15, Kindle.

14. Robert Arp, Barry Smith, and Andrew D. Spear, *Building Ontologies with Basic Formal Ontology* (Cambridge, MA, and London: MIT Press, 2015), 1, Kindle.

15. Arp, Smith, and Spear, *Building Ontologies*, 1.

16. Arp et al., *Building Ontologies*, 3.

17. Arp et al., *Building Ontologies*, 3.

18. Arp et al., *Building Ontologies*, 3.

19. Arp et al., *Building Ontologies*, 3 (emphasis in original).

20. Fredson Bowers, *Principles of Bibliographical Description* (Winchester, UK, and New Castle, DE: St. Paul's Bibliographies and Oak Knoll Press, 1994), 6.

21. Simsion, *Data Modeling*, loc. 795 of 9427.

22. David C. Hay, *Data Model Patterns: Conventions of Thought* (New York: Dorset House Publishing, 1996), as cited in Simsion, *Data Modeling*, loc. 744 of 9427.

23. Fred McFadden, Jeffrey A Hoffer, and Mary Prescott, *Modern Database Management* (Reading, MA: Addison-Wesley, 1999), as cited in Simsion, *Data Modeling*, 744 of 9427.

24. Heikki Topi and V. Ramesh, "Human Factors Research on Data Modeling: A Review of Prior Research, An Extended Framework and Future Research Directions," *Journal of Database Management* 13, no. 2 (2002): 3.

25. Arp et al., *Building Ontologies*, loc. 117 of 5515.

26. Arp et al., *Building Ontologies*, loc. 135 of 5515.

27. Arp et al., *Building Ontologies*, loc. 128 of 5515.

28. Bowers, *Principles of Bibliographical Description*, 23.

29. In the BFO, "continuants" are "entities that continue or persist through time," where "occurrents" are "entities that occur or happen, variously referred to as 'events' or 'processes' or 'happenings.'" Arp et al., *Building Ontologies*, loc. 2216 of 5515.

30. McGann, "The Socialization of Texts," 83.

31. McGann, "The Socialization of Texts," 83.

32. Jerome McGann, *A New Republic of Letters: Memory and Scholarship in the Age of Digital Reproduction* (Cambridge, MA, and London: Harvard University Press, 2014), 5, Kindle.

33. McGann, "The Socialization of Texts," 71–72.

34. McGann, "The Socialization of Texts," 77.

35. McGann, "The Socialization of Texts," 70.

36. McGann, "The Socialization of Texts," 75.

37. McGann, "The Socialization of Texts," 75.

38. McGann, "The Socialization of Texts," 82.

39. Arp et al., *Building Ontologies*, 13.

40. McGann, "The Socialization of Texts," 82–83 (emphasis in the original).

41. Google, s.v. "nearest pizza," autocompleted to "nearest Pizza Hut," Saturday, January 29, 2022, 8:16 pm in Goyang-dong, South Korea.

CHAPTER 11

1. John D. Kelleher and Brendan Tierney, *Data Science* (Cambridge, MA, and London, MIT Press, 2018), 19, Kindle.

2. Kelleher and Tierney, *Data Science*, 19.

3. Thomas Davenport and D. J. Patil, "Data Scientist: The Sexiest Job of the 21st Century," *Harvard Business Review*, https://hbr.org/2012/10/data-scientist-the-sexiest-job-of-the-21st-century, accessed August 5, 2023.

4. Barb Darrow, "Data Science Is Still White Hot, but Nothing Lasts Forever," *Forbes*, http://fortune.com/2015/05/21/data-science-white-hot/, accessed August 5, 2023.

5. Ryan Swanstrom, "Colleges and Universities with Data Science Degrees," http://datascience.community/colleges, accessed May 15, 2017. As of February 2022, Swanstrom lists 632 programs.

6. Gil Press, "A Very Short History of Data Science," *Forbes*, https://www.forbes.com/sites/gilpress/2013/05/28/a-very-short-history-of-data-science/#55cfc05c55cf, accessed August 5, 2023; Kelleher and Tierney, *Data Science*, 17.

7. Kelleher and Tierney, *Data Science*, 6.

8. Kelleher and Tierney, *Data Science*, 6–7.

9. Kelleher and Tierney, *Data Science*, 6–7.

10. Kelleher and Tierney, *Data Science*, 6–7.

11. Wiebke Denecke and Zhang Bowei, "Reclaiming Bibliography, from East to West," unpublished manuscript, last modified August 16, 2021.

12. "'Thus the call number issues from its location.' Just as the conscription number is aimed at establishing the possible location of a respective recruit, so the call number of a book ideally carries the address of its regular storage place." Markus Krajewski, *Paper Machines: About Cards & Catalogs, 1548–1929* (Cambridge, MA, and London: MIT Press, 2011), 29, Kindle.

13. Kelleher and Tierney, *Data Science*, 6.

14. Kelleher and Tierney, *Data Science*.

15. Kelleher and Tierney, *Data Science*, 7–8.

16. E. F. Codd, "A Relational Model of Data for Large Shared Data Banks," *Communications of the ACM* 13, no. 6 (1970): 377.

17. Kelleher and Tierney, *Data Science*, 7–8.

18. Rob Kitchin and Gavin McArdle, "What Makes Big Data, Big Data? Exploring the Ontological Characteristics of 26 Datasets," *Big Data & Society* 3, no. 1 (2016): 1.

19. Doug Laney, "3D Data Management: Controlling Data Volume, Velocity, and Variety," Application Delivery Strategies (Stamford, CT: Meta Group), February 6, 2001, viewed through the Internet Archive's Way Back Time Machine, https://web.archive.org/web/20120304154148/https://blogs.gartner.com/doug-laney/files/2012/01/ad949-3D-Data-Management-Controlling-Data-Volume-Velocity-and-Variety.pdf.

20. Kitchin and McArdle, "What Makes Big Data, Big Data?" 1.

21. Kitchin and McArdle, "What Makes Big Data, Big Data?" 1.

22. Kitchin and McArdle, "What Makes Big Data, Big Data?" 1.

23. Laney, "3D Data Management."

24. Laney, "3D Data Management."

25. Laney, "3D Data Management."

26. Laney, "3D Data Management."

27. Laney, "3D Data Management."

28. Laney, "3D Data Management."

29. See Michael Buckland, "Information as Thing," *Journal of the American Society for Information Science* 42, no. 5 (1991): 351–360.

30. Laney, "3D Data Management."

31. Laney, "3D Data Management."

32. Laney, "3D Data Management."

33. Laney, "3D Data Management."

34. Laney, "3D Data Management."

35. Bernhard Rieder, "Reading Technology 1: Edgar F. Codd, a Relational Model of Data for Large Shared Data Banks, 1970," *The Politics of Systems: Thoughts on Software, Power, and*

Digital Method, posted September 30, 2010, http://thepoliticsofsystems.net/2010/09/reading-technology-1-edgar-f-codd-a-relational-model-of-data-for-large-shared-data-banks-1970/.

36. Laney, "3D Data Management."

37. Kitchin and McArdle, "What Makes Big Data, Big Data?" 1. Also see Viktor Mayer-Schönberger and Kenneth Cukier, *Big Data: A Revolution That Will Change How We Live, Work, and Think* (London: John Murray, 2013); Martin Dodge and Rob Kitchin, "Codes of Life: Identification Codes and the Machine-Readable World," *Environment and Planning D: Society and Space* 23, no. 6 (2005): 851–881, https://doi.org/10.1068/d378t; danah boyd and Kate Crawford, "Critical Questions for Big Data," *Information, Communication & Society* 15, no. 5 (2012): 662–679, https://doi.org/10.1080/1369118X.2012.678878; Nathan Marz and James Warren, *Big Data: Principles and Best Practices of Scalable Realtime Data Systems* (Westhampton, NJ: Manning, 2012); Bernard Marr, "Big Data: The 5 Vs Everyone Must Know," LinkedIn, March 6, 2014, https://www.linkedin.com/pulse/20140306073407-64875646-big-data-the-5-vs-everyone-must-know; Eileen McNulty, "Understanding Big Data: The Seven V's," Dataconomy, May 22, 2014, http://dataconomy.com/seven-vs-big-data/.

38. Deborah Lupton, "The Thirteen Ps of Big Data" (created May 11, 2015), *This Sociological Life*, https://simplysociology.wordpress.com/2015/05/11/the-thirteen-ps-of-big-data/, accessed June 26, 2019.

39. Lupton, "The Thirteen Ps of Big Data."

40. Lupton, "The Thirteen Ps of Big Data."

41. Christine L. Borgman, *Big Data, Little Data, No Data: Scholarship in the Networked World* (Cambridge, MA, and London: MIT Press, 2015), loc. 378–385 of 9460, Kindle.

42. Borgman, *Big Data, Little Data, No Data*, loc. 378–385 of 9460.

43. Kelleher and Tierney, *Data Science*, 10 (emphasis in original).

44. William Playfair, *Lineal Arithmetic; Applied to Shew the Progress of the Commerce and Revenue of England During the Present Century; Which Is Represented and Illustrated by Thirty-three Copper-plate Charts Being an Useful Companion for the Cabinet and Counting House*. Printed for the author, and sold by A Paris, Roll's-building, Fetter-lane, 1798, 6. Scanned by Google and downloaded June 26, 2019. A stamp on page 15 of the PDF downloaded suggests that the copy scanned by Google was held by the British Museum.

45. Kelleher and Tierney, *Data Science*, 14.

46. Graham Upton and Ian Cook, *A Dictionary of Statistics*, revised ed. (Oxford and New York: Oxford University Press, 2008), 373.

47. Mariya Yao, Adelyn Zhou, and Marlene Jia, *Applied Artificial Intelligence: A Handbook for Business Leaders* (TOPBOTS, 2018), 8.

48. Meredith Broussard, *Artificial Unintelligence: How Computers Misunderstand the World* (Cambridge, MA, and London: MIT Press, 2018), loc. 603 of 4633, Kindle.

49. Broussard, *Artificial Unintelligence*, loc. 606–607 of 4633, Kindle.

50. Broussard, *Artificial Unintelligence*, loc. 606–607 of 4633, Kindle.

51. Kelleher and Tierney, *Data Science*, 14.

52. John D. Kelleher, Brian Mac Namee, and Aoife D'Arcy, *Fundamentals of Machine Learning for Predictive Data Analytics: Algorithms, Worked Examples, and Case Studies* (Cambridge, MA, and London: MIT Press, 2015), loc. 475–476 of 13053, Kindle.

53. This is the decimal value in the UTF-8 standard.

54. I am describing "supervised learning" here.

55. Ian Goodfellow, Yoshua Bengio, and Aaron Courville, *Deep Learning* (Cambridge, MA, and London: MIT Press, 2016), 8, Kindle.

56. Goodfellow et al., *Deep Learning*, 10.

57. *Oxford English Dictionary Online*, s.v. "description," accessed July 31, 2023.

58. Fredson Bowers, *Principles of Bibliographical Description* (Winchester, UK, and New Castle, DE: St. Paul's Bibliographies and Oak Knoll Press, 1994), 23.

59. Other color models exist, of course; I make an example of RGB for simplicity's sake.

CHAPTER 12

1. D. F. McKenzie, *Bibliography and the Sociology of Texts* (Cambridge: Cambridge University Press, 1999), loc. 328 of 1568, Kindle.

2. See Charles Duhigg, "How Companies Learn Your Secrets," *New York Times Magazine*, February 16, 2012, https://www.nytimes.com/2012/02/19/magazine/shopping-habits.html.

3. See, for example, the work of Joy Buolamwini, such as Joy Buolamwini and Timnit Gebru, "Gender Shades: Intersectional Accuracy Disparities in Commercial Gender Classification," *Proceedings of Machine Learning Research* 81 (2018): 1–15, http://proceedings.mlr.press/v81/buolamwini18a/buolamwini18a.pdf.

4. McKenzie, *Bibliography and the Sociology of Texts*, loc. 56–63 of 1568.

5. McKenzie, *Bibliography and the Sociology of Texts*, loc. 56–63 of 1568.

6. McKenzie, *Bibliography and the Sociology of Texts*, loc. 56–63 of 1568.

7. McKenzie, *Bibliography and the Sociology of Texts*, loc. 56–63 of 1568.

8. Judea Pearl and Dana Mackenzie, *The Book of Why: The New Science of Cause and Effect* (New York: Basic Books, 2018), 35–36, Kindle.

9. McKenzie, *Bibliography and the Sociology of Texts*, loc. 63 of 1568

10. McKenzie, *Bibliography and the Sociology of Texts*, loc. 63–70 of 1568.

11. Pearl and Mackenzie, *The Book of Why*, 51.

12. McKenzie, *Bibliography and the Sociology of Texts*, loc. 67–68 of 1568.

13. Pearl and Mackenzie, *The Book of Why*, 7.

14. Pearl and Mackenzie, *The Book of Why*, 26.

15. Pearl and Mackenzie, *The Book of Why*, 28.

16. Pearl and Mackenzie, *The Book of Why*, 362.

17. Pearl and Mackenzie, *The Book of Why*, 6.

18. Pearl and Mackenzie, *The Book of Why*, 195.

19. D. F. McKenzie, "Printers of the Mind: Some Notes on Bibliographical Theories and Printing-House Practices," *Studies in Bibliography* 22 (1969): 60.

CODA

1. Jerome McGann, *A New Republic of Letters: Memory and Scholarship in the Age of Digital Reproduction* (Cambridge, MA, and London: Harvard University Press, 2014), loc. 68 of 5263, Kindle.

2. See "About," Internet Archive, https://archive.org/about/, and "About," Common Crawl, https://commoncrawl.org/about/.

3. David G. T. Barrett, Ari S. Morcos, and Jakob H. Macke, "Analyzing Biological and Artificial Neural Networks: Challenges with Opportunities for Synergy?" *Current Opinion in Neurobiology*, Machine Learning, Big Data, and Neuroscience (special issue), 55 (2019): 61, https://doi.org/10.1016/j.conb.2019.01.007.

4. Margaret Mitchell, Simone Wu, Andrew Zaldivar, et al., "Model Cards for Model Reporting," *Proceedings of the Conference on Fairness, Accountability, and Transparency*, January 29–31, Atlanta (Atlanta: Association for Computing Machinery, 2019): 220–229, https://arxiv.org/abs/1810.03993, unnumbered first page.

5. Timnit Gebru, Jamie Morgenstern, Briana Vecchione, et al., "Datasheets for Datasets," *Communications of the ACM* 64, no. 12 (2021): 86.

6. Gebru et al., "Datasheets for Datasets," 86.

7. Clifford Lynch, "Stewardship in the 'Age of Algorithms,'" *First Monday* 22, no. 12 (2017), http://dx.doi.org/10.5210/fm.v22i112.8097.

Bibliography

Adler, Melissa. "Classification along the Color Line: Excavating Racism in the Stacks." *Journal of Critical Library and Information Studies* 1, no. 1 (2017): 1–32. https://doi.org/10.24242/jclis.v1i1.1.

Akrich, Madeleine. "The De-scripting of Technical Objects." In *Shaping Technology/Building Society: Studies in Sociotechnological Change*, edited by Wiebe E. Bijker and John Law, loc. 2619–2901 of 4465. Cambridge, MA, and London: MIT Press, 1992. Kindle.

A. N. "Henry Bradshaw." *Nature* 33 (February 18, 1886): 366. https://doi.org/10.1038/033366d0.

Andersen, Jack, ed. *Genre Theory in Information Studies*. Bingley, UK: Emerald Group Publishing, 2015.

Arp, Robert, Barry Smith, and Andrew D. Spear. *Building Ontologies with Basic Formal Ontology*. Cambridge, MA, and London: MIT Press, 2015. Kindle.

Barad, Karen. *Meeting the Universe Halfway: Quantum Physics and the Entanglement of Matter and Meaning*. Durham, NC, and London: Duke University Press, 2007. Kindle.

Barney, Stephen. "Chaucer's Lists." In *The Wisdom of Poetry: Essays in Early English Literature in Honor of Morton W. Bloomfield*, edited by Larry Dean Benson and Siegfried Wenzel, 189–223. Kalamazoo: Western Michigan University Press, Medieval Institute, 1982.

Barrett, David G. T., Ari S. Morcos, and Jakob H. Macke. "Analyzing Biological and Artificial Neural Networks: Challenges with Opportunities for Synergy?" *Current Opinion in Neurobiology*, Machine Learning, Big Data, and Neuroscience (special issue), 55 (2019): 55–64. https://doi.org/10.1016/j.conb.2019.01.007.

Barthes, Roland. "The Death of the Author." Translated by Richard Howard. *Aspen* 5+6 (1967). https://www.ubu.com/aspen/aspen5and6/threeEssays.html#barthes.

Bates, Marcia J. "The Invisible Substrate of Information Science." *Journal of the American Society for Information Science* 50, no. 12 (1999): 1043–1050.

Belknap, Robert E. *The List: The Uses and Pleasures of Cataloguing*. New Haven, CT, and London: Yale University Press, 2004. Kindle.

Benjamin, Walter. *Illuminations*. Translated by Harry Zohn. New York: Schocken Books, 2007. Kindle.

Berg, Jeremy, Cathy Chapman, Gretchen Neidhardt, Stephanie Porrata, Jennifer Young, and Eric Willey. "Social Justice in Cataloging Annotated Bibliography." *Faculty and Staff Publications–Milner Library* 141 (2021). https://ir.library.illinoisstate.edu/fpml/141.

Bogost, Ian. *Alien Phenomenology, or What It's Like to Be a Thing*. Minneapolis and London: University of Minnesota Press, 2012. Kindle.

Bohr, Niels. "Quantum Physics and Philosophy: Causality and Complementarity." In *The Philosophical Writings of Niels Bohr*, edited by J. Faye and H. J. Folse, vol. 3, 1–7. Woodbridge, CT: Ox Bow Press, 1987.

Bök, Christian. *The Xenotext: Book 1*. Toronto: Coach House Books, 2015.

Borges, Jorge Luis. *Other Inquisitions, 1937–1952*. Translated by Ruth L. C. Simms. Austin: University of Texas Press, 1964.

Borgman, Christine L. *Big Data, Little Data, No Data: Scholarship in the Networked World*. Cambridge, MA, and London: MIT Press, 2015.

Borko, Harold. *The Conceptual Foundations of Information Systems*. Systems Development Corporation, Santa Monica, CA, May 6, 1965. (Report No. SP-2507)(AD-615 718).

Borko, Harold. "Information Science: What Is It?" *American Documentation* 19, no. 1 (1968): 3–5.

Bowers, Fredson. *Principles of Bibliographical Description*. Winchester, UK, and New Castle, DE: St. Paul's Bibliographies and Oak Knoll Press, 1994.

Bowker, Geoffrey, and Susan Leigh Star. *Sorting Things Out: Classification and Its Consequences*. Cambridge, MA, and London: MIT Press, 1999. Kindle.

boyd, danah, and Kate Crawford. "Critical Questions for Big Data." *Information, Communication & Society* 15, no. 5 (2012): 662–679. https://doi.org/10.1080/1369118X.2012.678878.

Bradshaw, Henry. *A Classified Index of the Fifteenth Century Books in the Collection of the Late M. J. de Meyer, Which Were Sold at Ghent in November 1869*. London: Macmillan and Co., 1870.

Broussard, Meredith. *Artificial Unintelligence: How Computers Misunderstand the World*. Cambridge, MA, and London: MIT Press, 2018. Kindle.

Buckland, Michael. *Information and Information Systems*. New York: Greenwood Press, 1991. Kindle.

Buckland, Michael K. "Information as Thing." *Journal of the American Society for Information Science* 42, no. 5 (1991): 351–360.

Buckland, Michael. "What Is a 'Document'?" *Journal of the American Society for Information Science* 48, no. 9 (1997): 804–809.

Buolamwini, Joy, and Timnit Gebru. "Gender Shades: Intersectional Accuracy Disparities in Commercial Gender Classification." *Proceedings of Machine Learning Research* 81 (2018): 1–15. http://proceedings.mlr.press/v81/buolamwini18a/buolamwini18a.pdf.

Burgon, John William. *The Revision Revised*. London: Clowes, 1883.

Butler, Judith. *Bodies That Matter: On the Discursive Limits of Sex.* New York: Routledge, 1993.

Butler, Pierce. *An Introduction to Library Science.* Chicago: University of Chicago Press, 1933.

Cajori, Florian. *A History of Mathematical Notation.* Dover ed. Mineola, NY, and New York: Dover Publications, 2012.

Ch'ŏn Hye-bong. *Han'guk sŏjihak* (Korean bibliography). Seoul: Minŭmsa, 2006.

Codd, E. F. "A Relational Model of Data for Large Shared Data Banks." *Communications of the ACM* 13, no. 6 (1970): 377–387. https://doi.org/10.1145/362384.362685.

Coker, Cait, and Kate Ozment, eds. "A Bibliography: Women in Book History." http://www.womensbookhistory.org/.

Consultative Committee for Space Data Systems. *Reference Model for an Open Archival Information System.* Washington, DC: Consultative Committee for Space Data Secretariat, 2012. http://public.ccsds.org/publications/archive/650x0m2.pdf.

Darrow, Barb. "Data Science Is Still White Hot, But Nothing Lasts Forever." *Forbes.* http://fortune.com/2015/05/21/data-science-white-hot/.

Davenport, Thomas, and D. J. Patil. "Data Scientist: The Sexiest Job of the 21st Century." *Harvard Business Review.* https://hbr.org/2012/10/data-scientist-the-sexiest-job-of-the-21st-century.

Decolonising through Critical Librarianship. "Bibliography for Cataloguing and Classification." https://decolonisingthroughcriticallibrarianship.wordpress.com/2019/09/09/bibliography-for-cataloguing-and-classification/.

de Fremery, Wayne. "The Future of Adan Mun'go's Digital Archive: Big Data and Artificial Intelligence at Adan Mun'go." *Muncha wa sasang* 3 (2018): 107–115.

de Fremery, Wayne. "Twenty-First-Century Pleasures—Some Notes on Form, Media Transformation, and Korean Literary Translation." *Translation Review* 108, no. 1 (2021): 78–103.

de Fremery, Wayne. "What Counts as Deep Learning in Korean Studies?" *Korean Studies* 47 (2023): 300–311.

de Fremery, Wayne, and Michael Buckland. "Context, Relevance, and Labor." *Journal of the Association for Information Science and Technology* 73, no. 9 (2022): 1268–1278.

de Fremery, Wayne, and Michael Buckland. "Copy Theory." *Journal of the Association for Information Science and Technology* 73, no. 3 (2022): 407–418.

Denecke, Wiebke, and Zhang Bowei. "Reclaiming Bibliography, from East to West." Unpublished manuscript, last modified August 16, 2021. Microsoft Word file.

Dodge, Martin, and Rob Kitchin. "Codes of Life: Identification Codes and the Machine-Readable World." *Environment and Planning D: Society and Space* 23, no. 6 (2005): 851–881. https://doi.org/10.1068/d378t.

Dousa, Thomas M. "Evolutionary Order in the Classification Theories of CA Cutter and EC Richardson: Its Nature and Limits." *North American Symposium on Knowledge Organization* 2, no. 1 (2011): 76–90.

Drucker, Johanna. "Excerpts and Entanglement." Unpublished talk for the Document Academy meeting at the University of California, Berkeley, School of Information Management Systems (SIMS), August 13, 2003.

Drucker, Johanna. *Humanistic Approaches to Display*. Cambridge, MA, and London: MIT Press, 2020.

Drucker, Johanna. *The Visible Word: Experimental Typography and Modern Art, 1909–1923*. Chicago and London: University of Chicago Press, 1994.

Duhigg, Charles. "How Companies Learn Your Secrets." *New York Times Magazine*. February 16, 2012. https;//www.nytimes.com/2012/02/19/magazine/shopping-habits.html.

Elden, Stuart. "The Textual Issues around Foucault's 'What Is an Author?'" *Progressive Geographies*. April 11, 2017, and updated November 2021. https://progressivegeographies.com/2017/04/11/the-textual-issues-around-foucaults-what-is-an-author/.

Emery, Doug. "The Galen Palimpsest and the Modest Ambitions of the Digital Data Set." *Manuscript Studies* 3, no. 1 (2019): 83–109.

Foucault, Michel. *The Archaeology of Knowledge and Discourse on Language*. Translated by A. M. Sheridan Smith. New York: Vintage Books, 2010. Kindle.

Foucault, Michel. *The Order of Things*. New York: Vintage Books, 1994. Kindle.

Furner, Jonathan. "'Data': The Data." In *Information Cultures in the Digital Age: A Festschrift in Honor of Rafael Capurro*, edited by M. Kelly and J. Bielby, 228–306. Wiesbaden, Germany: Springer VS, 2016.

Furner, Jonathan. "Dewey Deracialized: A Critical Race-Theoretic Perspective." *Knowledge Organization* 34, no. 3 (2007): 144–168.

Furner, Jonathan. "Information Science Is Neither." *Library Trends* 63, no. 3 (2015): 362–377.

Furner, Jonathan. "Philosophy and Information Studies." *Annual Review of Information Science and Technology* 44, no. 1 (2010): 159–200.

Gabler, Hans Walter. "Late Twentieth-Century Shakespeares." In *Cambridge Companion to Textual Scholarship*, edited by Neil Fraistat and Julia Flanders, 79–96. Cambridge: Cambridge University Press, 2013. Kindle.

Gaifman, Hiam. "Naming and Diagonalization, from Cantor to Gödel to Kleene." *Logic Journal of the IGLP* 14, no. 5 (2006): 709–728.

Gaselee, Stephen. "The Aims of Bibliography." *The Library* 13, no. 3 (December 1932): 225–258.

Gaskell, Philip. *A New Introduction to Bibliography*. New Castle, DE: Oak Knolls Press, 1995.

Gebru, Timnit, Jamie Morgenstern, Briana Vecchione, et al. "Datasheets for Datasets." *Communications of the ACM* 64, no. 12 (2021): 86–92. http://arxiv.org/abs/1803.09010.

Gibson, James. *The Ecological Approach to Visual Perception*. Boston: Houghton Mifflin, 1979.

Gleick, James. *The Information: A History, a Theory, a Flood.* New York and Toronto: Random House, 2011. Kindle.

Goldsby, Jacqueline, and Meredith McGill, eds. "Black Bibliography Project." https://blackbibliog.org/.

Goodfellow, Ian, Yoshua Bengio, and Aaron Courville. *Deep Learning.* Cambridge, MA, and London: MIT Press, 2016. Kindle.

Greene, Roland, Stephen Cushman, Clare Cavanagh, et al., eds. *Princeton Encyclopedia of Poetry and Poetics.* 4th ed. Princeton, NJ: Princeton University Press, 2012. Kindle.

Greetham, David. "A History of Textual Scholarship." In *Cambridge Companion to Textual Scholarship*, edited by Neil Fraistat and Julia Flanders, 16–41. Cambridge: Cambridge University Press, 2013, Kindle.

Greetham, D. C. *Textual Scholarship: An Introduction.* New York and London: Garland Publishing, 1994. Kindle.

Greg, W. W. "Bibliography—An Apologia." *The Library* 13, no. 2 (1932): 113–143. https://doi.org/10.1093/library/s4-XIII.2.113.

Greg, W. W. "What Is Bibliography?" *Transactions of the Bibliographical Society* 12, no. 1 (1913): 39–53. https://doi.org/10.1093/libraj/TBS-12.1.39.

Hale, Barbara. *The Subject Bibliography of the Social Sciences and Humanities.* Oxford, New York, Toronto, Sydney, and Braunschweig, Germany: Pergamon Press, 1970. Kindle.

Haraway, Donna. *Simians, Cyborgs, and Women: The Reinvention of Nature.* New York and Milton Park, UK: Routledge, 1991. Kindle.

Harman, Graham. *The Quadruple Object.* Winchester, UK: Zero Books, 2011.

Harré, Rom, and Jean-Pierre Llored. "Procedures, Products and Pictures." *Philosophy* 93, no. 2 (2018): 167–186.

Hartley, R. V. L. "Transmission of Information." *Bell System Technical Journal* 7 (July 1928): 535–563. https://archive.org/details/bstj7-3-535.

International Federation of Library Associations and Institutions. "Functional Requirements for Bibliographic Records: Final Report." September 1997, as amended and corrected as of February 2009. https://repository.ifla.org/bitstream/123456789/811/2/ifla-functional-requirements-for-bibliographic-records-frbr.pdf.

ISKO Encyclopedia of Knowledge Organization. https://www.isko.org/cyclo/.

Kejriwal, Mayank, Craig A. Knoblock, and Pedro Szekely. *Knowledge Graphs: Fundamentals, Techniques, and Applications.* Cambridge, MA, and London: MIT Press, 2021.

Kelleher, John D., Brian Mac Namee, and Aoife D'Arcy. *Fundamentals of Machine Learning for Predictive Data Analytics: Algorithms, Worked Examples, and Case Studies.* Cambridge, MA, and London: MIT Press, 2015. Kindle.

Kelleher, John D., and Brendan Tierney. *Data Science*. Cambridge, MA, and London: MIT Press, 2018. Kindle.

Kinderman, William, and Joseph E. Jones, eds. *Genetic Criticism and the Creative Process: Essays from Music, Literature, and Theater*. Rochester, NY: University of Rochester Press, 2009.

Kirschenbaum, Matthew, and Sarah Werner. "Digital Scholarship and Digital Studies: The State of the Discipline." *Book History* 17 (2014): 406–458.

Kitchin, Rob, and Gavin McArdle. "What Makes Big Data, Big Data? Exploring the Ontological Characteristics of 26 Datasets." *Big Data & Society* 3, no. 1 (2016): 1–10.

Krajewski, Markus. *Paper Machines: About Cards & Catalogs, 1548–1929*. Cambridge, MA, and London: MIT Press, 2011. Kindle.

Kraus, Kari. "Conjectural Criticism: Computing Past and Future Texts." *Digital Humanities Quarterly* 3, no. 4 (2009). http://www.digitalhumanities.org/dhq/vol/3/4/000069/000069.html.

Laemmle, Rebecca, Cédric Scheidegger Laemmle, and Katharina Wesselmann, eds. *Lists and Catalogues in Ancient Literature and Beyond: Towards a Poetics of Enumeration*. Berlin: Walter de Gruyter GmbH, 2021.

Laney, Doug. "3D Data Management: Controlling Data Volume, Velocity and Variety." Application Delivery Strategies, 1–4. Stamford, CT: Meta Group Inc, 2001. Viewed through the Internet Archive's Wayback Machine on June 27, 2023, https://web.archive.org/web/20120304154148/https://blogs.gartner.com/doug-laney/files/2012/01/ad949-3D-Data-Management-Controlling-Data-Volume-Velocity-and-Variety.pdf.

Leguay, Thierry. "Roland Barthes: Bibliographie Générale (Textes et Voix), 1942–1981." *Communications* 36 (1982): 131–171. https://doi.org/10.3406/comm.1982.1545.

Library of Congress. "Structural Overview of LCHS." Library of Congress Subject Headings: Online Training. Updated March 23, 2020. https://www.loc.gov/catworkshop/lcsh/PDF%20scripts/2-1-Structural-Overview.pdf.

Lievrouw, Leah A. "Materiality and Media in Communication and Technology Studies: An Unfinished Project." In *Media Technologies: Essays on Communication, Materiality, and Society*, edited by Tarleton Gillespie, Pablo Boczkowski, and Kirsten Foot, loc. 573–1208 of 7947. Cambridge, MA, and London: MIT Press, 2014. Kindle.

Lin, Yii-Jan. *The Erotic Life of Manuscripts: New Testament Textual Criticism and the Biological Sciences*. New York: Oxford University Press, 2016.

Liu, James J. Y. *Chinese Theories of Literature*. Chicago: University of Chicago Press, 1975.

Lupton, Deborah. "The Thirteen Ps of Big Data." *This Sociological Life* (created May 11, 2015). https://simplysociology.wordpress.com/2015/05/11/the-thirteen-ps-of-big-data/.

Lynch, Clifford. "Stewardship in the 'Age of Algorithms'." *First Monday* 22, no. 12 (2017). http://dx.doi.org/10.5210/fm.v22i112.8097.

Lyytinen, Kalle. “Two Views of Information Modeling.” *Information & Management* 12, no. 1 (1987): 9–19.

Machlup, Fritz, and Una Mansfield, eds. *The Study of Information: Interdisciplinary Messages*. New York, Chichester, UK, Brisbane, Australia, Toronto, and Singapore: John Wiley and Sons, 1983.

Marr, Bernard. “Big Data: The 5 Vs Everyone Must Know.” LinkedIn. https://www.linkedin.com/pulse/20140306073407-64875646-big-data-the-5-vs-everyone-must-know, March 6, 2014.

Marz, Nathan, and James Warren. *Big Data: Principles and Best Practices of Scalable Realtime Data Systems*. Westhampton, NJ: Manning, 2012.

Mayer-Schönberger, Viktor, and Kenneth Cukier. *Big Data: A Revolution That Will Change How We Live, Work, and Think*. London: John Murray, 2013.

McGann, Jerome. *A New Republic of Letters: Memory and Scholarship in the Age of Digital Reproduction*. Cambridge, MA, and London: Harvard University Press, 2014. Kindle.

McGann, Jerome. “The Socialization of Texts.” In *The Textual Condition*, 69–87. Princeton, NJ: Princeton University Press, 1991.

McKenzie, D. F. *Bibliography and the Sociology of Texts*. Cambridge: Cambridge University Press, 1999.

McKenzie, D. F. *Cambridge University Press, 1696–1712: A Bibliographical Study*. Cambridge: Cambridge University Press, 1966.

McKenzie, D. F. *Making Meaning: “Printers of the Mind” and Other Essays*. Edited by Peter D. McDonald and Michael F. Suarez, S.J. Amherst and Boston: University of Massachusetts Press, 2002.

McKenzie, D. F. “Printers of the Mind: Some Notes on Bibliographical Theories and Printing-House Practices.” *Studies in Bibliography* 22 (1969): 1–79. https://www.jstor.org/stable/40371475.

McNulty, Eileen. “Understanding Big Data: The Seven V’s,” Dataconomy, http://dataconomy.com/seven-vs-big-data, May 22, 2014.

Miller, Carolyn R. “Genre as Social Action.” *Quarterly Journal of Speech* 70, no. 2 (1984): 151–167.

Mitchell, Margaret, Simone Wu, Andrew Zaldivar, et al. “Model Cards for Model Reporting.” *Proceedings of the Conference on Fairness, Accountability, and Transparency*, January 29–31 (Atlanta: Association for Computing Machinery, 2019): 220–229. https://arxiv.org/abs/1810.03993.

Montoya, Robert D. *Power of Position: Classification and the Biodiversity Sciences*. Cambridge, MA, and London: MIT Press, 2022.

Netz, Reviel, and William Noel. *The Archimedes Codex: How a Medieval Prayer Book Is Revealing the True Genius of Antiquity’s Greatest Scientist*. New York: Da Capo Press, 2007. Kindle.

Pearl, Judea, and Dana Mackenzie. *The Book of Why: The New Science of Cause and Effect*. New York: Basic Books, 2018. Kindle.

Playfair, William. *Lineal Arithmetic; Applied to Shew the Progress of the Commerce and Revenue of England During the Present Century; Which Is Represented and Illustrated by Thirty-three Copper-plate*

Charts Being an Useful Companion for the Cabinet and Counting House. Printed for the author, and sold by A Paris, Roll's-building, Fetter-lane, 1798.

Pollard, A. W. "By Alfred W. Pollard." 151–162. In James Duff Brown, "Practical Bibliography." *The Library* s2–4, no. 14 (1903): 144–162.

Pollard, A.W. "Note by A.W. Pollard." 255–258. In Stephen Gaselee, "The Aims of Bibliography." *The Library* 13, no. 3 (December 1932): 225–258.

Press, Gil. "A Very Short History of Data Science." *Forbes.* https://www.forbes.com/sites/gilpress/2013/05/28/a-very-short-history-of-data-science/#55cfc05c55cf.

Prothero, George Walter. *A Memoir of Henry Bradshaw: Fellow of King's College, Cambridge, and University Library.* London: Kegan Paul, Trench & Co., 1888.

Recorde, Robert. *The whetstone of witte, whiche is the seconde parte of Arithmetike: containyng thextraction of Rootes: The Cossike practise, with the rule of Equation: and the woorkes of Surde Nombers.* London: J. Kyngstone, 1557. https://archive.org/details/b30333179/page/n9/mode/2up?q=equal.

Rieder, Bernhard. "Reading Technology 1: Edgar F. Codd, a Relational Model of Data for Large Shared Data Banks, 1970." *The Politics of Systems: Thoughts on Software, Power, and Digital Method,* posted September 30, 2010, http://thepoliticsofsystems.net/2010/09/reading-technology-1-edgar-f-codd-a-relational-model-of-data-for-large-shared-data-banks-1970/.

Rosenmeyer, Thomas. *Green Cabinet.* Berkeley: University of California Press, 1969.

Salminen, Airi. "Modeling Documents in Their Contexts." In *Encyclopedia of Library and Information Sciences.* 4th ed., edited by John McDonald and Michael Levine-Clark, 3105–3116. Boca Raton, FL: CRC Press, 2018.

Saracevic, T. "Information science." In *Encyclopedia of library and information sciences.* 3rd ed., edited by M. J. Bates, 2570–2585. New York: Taylor and Francis, 2009.

Saracevic, Tefko. "Information Science." In *Encyclopedia of Library and Information Sciences.* 4th ed., edited by John McDonald and Michael Levine-Clark, 2216–2231. Boca Raton, FL: CRC Press, 2018.

Schneider, Georg. *Theory and History of Bibliography.* Translated by Ralph Robert Shaw. New York: Columbia University Press, 1934.

Schutz, Alfred. "The Stranger: An Essay in Social Psychology." *American Journal of Sociology* 69 (1944): 499–507.

Sennett, Richard. *The Craftsman.* New Haven, CT, and London: Yale University Press, 2008. Kindle.

Shannon, Claude E. "A Mathematical Theory of Communication." *Bell System Technical Journal* (July and October, 1948): 379–423; 623–656. Accessed January 3, 2020, https://archive.org/details/bellsystemtechni27amerrich/page/n9.

Simmel, Georg. "The Stranger." In *The Sociology of George Simmel,* edited by Kurt Wolff, 402–408. Glencoe, IL: Free Press, [1908] 1950.

Simsion, Graeme. *Data Modeling: Theory and Practice*. Denville, NJ: Technics Publications, 2007. Kindle.

Star, Susan Leigh. "Misplaced Concretism and Concrete Situations: Feminism, Method, and Information Technology." In *Boundary Objects and Beyond: Working with Leigh Star*, edited by Geoffrey C. Bowker, Stefan Timmermans, Adele E. Clarke, and Ellen Balka, 142–166. Cambridge, MA, and London: MIT Press, 2015. Kindle.

Star, Susan Leigh, and Karen Ruhleder. "Steps toward an Ecology of Infrastructure: Design and Access for Large Information Spaces." *Information Systems Research* 7 (1996): 111–134.

Stonequist, Everett. *The Marginal Man*. New York: Russell and Russell, 1961.

Swanstrom, Ryan. "Colleges and Universities with Data Science Degrees." *Data Science 101* (blog). Accessed May 15, 2017. At time of writing (February 2022) the url http://datascience.community/colleges redirects to https://ryanswanstrom.com/colleges/.

Tanselle, G. Thomas. *Bibliographical Analysis: A Historical Introduction*. Cambridge: Cambridge University Press, 2009. Kindle.

Tanselle, G. Thomas. "The Work of D. F. McKenzie." *Papers of the Bibliographical Society of America* 98 (2004): 511–521.

Taylor, Robert. "Professional Aspects of Information Science and Technology." In *Annual Review of Information Science and Technology*, edited by C. A. Caudra, 15–40. New York: John Wiley & Sons, 1966. https://archive.org/details/annualreviewofin00cuad.

Topi, Heikki, and V. Ramesh. "Human Factors Research on Data Modeling: A Review of Prior Research, An Extended Framework and Future Research Directions." *Journal of Database Management* 13, no. 2 (2002): 3–19.

Toth, Michael, and Doug Emery. "From Decayed Parchment to 'Bit Rot'—Challenges in Digitizing Archimedes," January 22, 2009, Library of Congress, video recording, https://tile.loc.gov/storage-services/media/webcasts/2009/090122prv1300_640x480_800.mp4.

Turing, A. M. "On Computable Numbers, with an Application to the Entscheidungsproblem." *London Mathematical Society* s2–42, no. 1 (1937): 230–265. https://londmathsoc.onlinelibrary.wiley.com/doi/epdf/10.1112/plms/s2-42.1.230.

Turner, James. *Philology: The Forgotten Origins of the Modern Humanities*. Princeton, NJ: Princeton University Press, 2014. Kindle.

Turner, Katlyn, Danielle Wood, and Catherine D'Ignazio. "The Abuse and Misogynoir Playbook." In *The State of AI Ethics*, 15–34. Montreal: Montreal AI Ethics Institute, 2021. https://montrealethics.ai/wp-content/uploads/2021/01/The-State-of-AI-Ethics-Report-January-2021.pdf.

Uexküll, Jakob von. *A Foray into the Worlds of Animals and Humans: With a Theory of Meaning*. Translated by Joseph D. O'Neil. Minneapolis and London: University of Minnesota Press, 2010. Kindle.

Upton, Graham, and Ian Cook. *A Dictionary of Statistics*. Revised ed. Oxford and New York: Oxford University Press, 2008.

US Office of the Director of National Intelligence through the Intelligence Advanced Research Projects Activity. "MIST Molecular Information Storage." https://www.iarpa.gov/research-programs/mist.

Van Hulle, Dirk. *Genetic Criticism: Tracing Creativity in Literature.* Oxford: Oxford University Press, 2022.

Wang, Michelle C. "Thousand-Armed and Thousand-Eyed Avalokiteshvara." Object Narrative. In *Conversations: An Online Journal of the Center for the Study of Material and Visual Cultures of Religion* (2014). doi:10.22332/con.obj.2014.32.

Warren, Frederick Edward. "In Memoriam, Henry Bradshaw." *The Academy* 30, no. 721 (February 27, 1886): 147–149.

Warren, Michelle R. "The Politics of Textual Scholarship." In *Cambridge Companion to Textual Scholarship*, edited by Neil Fraistat and Julia Flanders, 119–133. Cambridge: Cambridge University Press, 2013. Kindle.

Whittaker, Elaine. "Artist Statement." https://www.elainewhittaker.ca/artist-statement.

Whymarrh. "Reading \r (Carriage Return) vs. \n (Newline) from Console with getc?" Updated April 7, 2012, https://stackoverflow.com/questions/10059142/reading-r-carriage-return-vs-n-newline-from-console-with-getc#:~:text=4%20Answers&text=%5Cn%20is%20the%20newline%20character,the%20enter%20key%20was%20pressed.

Williams, Martha E. "Defining Information Science and the Role of ASIS." *Bulletin of the American Society for Information Science* 14, no. 2 (1988): 17–19.

Williams, Raymond. *Keywords: A Vocabulary of Culture and Society*. New York and Oxford: Oxford University Press, 2015. Kindle.

Wilson, Patrick. *Two Kinds of Power: An Essay on Bibliographical Control.* Berkeley and Los Angeles: University of California Press, 1968.

Wimsatt, W. K., and M. C. Beardsley. "The Intentional Fallacy." *The Sewanee Review* 54, no. 3 (1946): 468–488.

Wright, Alex. *Cataloging the World: Paul Otlet and the Birth of the Information Age*. New York and Oxford: Oxford University Press, 2014.

Wu, Jiang, and Lucille Chia. "Introduction." In *Spreading Buddha's Word in East Asia*, edited by Jiang Wu and Lucille Chia, 1–14. New York: Columbia University Press, 2016. Kindle.

Yao, Mariya, Adelyn Zhou, and Marlene Jia. *Applied Artificial Intelligence: A Handbook for Business Leaders*. TOPBOTS, 2018.

Yeats, William Butler. "Among School Children." In *The Yeats Reader*, edited by Richard J. Finneran, 102–105. New York: Scribner Poetry, 2002.

Yi Sang. "Diagnosis 0:1." *Chōsen to kenchiku* (July 1932): 25.

Yi Sang. "Publication Law." *Chōsen to kenchiku* (July 1932): 26.

Index

Note: Figures are indicated by "f" following page numbers.